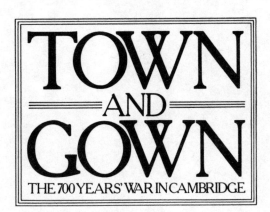

TOWN AND GOWN

THE 700 YEARS' WAR IN CAMBRIDGE

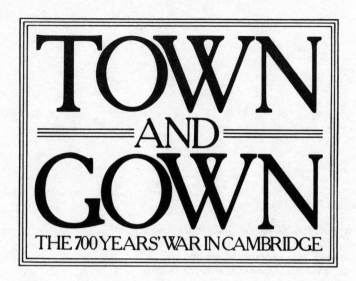

TOWN AND GOWN
THE 700 YEARS' WAR IN CAMBRIDGE

ROWLAND PARKER

 Patrick Stephens, Cambridge

First published in 1983

British Library Cataloguing in Publication Data

Parker, Rowland
  Town and gown.
  1. Public opinion—University of Cambridge
  I. Title
  378.426'59   LF103

  ISBN 0-85059-639-4

Photoset in 10 on 11 pt Times
by Manuset Limited, Baldock, Herts.
Printed in Great Britain on White Book Wove
90 gsm Vol 18, and bound, by The Garden City
Press, Letchworth, Herts, for the publishers,
Patrick Stephens Limited, Bar Hill, Cambridge,
CB3 8EL, England.

Contents

Preface   7
Introduction   9
Chapter 1   Unwelcome paying guests   13
Chapter 2   War and peace 1260-1280   23
Chapter 3   Stubborn resistance 1280-1323   32
Chapter 4   Change of tactics 1323-1380   38
Chapter 5   Away with the learning 1380-1381   45
Chapter 6   Fighting a losing battle 1382-1420   52
Chapter 7   Resignation 1423-1503   63
Chapter 8   Rebellious townsmen 1503-1534   69
Chapter 9   A near thing 1534-1546   76
Chapter 10 Licensed jetting 1547-1560   83
Chapter 11 Patronage and perversity 1561-1591   89
Chapter 12 Poor town 1591-1605   108
Chapter 13 If you cannot beat them 1605-1660   122
Chapter 14 Corruption and stagnation 1660-1820   133
Chapter 15 Revival and reform 1820-1894   142
Chapter 16 Peace in our time 1894-1982   157
Glossary   172
Index   174

Preface

The addition of yet another book to the long list of those dealing with Cambridge calls for explanation, indeed justification. It is simply that the full story of the long conflict between Town and Gown has, surprisingly, never been told. It has been mentioned countless times, usually with bias towards one side or the other, often with embarrassment and mostly with the suggestion that it was of little significance. It is true that local feuds within a community, or between two neighbouring communities, were a common feature of medieval life, that many of them persisted well into modern times and that few of them left a permanent imprint on people or places. Few of them, however, reached such intensity of passion and lasted so long or with such effect as the one which is the subject of my story.

A 'story' is what I have tried to tell. This is not meant to be a history of either the town or the university. Inevitably there is a lot of 'history' in it, but far more has been omitted in the desire to keep strictly to my theme and produce a straightforward readable tale. As always, I have written for the general reader rather than for the specialist student, so there are no footnotes or detailed references to sources and no bibliography, as such. I might have compiled an impressive list—well, a couple of pages—of books which I have consulted or which others might wish to consult. But I wanted to avoid the impression that this was simply a re-hash, as so many Cambridge books turn out to be. I have used original sources for most of the story.

My version of events from 1200 to 1530 is based largely on entries in the Rolls (Patent, Close, Charter, Hundred, Assize and Parliamentary), a total of well over 200 volumes. To have taken short cuts in the research on that period would have resulted in missing much and perhaps misinterpreting a lot more. Even so, I could have misinterpreted some of the facts. The one author on whom I have drawn heavily is C.H. Cooper, whose four volumes of *Annals of Cambridge* were published in 1842. He, too, used original sources, quoting in full just about every relevant document available in his day. While expressing my indebtedness and gratitude to him, I must point out that I have done what he failed to do, namely edit the material, summarising, synthesising, abridging and selecting—again in the interests of readability. As regards the town material I have taken Cooper very much on trust; as Town Clerk he was well placed to ferret out the facts and in that respect he did exercise some restraint.

As regards the university material for the 16th, 17th and 18th centuries, I preferred to explore for myself the manuscript documents in the University Archives, many of which Cooper evidently saw and many of which he either missed or neglected as not being relevant to his view of history. So there is a good deal of hitherto unpublished material in this book, and for this my warmest thanks are due to Miss E. Leedham-Green, Keeper of the University Archives, who kindly gave me access to a mass of documents and a lot of help in locating those most suitable to my purpose.

The 19th century documentation of the conflict is voluminous, as one would expect. I have drawn mainly on *The Cambridge Chronicle and University Journal* and latterly on *The Cambridge Reporter*. Mr Jim Brown saved me many tedious hours of searching through newspaper files, for which my thanks are due to him, also for the task of producing the maps used as illustration to the text.

The publishers and I wished to have the story brought right up to date. This has proved to be the most difficult and yet in a way the most enlightening part of the whole undertaking. It involved interviews with many people of widely differing age and status. I forget which Latin author, in connection with which subject, said that there were as many opinions as there were people, but I am sure that he was right. One point arising from these interviews was the confirmation that a lot of townspeople today know little or nothing about the history of Town/Gown relations which strengthens my excuse for writing the book. I ought to thank all those who gave their time and patience and especially those who supplied factual information. But many were unknown to me and some wished to remain anonymous—for it is still a delicate topic—so, while I do thank them all, I name none.

It might be said that in writing the book at all I have dug up a hatchet which was better left buried. In my defence I can at least claim total impartiality. Of course I have opinions and of course they colour the narrative at times. To write just the facts, the whole facts and nothing but the facts, apart from being an impossibility, makes for dull reading. I have tried to favour neither side, whilst being conscious of a debt of loyalty to both. Though not a member of the university, for the past 15 years I have had close connection with it and have benefited greatly from the courtesy and kind co-operation afforded me by its members. I lived in the town for five years and spent nearly the whole of my working life there; many of the townspeople are my personal friends. To hurt their feelings is the very last thing I would wish to do.

Rowland Parker
Foxton, December 1982

Introduction

From the files of the *Cambridge Chronicle and University Journal* of November 9 1850:

'TOWN AND GOWN!'

It is well known that the 5th of November in Cambridge is often the signal for the revival of this antagonistic cry and, what is worse, a number of encounters generally take place, in which the weapons used are not confined to fists. A variety of circumstances this year tended to induce a fear that the disturbances would be of a more desperate character than ordinary. It was expected that the feelings of the gownsmen against the recent aggressions of the Papacy would find vent in boisterous rejoicings; while the vexed questions now pending as to the University contribution to the expenses of the Town in various shapes would, it was thought, add to the violence of both parties. Vigorous measures were accordingly taken by the authorities of both the Town and University to prevent collision between the disorderly members of the two bodies; though it was evident that they did not act in concert. On the part of the University, the Undergraduates were 'gated' at nine o'clock, and a number of Masters of Arts paraded the streets, aided by the University constables, to exercise control over such gownsmen as were to be found in the streets after that hour.

About 10 o'clock a disorderly gang of the most disgraceful characters in the town adjourned from Parker's Piece and commenced parading the streets and hooting and yelling at every University man they met. It was impossible for the police to disperse this body; nor indeed did they attempt to secure a single member of it, though on any other occasion such conduct as these ruffians were guilty of would have secured them a safe night's lodging in the Station-house. This mob had the complete control of the streets all the evening and at last a collision took place in Green Street; here several University men had joined for mutual protection, and the cap of one of them was knocked off from behind by one of the mob, who immediately measured his length beside it on the ground. A general fight ensued, in which the gownsmen had for a short time the best of it; but five or six to 300 is long odds; and thinking that discretion is the better part of valour, those of the toga retreated into a house, so soon as the tide began to turn, and bolted the door on the other side, leaving several of their foes prostrate on the ground. The activity with which this manoeuvre was executed was admirable, and the exasperated mob, baulked of their prey, vented their rage upon two university constables who had arrived on the spot. Beset on all hands, one of these men, a servant of Trinity Hall, used his staff, and that not lightly, upon the head of one of the ringleaders named Dunn, a Falcon-yard hero, and drew blood; the mob immediately closed in, and the constables had to take to their heels; they took refuge in the yard leading to the new rooms of the Union Society, and were here run down, and much maltreated; their staves were secured by the mob, and the assailant of Dunn was most severely beaten. A sally then took place from the rooms of the Union Society, and the gownsmen, linked arm-in-arm, soon cleared the street of the mob, who set about parading the town.

Several gownsmen who had been ordered home to their colleges were afterwards proctorised in the streets, and the condition of one Johnian was really pitiable; he, having been ordered home, was caught by the Proctor again minus cap, his gown in ribbons, and exhibiting other unequivocal symptoms of having been engaged in a recent mêlée.

On Wednesday night the townspeople again attempted a riot, as did a body of gownsmen, who, smarting under the treatment of their fellows of the night before, turned out well armed. These, however, were hemmed in in Green Street by the authorities, and dispersed, but sundry skirmishes took place notwithstanding; and among the casualties may be recorded that a man of Christ's College had his front teeth knocked out; another gownsman had his spectacles broken on his face, which was severely cut by the pieces of glass, some of which there was great difficulty in extracting, but fortunately his sight was uninjured.

On Thursday night, during a rehearsal of the Choral Society, one poor solitary gownsman was set upon by a low mob outside the Town Hall; his cap and gown were destroyed; he was trampled on by the mob, and it was with some difficulty that he was rescued by the police.

In 1935 I came to live in Cambridge—not as a student, but as a young teacher. I had not been there long before I heard about the 'Town and Gown Riots', though nobody could tell me much about them other than that they occurred on November 5 and nobody knew why. Accordingly, on November 5, desirous of finding out for myself, and seeing no prospect of excitement in an evening spent in solitude in rather dreary digs, I strolled along to the market-place at about nine o'clock.

The market-place was poorly lit. Most of the lamps had been extinguished and no shop windows were illuminated, in fact many had been boarded up. In the semi-gloom, however, it was possible to distinguish large numbers of people in stationary groups, silent for the most part. Evidently many others besides myself were there as idle spectators. Then, for reasons difficult to determine, a group would suddenly become extremely mobile and noisy. A group of giggling girls screamed in mock alarm as a 'banger' exploded beside their legs, causing them to scatter; then they re-formed and rushed towards another part of the square, where a group of black-gowned youths could be vaguely seen in a scuffle with a bunch of policemen. Before they reached the spot, that scuffle had ceased, and another one had broken out elsewhere. When the police converged upon a group of students, attracted by a bang or a volley of shouts, that group vanished into the crowd of bystanders, or fled at top speed along Petty Cury, Rose Crescent or Market Street. Who was attacking whom, or who was shouting what, or why, I could not make out. Having seen one policeman's helmet knocked off, and one youth shin up a lamp-post to place a helmet on top of it amid rousing cheers, I concluded that this must have been the object of the exercise.

When the proctor, resplendent in his working clothes and flanked by two burly top-hatted 'bulldogs', appeared I thought I was going to see a bit of real excitement at last and witness a slice of traditional university pageantry, or something. But the undergraduates just stood still in silence, or disappeared even more rapidly than they had at the approach of the police.

The utter silliness of the whole affair suddenly struck me. I returned to my digs, still wondering. Was *this* what Town and Gown riots were all about? A lot of immature students—they were two or three years younger than me—who indulged in a bit of rowdy horseplay? Over the years I have discovered that a great many people shared that view. Forty-five years later I decided to find out what the Town/Gown conflict really was about. This book is the result.

Note on the maps in this book
These are intended solely to illustrate the text—accuracy of detail, even where it might have been possible, has been sacrificed in the interests of clarity and simplicity.

Chapter 1

Unwelcome paying guests

'We were here first—go away and leave us alone!'. The sentiment behind that anguished cry has been the basis of countless childish squabbles, fuelled many a local feud and caused national conflicts lasting on and off for centuries, some of them so long that animosity has become a matter of habit and tradition rather than one of reason. Such was the seemingly sense-less conflict between the town and the university at Cambridge, a 'war' which began over 700 years ago and only ended within the memory of some people now living. As with most wars, there was never much 'sense' in it; yet there were many reasons for it and they changed as time went on. Basically, in the beginning, it was a case of a settled community feeling a sense of outrage at the invasion of their territory by a band of outsiders who did not fit the established pattern of life there, and whose presence, many of the townsmen thought, threatened their security, prosperity and peace. That attitude will perhaps be easier to understand if we review briefly the history of the townsmen during the thousand or so years prior to the arrival of the last wave of intruders, for that was the margin by which they 'got there first'.

The story of the first half of that period must be more speculation than history, little light being cast on it by archaeology, even less by documentation. There was, from the first century to the fifth, a Romano-British town of sorts, 20 odd acres in extent, partly if not wholly walled, sitting astride a crossroads to the north-west of the river-bend. Whatever importance it had, or was intended to have, has been wholly buried by time and the overlying strata of later occupation, some of it very recent. There were two Anglo-Saxon settlements: one Saxon on the ruins of the old town, called *Grantaceastr* in the seventh century; the other, Anglo, on the lower ground south and east of the river. They became united, with or without their consent, under Mercian domination, into a single settlement, a 'port' of some significance bearing the name of *Grantebrycge* in the ninth century. The Danes left their mark on this small but growing 'town' in more ways than one; they 'rode through' it in 870 and 'sat' in it for a whole year in 875 which cannot have been good for morale or the food supply but doubtless boosted the birth-rate quite a bit. Three years later it came under official Danish rule for a period of 40 years during which it acquired certain Scandinavian features, such as government by 'lawmen' and a lasting aversion to interference by outsiders in its affairs. In 921 the town swore allegiance to the English king, a loyalty which, apart from one brief lapse, it was to maintain for ever and which helped to earn it recognition as the county-town. It also had the frightening experience of a final visitation by the Danes in 1010, when it was looted and burnt.

A half-century of peace allowed the little town to grow and thrive (see opposite). Then once again outsiders took control—Frenchmen this time. Twenty-seven houses were destroyed to clear a site for the Norman castle in the middle of what was once the Roman town. The sheriff, managing the town for the king, treated it as if it were his own, installing his own mills, annexing pasture for his own use, demanding three times as much ploughing and carting service as his predecessors had done and increasing inheritance fees eightfold. The burgesses—the majority of whom were farmers, though traders and artisans were on the increase—craved for independence almost as much as they wanted wealth and security. They knew moreover—constant reminders did not allow them to forget—that independence had to be paid for in hard cash, like all privileges.

Their early overtures to King Henry I met with little response, but in 1120 or thereabouts the king did make a concession of some significance for the town. He ordered that no boats should load or unload anywhere in the county except at 'my borough of Cantebruge', that carts be laden there only and tolls taken nowhere else. Thus was established the commercial pre-eminence of Cambridge as a market town, particularly as regards the carrying trade between there and Lynn, a river-route carrying more merchandise, especially corn, than any of the roads in the area.

Successive sheriffs continued to harass the townsmen. Some had an eye to the salvation of their own souls by endowing religious houses, an investment to which the townsmen raised no objections. All seemed to take their duties as money-collectors too seriously and, as keepers of law and order, too lightly. The fee-farm rent—which the townsmen paid annually to the king, via the sheriff, for their town—came to £60, plus various 'aids', 'gifts' and 'tallage' from time to time. They reckoned that they and the king would be better off if they collected the money and accounted for it themselves. With this end in view, in 1185, they made a bid of 300 silver marks (£200) and one gold mark (£6) to become tenants of the Crown and be free of the sheriff's interference in this and other matters. Granted vaguely what they had asked for, they found great difficulty in paying what had been promised. So they struck another bargain with King Richard I, whose concession was equally vague—'the king will do with the town according to his will'.

With commendable perseverance they tried again with King John in 1201, securing a charter of sufficient substance to form the basis of many a legal stand to be taken in the centuries to come. It granted them the right to have a guild of merchants, the right that all law-suits involving the burgesses should be heard within the borough and be conducted in accordance with

Cambridge just before the Norman Conquest
This map is of necessity largely conjecture and inference. The only completely certain features are the river and the bridge. There was most probably a defensive ditch, but not called King's Ditch as it was later. Of the seven churches shown, three—All Saints, St Benet's and St Peter's—are almost certainly pre-Conquest, one (St Edward's) very probably so and the other three possibly so. The street-plan is wholly conjectural and no street-names of this date are known. The diagrammatic distribution of dwellings shown here roughly reflects the statistics supplied by the Domesday Survey of 1086.

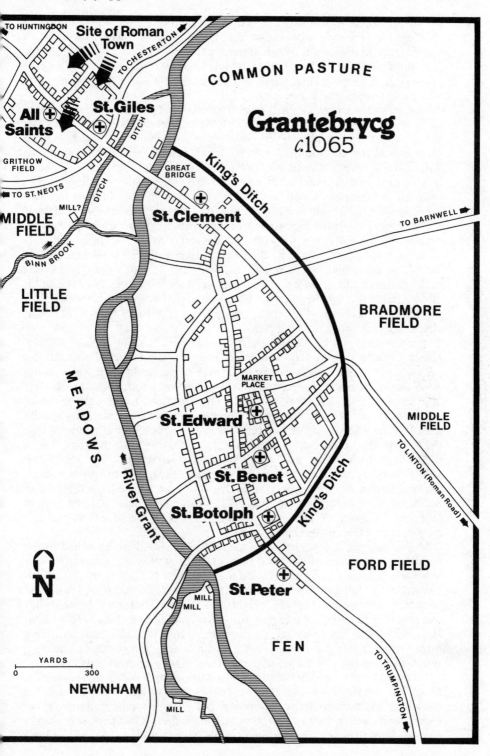

TO HUNTINGDON

Site of Roman Town

TO CHESTERTON

COMMON PASTURE

St. Giles

Grantebrycg
*c.*1065

All Saints

GRITHOW FIELD

TO ST. NEOTS

GREAT BRIDGE

King's Ditch

DITCH

DITCH

MIDDLE FIELD

MILL?

St. Clement

TO BARNWELL

BINN BROOK

LITTLE FIELD

BRADMORE FIELD

M E A D O W S

MARKET PLACE

St. Edward

MIDDLE FIELD

TO LINTON (Roman Road)

River Grant

St. Benet

St. Botolph

King's Ditch

N

FORD FIELD

St. Peter

MILL
MILL

F E N

YARDS
0   300

TO TRUMPINGTON

NEWNHAM

MILL

the custom already established, freedom from all tolls everywhere (a hollow privilege, for the same concession was made to most towns), the right to hold a fair in Rogation Week (later, somehow, transferred to Reach), freedom from 'scot-ale' and other devices used by royal officials to extract money for favours granted, and special protection for visiting merchants who paid the customary dues.

That cost the townsmen a further 250 marks. The outlay of such large sums either indicates the magnitude of the commerce of the town, or the farsighted and not altogether disinterested generosity of the leading members of the community, who by now probably numbered about 40, stiffened by several families of knightly class. The constant customary income of the town consisted of rents, known as 'hagable' and 'landgable', paid by householders and landholders, and had not altered for two centuries—in fact it remained unaltered for a further two centuries. Half of this amount thus raised consisted of more than 150 separate payments, ranging from a halfpenny to twopence; the rest consisted of three payments by large landholders, including the Prior of Barnwell. The total came to less than £8 a year, which would not go far. Mill rent, tolls on river-traffic, tolls in the market and fair, sale of municipal freedom, subscription to the guild, etc, probably brought in a further £70 a year. That would just suffice to pay the fee-farm rent, provide stocks and pillory and a few barrels of ale at election time or when the king called.

The shortcomings of the new charter were soon apparent; it did not specifically exclude the sheriff from interference in the town's financial and judicial affairs and it lacked any guarantee of perpetuity. However, King John was quite ready, indeed anxious, to grant yet another charter (for yet another fee of 250 marks) in 1207. This confirmed the previous one, particularly that the £60 rent should be paid (in two instalments) annually direct to the Exchequer. It granted 'for ever' the additional privilege that the townsmen should elect as reeve (prefect, provost, later mayor) 'whom they will and when they will' and also granted what was to prove, all too soon, the pious hope that they and their heirs might hold the town with all its appurtenances 'well and peaceably, freely and quietly, entirely and honourably'. Cambridge, in the eyes of the law, was a fully-fledged independent town at last, not a 'manor', not a 'hundred' containing manors, but a free borough of free men.

More than just a few barrels of ale and wine would be broached in the guildhall and taverns of the town throughout that May week in 1207 as the newly-elected mayor and bailiffs and the 'four-and-twenty' men of the town council led the celebrations in honour of their new status with a very real sense of achievement and civic pride, heightened by the realisation that what they had got, they had worked and paid for—they, and their fathers before them. It would be churlish to belittle their achievement or deride their justifiable pride therein, but one must be realistic. Their 'borough' was still—by modern standards, and even by the standards of the day—a wretched little town.

It consisted of some 500 buildings—twice as many if one included stables, pig-sties, cowsheds, barns, etc—only one of which, apart from the churches, was built of stone. There was not a single public building, again excepting churches, in the town, though the Tollbooth was probably then in course of construction and within a couple of decades the town would have its own gaol. The modest size of those churches, of which there were, or soon would be, a dozen, can be gauged even today by looking at the (reconstructed) St Peter's, the chancel-arch of St Giles' and the tower of St Benet's. There were only two main streets—though plenty of narrow, twisting 'lanes'—supposedly 'paved' with gravel, in fact paved with dung and filth and frequented as much by animals as by humans. When the river was in flood, which meant a rise of only a few feet, large areas of the town reverted to swamp, with only the 'hills' (Market Hill, Peas Hill, St Andrew's) relatively high and fairly dry. That river, the town's commercial artery, was also its main sewer. The King's Ditch was more of a rubbish-dump than a defence. Ten minutes' walk from the market-place in any direction would have brought one into the fields surrounding the town.

The power wielded by the mayor and bailiffs was largely one of control over buying and selling; their legal jurisdiction stopped far short of dealing with serious crime, which was still the concern of the sheriff and the county justices of the peace. However, buying and selling—not merely local produce, but commodities brought from afar as well—was the mainstay of the town. Given the position it had now reached, and the potential of its situation, there was every reason to suppose—as I do not doubt those burgesses did—that its prosperity and fame would increase. And so it would, so it did, but in a manner wholly different from what they had supposed. For, within two years of those celebrations, a new element was introduced into the human structure of the town; one which, I am sure, those junketing burgesses had never for one moment envisaged and one whose influence they could not have assessed.

*   *   *

Attempts to discover or invent explanations of its origin cannot alter the fact that nobody really knows when Cambridge University was founded, or by whom, or indeed whether it was ever founded at all but, like the town, just happened. Early universities grew naturally, often fortuitously, out of 'schools'. Some schools had existed since the days of King Alfred, even earlier. They were mostly sponsored by monasteries or bishops whose aim was to supply the Church with literate recruits, able, that is, to read and write Latin. Learning for its own sake did exist, however, giving rise to scholars who tended to congregate in small groups. Where they congregated, there was automatically a 'school', if only for as long as the scholars found it convenient to live there. It is quite certain that schools existed at Oxford in the latter part of the 12th century and that, taking their cue from the merchants who formed guilds for their mutual protection and advantage, the scholars there formed themselves into an organised guild which soon became known as a 'university'—another way of saying 'community'—after the model of those already established at Paris, Bologna and elsewhere.

The only clue we have as to the beginning of the university at Cambridge is the account given by the monastic chronicler, Roger of Wendover, of an incident at Oxford which occurred, he says, in 1209.

About that time a certain clerk at Oxford, absent from his studies, killed a woman by chance, and fled when he realised that she was dead. When the mayor of the town with many others ran to the scene and found the dead woman, they went to look for the killer in the lodging which he occupied with three other students. Failing to find the guilty man, they took his three fellows, who knew nothing whatever of the murder, and cast them into prison. A few days later, on the orders of the King of England, and in violation of ecclesiastical privilege, they were taken outside the town and hanged. After that, there departed from Oxford upwards of 3,000 of the clerks, masters as well as pupils, so that not one of the whole university remained. Some of them, quitting their studies, went to Cambridge, some even to Reading, leaving the town of Oxford empty.

Exaggerated, of course; most monastic accounts were, especially as regards numerical statements, and biased—in this case coloured by Roger's righteous indignation at the violation of ecclesiastical privilege by the civil authorities. Cantabs may find it slightly embarrassing to admit that the University of Cambridge probably owed its origin to the murder of a prostitute by an Oxford student, but the alternative explanations are far less credible. The fact is that students *did* come to Cambridge at about that time—not 3,000 of them, more likely 300—and a university *was* established there soon afterwards. It is on record, with a 'chancellor' at its head, by the year 1226 (in the 'Black Book' of New College, Oxford).

Roger's account, true or not, prompts questions to which imagination alone provides answers. A mass exodus like that suggests conditions of panic that the mere hanging of three students was unlikely to have caused; tension must have been building up for some time. Did the masters and students all leave at once, all together? If so, how did they manage for food and accommodation on what must have been at least a three-day journey? The question may be superfluous as regards the masters, who would have had money and horses; as for the students, they were no doubt as adept then at travelling long distances without any money, as are their modern counterparts, and even more adept at extracting the contents of larders and henhouses. Did they all arrive in Cambridge at once or in small bands over a period of weeks, months or years? There were a dozen other towns to which they might as easily have gone—why did they pick on Cambridge?

I do not think that, as has been suggested, the proximity of the great Fenland abbeys had anything to do with it. They are not all that near and later events show that, apart from some of the friars, the monastic fraternities were not very interested in the university. The only explanation that makes sense, apart from pure chance, is that 'schools' already existed at Cambridge—not just the ordinary 'grammar' schools, but cells of advanced studies—and that the fugitive masters, knowing this, decided to settle there. I would not rule out the possibility that another attraction of Cambridge was its reputation as a place where there were ample supplies of food and drink.

We can only guess at the initial effect on the town of this 'invasion'. One of the first results, I imagine, would be an unprecedented fluttering in the hearts of several hundred girls and young women, quickly followed by the fitting of more secure bolts and locks on doors by several hundred apprehensive fathers and husbands, then the flocking in from the surrounding villages of other females keen to ply a trade unfettered by the rules of any guild. Those members of the community who owned or rented house-room beyond their own needs, as well as those who were content to sleep on the rushes or straw themselves in order to make beds available for paying guests, would rejoice in the prospect of reaping a golden harvest—until they found out how little money the students had. Innkeepers and taverners could be sure of a trade boom, and brewers would quickly learn to produce an inferior brew, at standard price, which, served to their ordinary customers, would have landed them in the pillory or tumbril.

All is not guesswork concerning the early days of the university. One certainty is that the king, Henry III, was wholly in favour of it. He probably granted its first charter, though it has not survived; if he did, it is not likely to have cost the scholars a fraction of what it had cost the townsmen. In 1229 he sent a cordial invitation to the students of Paris, on whom 'unjust laws' were inflicting 'tribulations and distress', to come and pursue their studies in English towns (not specifying Cambridge, or any other town) where he assured them of freedom and peace. How many came, we do not know but those who came were not likely to have found much peace, more likely to have destroyed such peace as there was. For another certainty is that where there were students, there was trouble. This is revealed by letters which the king addressed to the sheriff of Cambridgeshire and the Bishop of Ely in May 1231: 'In our town of Cantebrigge is gathered a multitude of students—many of them are rebellious and incorrigible. They are not under the tutelage of any master but claim to be scholars when in fact they are not'.

The sheriff was ordered to take a strong body of armed men to Cambridge in order to expel from the town all such rebellious students as were notified to him by the chancellor, masters and the bishop and to imprison any still found there after proclamation and the lapse of 15 days. It is evident, then, that there were a lot of students at Cambridge, although the exact size of a 'multitude' is difficult to determine, and that the university authorities had no control over those who chose not to be controlled. The presence of these latter presented the mayor and bailiffs with a problem which they did not even try to solve—to be fair, they lacked adequate means and authority, and had a lot of other problems to tackle—but hastily passed to the king and sheriff, even though it meant tolerating the interference they had sought to get rid of.

At the same time the king sent the mayor and bailiffs a letter which, besides confirming several things stated above, reveals something of the other side of the picture:

A multitude of students, from this country and overseas, come to our town of Cantebrigge, which pleases us very much, for it benefits our kingdom and does us honour, and you must be pleased to have the students among you. But we hear that the charges in your inns and lodging-houses are so exorbitant that, unless you do something to moderate them, the students will be obliged to leave your town, and we do not want that to happen.

The king issued a strict order that the lodging-charges be supervised 'as is customary in a university' by two masters and two honest townsmen, and a fair rate fixed and maintained. This fleecing of students by lodging-house keepers was not peculiar to Cambridge, a copy of that same letter was sent to the mayor and bailiffs of Oxford, and the reference to university custom seems to imply that it was universal practice, as indeed one would expect.

Now, the presence of a few (or even 'many') wild young men in the student body—their wildness almost certainly overstated by thwarted masters and timid burgesses alike—and the over-charging for lodgings could not possibly constitute a cause of war. True, they represented real grievances, one on either side. They ought to have been capable of rapid settlement. But subsequent events, the detailed reporting of which begins some 30 years later and continues with ever increasing detail and only occasional intermission for the next six and a half centuries, reinforce the belief that there was bitter animosity between the university and the town from the very first moment that the two began to live together. Let it be said at the outset that not *all* the townspeople hated *all* the university men all the time. Nevertheless it seems pertinent to ask why should any of them have hated any of the other party, when there was mutual gain for all of them in living together peaceably? What did Cambridge townspeople in general have against students in general?

Firstly—and foremost, I believe—students were disliked as they were 'foreigners', outsiders, interlopers; some of them foreigners in the modern sense that they came from foreign countries like France, Italy, Scotland, Wales, etc, all of them foreigners in that they came from outside Cambridge. They were not known, did not belong and could not be traced if and when they departed. Unlike the other foreigners who came regularly to the fairs— and they likewise were the object of profound suspicion and mistrust— students could not be 'attached', in the event of misdemeanour, by distraint of their possessions, for the majority of them had none except what they carried on their persons.

Being young did not count in their favour, as it might today. Many of them were very young when commencing their studies, mere boys of 14 or 15 years, though seven years older by the time they had completed their studies, if they ever did. Being boys, they behaved like boys. Town lads were kept more or less under control by being compulsorily in a 'tithing', that is, being enrolled in a recognised group, the other members of which could be held responsible for their behaviour, or by being apprenticed to masters who accepted responsibility for them as well as teaching them their trade. The academic masters, in theory at least, had similar responsibility for their pupils, but no other means of enforcing discipline than by caning, which never did produce the results claimed for it. The town watchmen were there to prevent night wanderers, but preferred to keep out of sight when a gang of roistering students appeared on their beat.

Other writers on this topic have explained the Town/Gown conflict in a single word—'jealousy' (on the part of the townsmen, of course). It would be pointless to deny that a lot of people did (and still do) resent those with intellects and faculties superior to their own and that their resentment took the form of an expressed contempt for 'learning'. Whatever one feels about that, it must be admitted that in one respect the townsmen's jealous resentment was excusable, namely the privilege enjoyed by the students as 'clerks' or 'clerics'. The mere fact that they were students entitled them to 'benefit of clergy'; they could be tried for an offence by a civil court, but only punished by an ecclesiastical court and, since the Church did not condone the death penalty, a student could 'get away with murder'. Coupled with resentment of that privilege was a growing mistrust of the 'religious', in which category the students were placed (and which indeed was the aim of most of them) despite the irreligious conduct of some of them.

Add to all that a few youthful pranks attributable to high spirits, cunning tricks to make the odd penny or avoid parting with it, the consumption of ale beyond their holding capacity, the swaggering gait and loud guffaws of boys who thought they were men, insolent remarks about 'peasants' addressed to no one in particular but falling on the ear of some highly respectable merchant—and the unpopularity of the students needs no further explanation; of some of them, that is.

As for the attitude of the students towards the townsmen, we have absolutely nothing to go on at this early stage. Later, much later, it is well attested and can be summed up in one brief phrase—arrogant contempt. If it was any different in the beginning the only modification I would suggest would be 'amused contempt'.

King Henry unwittingly helped to foster this antipathy between the university and town by a measure which was intended to promote more peaceful relations. In response to a request from the chancellor he banned a tournament which had been arranged to take place at Cambridge in 1225, did the same thing again in 1234 and four times more in the course of the next few years. The reason given for the ban was that the studies of the scholars would be disturbed. They certainly would, for these local tournaments—popularly supposed to be gatherings of the nobility and gentry for the display of valour and chivalry—attracted all the rogues, riff-raff and loose women from miles around, just like a fair; gambling, brawling and drinking were the order of the day and night. The students would not have missed it at any price—especially those young bloods who, 'rebellious and incorrigible', were only at the university for the fun of it. In actual fact, the tournaments *did* take place, despite the ban. Various knights had their lands seized 'because they took part in a tournament at Cambridge' and only got them back on payment of a fine and the town itself was stripped for a time of all its franchises which were restored on payment of 100 marks. This did nothing to endear them to the students. And if the tournements had not been held, the townsmen would still have had a grudge against the university, for an event like that brought in a lot of money, especially to innkeepers and victuallers.

I never found the study of Latin all that irritating myself, but there must have been something particularly provoking about that early university regime—was it the corporal punishment?—for it seems that when the students were not annoying the townsmen they sought light relief in fighting among themselves. This probably did not worry the townsmen much. It worried the chancellor—not so much that his charges were prone to sticking daggers in each other as that, when they did, they might have to go all the way to Rome to get absolution for their transgressions, thereby missing their studies for quite a long time. So in 1233 he and the Bishop of Ely petitioned Pope Gregory IX and obtained permission for absolution to be granted by the bishop. They went a step further and secured authorisation that sinning students should not be tried in any court outside the diocese of Ely, so long as they were willing to be tried by the chancellor or the bishop. This was the first step on the long road leading towards exclusive university privilege.

The next came in 1242, this time prompted by the king, and the excluded party was the town magistrature, the mayor and bailiffs—though the term 'magistrates' hardly applies as yet. The king wrote to the sheriff as follows (I have simplified, condensed and modernised all those documents quoted; the full text in translation is rather tedious, and not always very comprehensible): 'Quarrels have arisen between clerks and laymen—mischiefs perpetrated against the Crown and others. If any scholar is involved in an offence meriting imprisonment, and the burgesses are powerless or negligent to deal with it, you, on the order of the chancellor, shall imprison the culprit and keep him until the chancellor orders his delivery.'

It was less than 20 years since the burgesses had paid a huge sum of money to be confirmed in their freedom from interference by the sheriff and here was the king ordering the sheriff to interfere! And on the orders of the chancellor, who had hardly been in the place long enough to know what was what. No wonder they protested!

A few years later, during Lent in 1249, there was a serious outbreak of violence in the town. Houses were broken into and looted; several people were killed and more wounded. A number of the students, in fear or disgust, left Cambridge and went to Oxford—that in itself speaks volumes for the state of affairs at Cambridge, though they probably soon had reason to regret the move. The king countermanded his previous order to the sheriff and told him to provide an armed force for the protection of two justices appointed to go to Cambridge to inquire into the offences committed by both students and townsmen. The findings of the inquiry are not on record.

It seems, then, that the king was well wide of the mark in thinking that the burgesses of Cambridge were 'glad to have the students among you'. A state of affairs with which the mayor and bailiffs could barely cope, even had there been no university, was rendered even more difficult by its presence. The town was growing in size—it now had 15 parish churches and nine religious houses within its bounds—although its bounds, as regards the actual town, were still only ten minutes away from its centre. It needed peace and stability if it was to develop into a really prosperous town. Alas, peace and stability was precisely what it was not going to get.

Chapter 2

War and peace 1260-1280

Events already described, as well as those to be outlined in following chapters, tend to give the impression that Cambridge in the 13th and 14th centuries was a little hell-on-earth, devoid of all law and order. Whereas the truth is that Cambridge was not very much worse in this respect than anywhere else. Murder, robbery, rape and pillage were common features of medieval life everywhere. They appear to have been more common in towns because people were more numerous there and crime more difficult to detect. When detected, it was more difficult to establish guilt. Against the elaborate machinery of hue-and-cry, watch and ward, coroner's inquests, theoretical collective responsibility, personal pledges and so on, is to be set the protection afforded the criminal by unlit streets, deserted stretches of countryside only minutes away from the town centre, the principle of sanctuary upheld by the churches which put mercy before justice, and the universal mistrust of the law which made many turn a blind eye to crime, to the point of removing a dead body on to a neighbouring property rather than report it.

All this is graphically illustrated in the prosaic entries on the official record of the Assizes held at Cambridge in the year 1260. I here quote from it, briefly, only those incidents relating to the town, and then only those in which students were involved. And this, let me emphasise, was for a period of several years during which no serious trouble had been officially reported in the town:

David de Boyton of Warwicks killed William de Boyton, his friend, between Cambridge and Newnham, and immediately fled. Outlawed. No chattels, being a stranger clerk.
Robert FitzWalter of Middlesex, Thomas Lasham and John Lowe wounded Gilbert Swan in the parish of All Saints, so that he died. They fled and are outlawed. They had no chattels, and were not in a tithing, being stranger clerks.
Malefactors unknown met John Smith at Bridge Street and killed him. The hue-and-cry was raised in the whole town, but the town did not arrest them, so is fined. On the night when this happened John, with many others, was on watch duty. The coroner did not arrest the other watchmen, so he is fined.
Malefactors unknown killed John Betun in St Mary's churchyard. John Saleman and Simon Ely were arrested for the crime and gaoled. They were later bailed by royal writ with 24 men as pledges, but the bailiff lost the writ. John and Simon now appear to defend themselves and elect trial by a jury of 12, who say they are not guilty. The jury say that Bernard le Suer was guilty of the murder and that he has fled. So he is outlawed. He had no chattels and was not in a tithing.
Aunger, son of Simon Baker, and John, the clerk of Master Guy, had a quarrel on

the bridge of Cambridge. Aunger struck John in the belly with a knife so that he died at once. He fled to sanctuary in St Clement's church and abjured the realm. He had no chattels and was not in a tithing, being a clerk. Later it was testified that Ralph le Bernicus with other clerks by night . . . [unfinished].

Roger Ely accused Richard, son of Hugh le Rus that when he was peaceably in his own house on the evening of January 18 1257, Richard came and gave him a wound in the left breast three inches long and three inches deep, and another wound in the right arm, one inch long. Richard comes and says that he ought not to answer here as he is a clerk. The bishop's officer, present in court, claims him as a clerk. But that it may be known how he is to be delivered, as guilty or not guilty, to the bishop, let the truth of the matter be decided by the jury. They say he is guilty, so let him be delivered to the bishop as such.

Those cases, while illustrating the readiness of students to settle arguments with the knife, point to the cumbersome and ineffective nature of the legal machinery of the time. The others, which I have not quoted, underline the utter inadequacy of the authorities, especially in the town, to operate that machinery. There were 26 cases heard at that Assize, concerning three murders, 14 thefts, two accidental deaths, four robberies with violence and three assaults. In five cases the plaintiff did not appear, in 17 cases the defendants did not appear; more than half of them had sought sanctuary in one or other of the town churches, then abjured the realm. Five people escaped from the town gaol and of a total of 40 people charged (plus a number not charged because not known) only two were sentenced, both to a further spell in gaol. Even while that court was in session a fresh outburst of violence was brewing. It began, as was not unusual, with a dispute amongst the students themselves.

The townsmen lumped all the students together as 'foreigners'. They grouped themselves into 'nationalities'; those coming from north of the Trent were 'Northerners', those from south of it were 'Southerners'—at Oxford there were Easterners and Westerners as well—and, of course, the Welsh and Scots formed separate groups. What began as a North v South skirmish developed into a free-for-all, involving townsmen and gownsmen alike. Into the fray plunged jubilantly every idle beggar, professional thief and cut-throat living in the town and neighbourhood. There were plenty of this sort, constantly attested but rarely identified and their role in the war must not be overlooked. For several days the town was in a state of confusion and terror. Houses were attacked and plundered indiscriminately. Heads were broken and corpses left lying in the streets.

News reached the king in the form of a complaint in 1265 by Master Robert de Driffield and his fellow scholars that 'certain malefactors, cleric as well as lay, of the town of Cambridge broke their inns, beat them and plundered them of their goods'. Some authorities have said that the 'goods' included valuable university records, but I can find no confirmation of this. On November 24 two justices were commissioned to deal with the matter. On January 13 the king instructed the Justices in Eyre in the county that, in addition to the ordinary cases, they were particularly to 'look into the contentions which have arisen between the university and the people of Cambridge', to deal with any further excesses without waiting for other justices to be sent and to impose due fines at their discretion.

The local magistrates had apparently already acted with exceptional promptitude and perhaps rather more zeal than was consistent with justice. Taking the view that the fracas was entirely the fault of the students, they had hanged several and fined and imprisoned others, including several of the masters. It must not be assumed that the learned doctors and masters stood aloof from these unseemly brawls; they were as adept at wielding cudgels or swords as any of their pupils. Because of this, on February 11, two itinerant justices were sent specifically to Cambridge 'because the king wishes justice to be done for both sides'. They were ordered to appoint local juries 'so that they do not proceed to hanging or mutilation of the clerks, but punish them in some other way by the counsel of the university'. They were also to cause proclamation to be made by the sheriff of Norfolk and Suffolk that 'all clerks of those counties might safely come to Cambridge and peacefully pursue their studies there as in former times'. So it would seem that there had been a mass exodus from Cambridge of the East Anglian students.

In mid-March pardon was granted to Master John de Depedale, Master Hugh de Thornham and 16 scholars of Norfolk and Suffolk, also to Roger Parleben, son of the Cambridge coroner, and nine other townsmen 'for the assault lately made upon certain northern scholars of the university of Cambridge' of which they had been found guilty by the local magistrates. One account of the affair states that 16 of the townsmen were hanged, but I think that the author (Fuller) probably overlooked the pardons.

Neither side could rightly claim victory in the battle, though no doubt both sides did. A number on the university side were more than ready to quit the field of battle. Seeing no hope of a peaceful existence at Cambridge, a contingent of the more serious-minded students, with the king's consent, left the town and went to Northampton where, with a similar party from Oxford, they established a new university. It was short-lived, however, mainly because of the disapproval of the chancellor and masters of Oxford. On February 1 1265 the king wrote to the mayor and citizens of Northampton:

As a result of certain great contention at Cambridge three years ago some of the clerks withdrew and transferred to our town of Northampton to establish a new university there. Believing that the town would benefit as well as ourselves, we agreed to their request at the time . . . now we understand that, if this university remained there, it would greatly prejudice our town of Oxford . . ..

It was definitely not the townspeople of Oxford who pleaded for the return of the students and even more definitely not the townspeople of Cambridge. In fact it was 'all the bishops' who urged that the nascent new university be nipped in the bud. Accordingly it was and the crest-fallen refugees trooped back to Cambridge.

History does not record, as far as I know, whether the townspeople of Northampton counted that as a fortunate deliverance or an unfair deprivation. I cannot help thinking that the attitude of the bishops and magnates and the ready acceptance of their advice by the king was rather short-sighted. I would have thought that the dispersal of the students in smaller numbers to a greater number of towns was one possible solution to the problem of the incessant strife which now racked the two university towns. On further reflection, it might equally have meant the creation of yet more trouble-centres. It is evident that the chancellors of both universities were intent on maintaining their position of unique privilege; and likely that the bishops were determined that no more such privileged positions should be created.

Two years later, in the spring of 1267, the king himself came to Cambridge with a large army, not to subdue the militant students but to put a stop to the depredations of the insurgent barons entrenched in the Isle of Ely. He failed in that and, as soon as he had gone, the town was subjected to a violent raid by the barons who demonstrated the near-impossibility of defending it. He did, however, get a clearer picture of the situation at first hand, from the university point of view, and a year later issued a charter, the most specific and comprehensive so far, aimed at 'the peace and tranquillity as also the utility of the scholars of the university of Cambridge'. This is how it was to be achieved:

1 Two aldermen were to be appointed, associated with four of the more discreet and lawful burgesses, who should all swear loyalty to the king, and assist and consult with the mayor and bailiffs to keep the peace, hold the assizes, search out malefactors and disturbers of the peace, night-wanderers and harbourers of thieves and rogues.

2 In every parish of the town two men should be elected from among the more law-abiding parishioners, sworn to inquire diligently every two weeks as to suspected persons lodged in the parish. Householders should be held responsible for anyone lodged for three nights in their houses.

3 No shopkeeper or stallholder should buy foodstuffs in Cambridge or on the way to the town, or buy anything for re-sale before 9 am, on pain of a fine according to the nature of the offence.

4 If a layman inflicted a wound on a clerk, he was to be arrested at once; if the injury was serious, the layman was to be put in prison and kept there until he made reasonable satisfaction to the clerk.

5 If a clerk seriously wounded a layman, he should be imprisoned in the town gaol until the chancellor should demand him.

6 Bakers and brewers who contravened regulations governing weight, quality and price should be fined for the first offence, forfeit their bread or ale for the second and for the third offence be punished by standing in the pillory or being led round the town in a tumbril (and subjected to various indignities on the way).

7 Every baker should have his own seal (a wooden stamp) and mark his bread with it so that it be known whose bread it was and be heavily fined for failure to comply.

8 Every ale-brewer should hang out a sign or else forfeit his ale.

9 Wines should be sold commonly and without discrimination as between layman and clerks once the barrel had been broached.

10 The assize of bread was to be made twice a year, ie, within a fortnight of Michaelmas and on the Feast of St Mary in March; the assize of ale to be made at the same time, according to the price of corn and malt. Whenever an assize was made, the chancellor of the university or his deputy was to be present if they so wished; if not present, then the assize should be considered invalid.

11 'Moreover the king wills that the town of Cambridge be cleansed of dung and filth and be kept clean and that the conduits be opened as of old they used to be, and be kept open, in order that filth may flow away through them, unless some other use or need stand in the way and that obstacles impeding their passage be removed and especially that the great ditch of the town be cleansed. For the observing of which things there shall be appointed two of the more lawful burgesses in every street, sworn before the mayor and bailiffs, the chancellor and masters being invited to this if they wish to be present.'

I think you will agree that there was little in that document—it can hardly be called a 'charter'—that was likely to put a stop to armed gangs of young men roaming the streets by day and night in search of trouble. It was clearly inspired by complaints from the chancellor who was anxious mainly to ensure an adequate, fairly-priced supply of food and drink for himself and his students, safer lodgings and a less obnoxious environment. As such it was highly commendable, especially on the latter point. At the assizes of 1260 a complaint had been made against one Golda of Ditton who had built a hithe 'on the river of Heneya [a branch of the river roughly opposite Trinity Hall] so that whereas the water of the river used to run through the gutters of the town for the convenience of the inhabitants, it is now obstructed'. It was not until three and a half centuries later that this method of street-cleansing was to operate successfully again.

But the more progressive of the burgesses were not likely to thank the king for giving them an elementary lesson in the rudiments of town-management. Even the most dull-witted amongst them must have seen at once that the 'charter' was the thin end of the wedge of university privilege being adroitly inserted into the mass of municipal authority, a mass as yet far from solid or stable. As a legal document, the charter had so many loop-holes in it that the town authorities could not have made it a sound constructive basis for lasting peace even if they had wanted to, which they certainly did not. Hostilities were renewed almost at once, as soon as the aftermath of the barons' war had been dealt with. In July 1269 the king was obliged to fall back on the method he had used 38 years before:

Because the bailiffs and burgesses of Cantebrigge are not only negligent but incompetent in the suppression of the insolences of malefactors and other things harmful to the masters and scholars of the university, the king orders that, whenever the bailiffs and burgesses are thus negligent or incompetent, the sheriff of Cantebrig-geshire shall come with a sufficient posse of the county and cause such harmful things to be suppressed whenever he is so requested on behalf of the university.

I do not know whether the king realised that that order was a direct contra-diction of the charter which he had granted to the townsmen. I am quite certain that the burgesses did. They, or their fathers, had paid dearly for the right to exclude the sheriff from their town (they could not keep him away from the castle) and now the king was saying that the chancellor of the university should invite him in. It was an insult even harder to swallow than 'negligent' or 'incompetent'. The simple truth of the matter was, of course, that neither town nor university was equipped with adequate means of keeping law and order and, all things considered, it was just as well; the university was sufficiently threatened as it was, without trained bands being brought into the fight.

The King was determined that 'his' university should survive. In April 1270 he again visited Cambridge (Barnwell Priory alone made these early royal visits possible) accompanied by Prince Edward, who personally assumed the role of mediator between the conflicting parties, and a sort of treaty or 'composition' was drawn up, agreed and sealed with the common seals of the university and the town and with the royal seal. The object of the exercise was again to secure 'peace' of both university and town, but again with a bias towards the university:

Each year, within a fortnight of the time when the masters resume their lectures after Michaelmas, there shall be chosen five scholars of discretion from any of the English counties, three from Scotland, two from Wales and three from Ireland, and ten burgesses, ie, seven from the town and three from the suburb [not altogether clear, but I think this means that part of the town north of the river] who shall swear a personal oath that, cleric or lay, on behalf of all, they will keep the peace and tranquillity of the university, and cause others to do the same.

Likewise all other clerks and laymen shall take oath to remain peacefully at their studies and, if any rebellious students or laymen be found who, having first been warned, will not behave themselves, then the scholars, in so far as is becoming their status and clerical orders, shall assist the burgesses in arresting them.

There shall be chosen also certain masters, who shall write down the names of all principals, all houses and all occupants of the same; they shall likewise swear that they will not admit any known trouble-makers in their houses and that they will report those found to be trouble-makers. Laymen having servants or lodgers in their houses shall take a similar oath and require the same of their servants and lodgers.

If rebels are discovered, either by clerks or by laymen, they shall be expelled from the university or from the town. If they are so numerous that they cannot be expelled by the burgesses with the help of the clerks, they shall be reported to the king.

If it happen that any of the elected clerks or laymen be absent, others shall be co-opted in their place. Before the election, each party shall swear to uphold the privileges of the university and to observe the terms of this agreement.

Thus was born an institution—it later acquired the names of 'Great Congregation' and 'Black Assembly'—which was to endure in modified form for six centuries and give rise to endless bickering. Again it was the thin end of the wedge, tapped a bit more firmly. Yet, apart from perhaps too much reliance on the binding-force of a personal oath, it was a sensible agreement, which did usher in a period of (almost) peace lasting for nearly 20 years. Three months later the king 'for the peace of the masters and scholars' imposed a complete ban on tournaments in the town or within five miles of it, on pain of forfeiture of all their possessions by the knights and barons. This time the ban proved effective, aided by the departure of many of the said knights on a crusade.

By 'almost peace' I meant as between university and town. Each side had

Cambridge c 1280
There is a good deal of conjecture about this map but most of the features shown are well documented by the Hundred Rolls and other records. It shows two significant features: 1 The extraordinary extent to which the town and its immediate environs have been 'invaded' by religious fraternities—the largest, Barnwell Priory, is just off the map to the east—with the evident concurrence of the townspeople, despite the fact that within the town were no less than 15 parish churches and 2 The fact that, although the university had been in existence for about 70 years, it had acquired no 'territory' of its own in the town by this date.

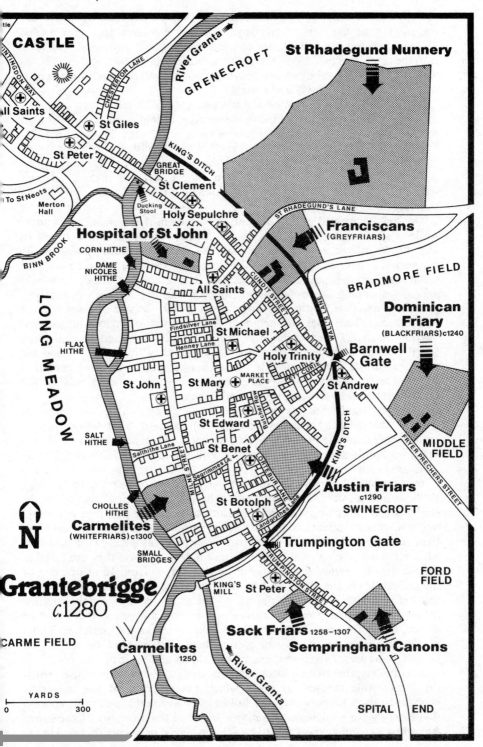

CASTLE

River Granta

GRENECROFT

St Rhadegund Nunnery

CHESTERTON LANE

HUNTINGDON WAY

All Saints

St Giles

St Peter

KING'S DITCH

GREAT BRIDGE

To St Neots

Merton Hall

Ducking Stool

St Clement

Holy Sepulchre

ST RHADEGUND'S LANE

Franciscans
(GREYFRIARS)

Hospital of St John

CORN HITHE

DAME NICOLES HITHE

BINN BROOK

All Saints

CUNDITSTREET

BRADMORE FIELD

WALL'S LANE

Dominican Friary
(BLACKFRIARS) c1240

Findsilver Lane

St Michael

Henney Lane

FLAX HITHE

Holy Trinity

Barnwell Gate

L O N G   M E A D O W

St John

St Mary

MARKET PLACE

PETY CURIE

St Andrew

St Edward

KING'S DITCH

FRYER PRECHERS STREET

MIDDLE FIELD

SALT HITHE

Salthithe Lane

St Benet

Segrimmes La.

MILNE STREET

Austin Friars
c1290

CHOLLES HITHE

St Botolph

SWINECROFT

OAREBUR LANE

Landgrythes Lane

Carmelites
(WHITEFRIARS) c1300

SMALL BRIDGES

Trumpington Gate

N

Grantebrigge
*c.*1280

KING'S MILL

St Peter

TRUMPINGTON STREET

FORD FIELD

CARME FIELD

Carmelites
1250

Sack Friars 1258–1307

River Granta

Sempringham Canons

YARDS

0   300

SPITAL   END

its own troubles, mostly of a minor nature, stemming from other sources—
the ringing of the bell of St Benet's to summon students to lectures,
arguments over tithes, the duties of the 'rectors' (later 'proctors'), disputes
over the respective jurisdiction of archdeacon and chancellor, and arguments
with the merchants of Lynn over payment of toll—all of which were settled
without recourse to knives and cudgels.

It so happens that in this period of calm an inquiry into every aspect of
the town's affairs was made. From the answers to this inquiry can be drawn
the first complete picture of the town and its occupants. The year is 1278.
The material is the survey known as the Hundred Rolls. From it one learns
the names of most of the inhabitants of the town, what property they owned
or rented, for how much, from whom, where some of them lived, and
scores of other details. Map 2 conveys some of the information given. The
rest may be summarised thus:

The town consisted of 15 parishes, two of them (Holy Sepulchre and St
Andrew's) very small, with only six houses each; the rest with between 16
and 40. In all there were 500 houses, 84 shops (including stalls in the
market), 16 inns, 11 large barns or warehouses and 41 vacant sites (the
result of fires perhaps). From the 287 house-holders listed, it would
appear—assuming a proportion of families who did not own property—
that the population of the town was about 2,000, the size of a fairly large
village today. That does not include the university, the religious houses, the
vagrant element (which might run into hundreds, thousands in fair-time)
but it does include the large suburb of Barnwell with 90 houses and the
small suburb of Newnham with nine. About a quarter of the population
were farmers, mostly with holdings of 18 acres or less. The bulk of the
inhabitants lived by trading, services and crafts.

The most significant feature arising from an analysis of this mass of
detail is that an extraordinary number of people—at least 60—owned or
rented more than one or two houses. There were wives and widows with five
each, husbands and wives with seven, and one couple, John and Sabina
Aylsham, with *nine*. The inference is clear; these extra houses—apart from
a few housing labourers, servants and artisans—were being used to lodge
students and masters. I do not know what rent was being charged to the
students (probably no more than a penny or twopence per head per week)
nor how many students could be packed into one small house (never less
than four, I would think, and frequently as many as a dozen). I do know
what rents were being paid by the house-holders, because they are listed in
precise detail. *Annual* cash rents for houses ranged from 1d at one end of
the scale to 15s at the other, with the average somewhere around 4s. A large
number of houses, as well as parcels of land, were held on purely nominal
payments of a rose, a pair of gloves (value ½d), a peppercorn, a root of
ginger, or the furnishing of a candle or lamp in one of the churches. Those
nine houses of the Aylshams were costing them, each year, a total of 15s 8½d
in cash, two roses, two cloves, one pair of gloves and ½ oz of cummin.

It is obvious, therefore, especially if one adds to the lodging-house profits
the incalculable amount of trade which the presence of the university
brought to shop-keepers and stall-holders—to say nothing of innkeepers—
that catering for students was a major factor in the economy of the town.
Anyone who would expect this to be acknowledged or openly revealed in the

50 closely-written pages of the Hundred Rolls would be very disappointed. The 14 leading townsmen who constituted the 'jury' supplied information in minute detail as to every building, every plot of land, every half-penny paid, every church and monastery (not just the nine religious houses in the town, but the 26 others all over the country which had a financial stake in the town) and also the mills, fisheries, markets, fairs, ditches and bridges. They refer to their charters and liberties, record the fact that they have gallows, tumbril, pillory and 'all other instruments for doing justice'. And what do they have to say about the university? Just this (quoted verbatim):

The chancellor and masters of the university of Cambridge hold three messuages in the town, two of which they had by gift of Nicholas de Hedon, clerk, the other by gift of John of Thriplow, chaplain. But what rent they pay for the said houses the jury do not know and cannot find out.

They say that the chancellor and masters of the university of Cambridge have appropriated to themselves of their own authority more liberties than are granted in the charters which they hold of the king's predecessors, by sentences of excommunication compelling the bailiffs of the town to take a bodily oath against those who are the concern of the king and his bailiffs, to the prejudice of the king and contrary to the charters.

They also reveal that five masters each hold one house, all in the parish of St Michael's; one is the rector of the parish, another the Archdeacon of Ely. Apart from that, *not one word* about the university. It almost looks as though those 14 good and honest burgesses—nine of whom held 29 houses and 17 shops between them—were trying to pretend that the university was not there. Or perhaps they were hoping that it would go away, whilst knowing full well that, if it did, a fair slice of their livelihood would go with it.

Chapter 3

Stubborn resistance 1280-1323

The university did not go away. Firmly backed by royal authority and with a bit of belated, but very practical, help from the bishop, it was enabled to gain a foothold of a new kind in 1284. The Bishop of Ely, Hugh de Balsham, had proposed in 1280 to replace the monks of his Hospital of St John with scholars who should 'dwell together in the university of Cambridge according to the rule of the scholars at Oxford who are called of Merton', on condition that the alms of the poor coming to the said hospital were not thereby diminished. King Edward I heartily approved. As he put it: 'It befits the king's excellence, informed by the best examples, to assent willingly to deeds whereby men may be made wise for the utility of the commonwealth, and by their prudence advantage accrue in the rule of the realm and of the priesthood etc'. That is the first reference I know of to the university as an asset in the governance of the realm; it rapidly became an accepted belief, and was given practical application 15 years later when both universities were asked to send two or three of 'the more discreet and most expert in written law' to the parliament at Lincoln to give advice on matters of State.

The brethren already established in the hospital did not approve of the bishop's plan. Monks and students apparently did not mix very well. After four years most of the students, still under the bishop's patronage, were removed to two houses near the church of St Peter's outside the Trumpington Gate and endowed with perpetual possession of the property, the church of St Peter and two mills. The hospital was compensated by the gift of other property and a few years later the king ordered that all the food-stuffs confiscated for breach of the regulations concerning forestalling should, with the assent of the chancellor and mayor, be delivered to the master of the hospital for the maintenance of the poor scholars and others there. Thus was founded the first Cambridge college, *St Peter's House*. At last, nearly 80 years after the beginning of the university, some of the scholars—a mere handful, it is true—were housed in such a way that they could be locked in at night. Why the scheme was not followed up by the wholesale adoption of 'colleges' immediately is one of the mysteries of university history. Perhaps it was simply a matter of finance and architecture. Those houses which the first Peterhouse scholars occupied would be simple structures like the rest of the houses in the town, made of a timber frame with infilling of wattle and daub. Stone-faced walls, with a core of flint and rubble, were very costly to build. Those of Peterhouse, often pointed out as the oldest part of the university, date from much later.

The example set by the bishop did not go unheeded. A few years later Roger de Redingfield, chaplain, granted all his property in Cambridge—three houses, 26 acres of land and the church of the Friars of the Penitence of Jesus (already suppressed)—to the university and Matilda de Walde gave them the advowson of St Michael's church. Both acts were done for the benefit of the souls of the king and queen and of other benefactors of the university, for the payment of expenses incurred in the defence of its liberties and for the sustenance of poor scholars. I shall not attempt to enumerate the many hundreds of similar pious endowments which follow on from this time. They are probably no more numerous than in preceding centuries, only appear so because each one had to be recorded and licensed (and paid for) in accordance with the provisions of the Statute of Mortmain (designed to curb the excessive acquisition of property by religious foundations, which included colleges). The point of mentioning them at all is that they indicate a growing support for the university, from both within and without the town. They are also, incidentally, one of the causes of the increasing friction between the university and the religious houses, which were also at this time thriving on benefactions, still coming into existence, in fact. The Gilbertine priory was founded in 1293 by Cicely St Edmund with a gift of 60 acres of land and property worth £2 a year. The town was not too pleased, for its revenue from the property dropped by 10s. But laymen did not make a fuss because some people decided to invest all their wealth in spiritual salvation. It was bodily conflict that caused a sudden flare-up of the war in 1290.

At the centre of the drama was one Bartholomew Gogging. He had been, initially, a draper, one of four in the town, all of whom in 1260 were accused of selling cloth which did not comply with regulations. He was also, in 1278, a farmer of 23 acres which he had acquired by marrying Joanna, the daughter of John Porthors, one of the wealthiest men in the town, who lived in the manor-house later called (for no very good reason) 'School of Pythagoras'. He owned a stall in the market-place and five houses in three different parishes—a man of some substance. With him was associated Richard Lawrence, who also owned five houses. Both men were 'clerks' in 1290; both, that is, members of the university and burgesses at the same time, the earliest examples known of a breed of opportunists who believed in having a foot in both camps when hostilities broke out. The advantage of this was demonstrated when Geoffrey de Grislee, one of the many students being lodged by either Gogging or Lawrence, was killed in a brawl. Gogging, Lawrence and a third bailiff, Roger de Withersfield, were arrested and charged with murder. All were found guilty and Withersfield was hanged. The other two claimed benefit of clergy and both satisfied the bishop of their innocence (to be more precise, both were able to find sufficient compurgators to swear to their innocence). But both, as a result of the charge, had forfeited their goods and chattels to the Crown, Gogging to the value of over £42, Lawrence £26, and both were still vainly petitioning for the restoration of the forfeits seven years later, despite repeated orders authorising it. I doubt whether they ever got their money back and I am surprised that the word 'Gogging' did not enter into the local vocabulary as did 'Quisling' very much later, nationally.

The disturbances, of which that incident was a part, caused the appointment of two justices to go to Cambridge to deal with 'robberies, homicides and other trespasses committed by the scholars and the burgesses upon one another'. I do not know all the details and if I did I would not inflict them upon you. The odd brawl now and then can be exciting; incessant brawling, like incessant anything, becomes a bore. That commission was followed a year later by another, this time 'touching discords between the rich and poor of the town of Cambridge as to the many taxes levied by the rich upon the poor without reasonable cause'. Well, it made a change.

That was not the first insance, and far from being the last, of the town authorities damaging their own cause by their injustice, unfairness and incompetence. In mitigation of their shortcomings, perhaps it ought to be said that the legal documents on which their authority was founded were only concerned with rights and privileges. They said nothing about duties and responsibilities to the community. This could be because they were taken for granted, because nobody envisaged them, or because there was never any money available from the communal chest for the provision of public amenities, or because to have provided them on a communal basis would have deprived individuals of the opportunity to safeguard their souls by acts of charity. None of those reasons, though, justified the imposition of tallage on those who could least afford to pay it, nor the misappropriation of money collected, with royal sanction, for some specific urban amenity, such as 'pavage', which enters the picture at about this date and stays there for a very long time.

Pavage was authorisation for a tax on all commodities sold to provide money to 'pave' the streets (ie, in the case of Cambridge, surface them with coarse gravel, no paving-stone being available). When, after several years of failure to collect the tax, the streets got worse rather than better, the chancellor, tired of stepping in and out of ruts filled with filth, and seeing an opportunity to strike a blow at the enemy on a new front, had a word with the king on the subject. As a result, the accounting of the mayor and bailiffs was made subject to the audit of the chancellor and a colleague. Subsequent to that, no 'paving' was done, or very little; for 40 years the pretence of improving the streets went on as before, until, eventually, the former practice was adopted of making every householder responsible for the stretch of street fronting his property and then even less paving was done. It is difficult to avoid the impression that the town authorities sometimes tried to make the town as uncomfortable as possible in the hope that the university would be driven elsewhere in disgust.

In 1294 the king renewed his father's order to the sheriff about going into the town with armed force to deal with rebellious students 'when the burgesses cannot or will not imprison them', subject to the wishes of the chancellor. The following year saw the appointment, for the first time, of two members to represent the borough in parliament. If the burgesses thought, as they probably did, that that would give them an advantage over the university (which had to wait more than 300 years for similar represent- ation) they were mistaken. The only advantage to the town was that its members now had more frequent contact with some of the influential men of the realm and it could have been such contact that resulted in Cambridge becoming the chief source from which the royal household obtained its supply of fish for the next three centuries.

After several minor skirmishes between university and friars or between town and Barnwell Priory, the major campaign was resumed in earnest in 1305. The formula is familiar: 'persons unknown, contriving to disturb the discipline of the scholars, broke the doors of the hostels of the masters and scholars and assaulted them'. At the same time as the justices were sent to inquire into the complaints of the university, the latter was granted the privilege that 'for all personal actions they may cite the burgesses and other lay persons of our town of Cambridge before the chancellor, and they shall not be hindered in that by the king's prohibition'. Another tap on the wedge.

It seems to be established beyond question that there was a connection between trouble in the town and tournaments in the neighbourhood, for in that same year of 1305 it was found necessary to repeat the prohibition of tournaments within five miles of Cambridge and imprison several knights who had disregarded it. The ban was repeated four years later. Tournaments would appear to have been part of a long historical tradition of trouble-agencies beginning, I suppose, with a gladiatorial contests and continuing on through bull-baiting, cock-fighting and prize-fighting, interspersed with political elections, to the football matches of today.

Even more potent as a trouble-fomenter, however, was a weak king. Edward II had not been on the throne more than two years when tension mounted everywhere and nowhere more than at Cambridge. On two occasions in 1310 the townsmen, led by the mayor and bailiffs in the company of the Bishop of Coventry and Lichfield (an unwilling participant, surely) attacked visiting merchants and 'robbed' them of their goods, substituting force for law. The university became alarmed, especially when the burgesses secured several additional privileges by the renewal of their charter, and pleaded for a confirmation of their own privileges and protection.

It was only too obvious that they were going to need it and equally obvious that it would be little more than a formality when they got it, for the town authorities seemed either to have gone mad or to have surrendered to mob-rule. The situation was exacerbated, if not wholly explained, by a disastrous harvest, scarcity of corn and sharply rising prices, plus a general slump in commerce. The university felt the pinch, but escaped the immediate onslaught of the townsmen's fury. It seems that Henry Hastings, a kinsman of the Earl of Pembroke, had sent two of his servants from Cambridge to buy cloth and other commodities at the market of St Ives and that the Cambridge shopkeepers thought that he ought to have made the purchases in the home town. Instead of politely telling him so, the mayor and bailiffs, with an army consisting of all the leading townsmen, marched out along the Huntingdon Road to Girton, where they met the returning servants, 'followed them in hostile manner to Cambridge where all the people were assembled, took the servants and put them in prison and took away the cloths'.

Nothing came of the affair. No one was injured, no blood shed and the confiscated goods were returned in due course. The fact that the names of all the 71 participants in the affair were known suggests that it was a concerted gesture which the town authorities considered right and proper, in fact 'legal' by their standards. It was also a demonstration of what could be done with a bit of organisation and leadership. The process was repeated a few months later. This time Thomas Baynard, clerk, and his servants were confronted at Chesterton by a crowd of two dozen townsmen—the number had increased to 172 by the time the justices came to consider the matter—and were relieved of goods they had purchased in a manner and place of which the townsmen disapproved. The same technique was applied by the vicar of Holy Sepulchre and a gang of supporters to secure the return of an infant ward to what they considered his rightful guardianship.

If this sort of thing were to become regular practice, all the local villains—such of them, that is, as were not actually part of the mob intent on securing 'justice'—would be quaking in their shoes, even more so the chancellor and masters of the university, against whom all manner of offences could be conjured up and dealt with by an avenging horde. Their only defence was to have their charters confirmed and amended where possible to strengthen their position at law, in the hope that law would prevail before long. There was not a great deal to be done in that respect. The three new charters, which followed in rapid succession between February 14 and June 3 1317, contained little that was new. Three days later the laws concerning the government of the town were amended. Whereas the king had lately agreed that offenders in the town should only be tried by their fellow burgesses acting as magistrates, now 'considering the dissensions which frequently arise between townsmen and scholars and the ill effects which may follow if inquisitions are made only by men of the town', the king had decided that 'foreigners' (ie, not natives of Cambridge) should conduct the business. Moreover, to put a stop to the severity of the punishments meted out to delinquent students and the leniency reserved for townsmen similarly offending, all should in future be imprisoned at the castle, not in the town gaol.

The castle had lately (since 1283) been rebuilt and strengthened, and so was a more suitable place of detention for criminals. Another reason for the change of procedure was that the town gaol was wanted for a special purpose. As this order of July 7 1317 shows:

No *public women* shall be allowed to remain in the town of Cambridge or its suburb. At the request of the chancellor of the university of Cambridge, a proclamation to this effect shall be made by the mayor and bailiffs four times a year at least, and any such women who shall be found staying in the town or suburb three days after such proclamation shall, at the request of the chancellor or his vice-gerent, be taken and put in the prison of the town until they shall be delivered by the chancellor or his deputy.

The wishful thinking that prompted the order is obvious enough, and, I suppose laudable enough in the circumstances; its hope of fulfilment, I would have thought, negligible—and subsequent developments support my view. For one thing, every proclamation by the town-crier, if they were made, would be greeted by a chorus of hoots and ribald laughter from students and townsmen alike (but not townswomen). A more practical and peaceful solution to the problem would have been to encourage the prostitutes, like the ale-sellers, to display a sign. No doubt the town gaol was so adorned before long.

In 1318, by papal decree, the university became a *studium generale*, a truly universal university whose doctors could read their lectures anywhere in Christendom instead of being restricted to their own schools. Moreover, and of far greater significance, it was granted complete exemption from the spiritual authority of bishop and archbishop. The chancellor became absolute head of his domain. His authority still continued to be challenged, by the bishops, by his own scholars and masters and, of course, by the townsmen. They were not much concerned with spiritual matters. False weights and measures, filthy unpaved streets, illegal toll-collecting, abuse of the prison—these were some of the matters about which the chancellor maintained a steady stream of complaint while all around him, all over the country, was rising up a tide of anarchy and lawlessness with which the law was powerless to cope. Those in authority openly resorted to acts for which there was no authorisation other than that conferred by armed force at one's back. The Prior of Barnwell, the bailiffs of Cambridge, even some of the masters, were converted to the general belief that might was right, while armed gangs roamed the country practising that creed.

In 1322 the dispatch of 20 men and two ships northwards to help the king in his wars left the townsmen no less well equipped to wage their own, which broke out, as usual, in the spring. Its nature is summed up in the commission given to *six* justices sent to deal with it:

Simon de Reepham, mayor, William de Sledmere, John Pourfisshe and Robert de Bury, bailiffs, and about 200 men of the town and county, as well as being involved in other affrays . . . acting in the name and with the authority of the town of Cantebrigg, attacked and spoiled various inns of the masters and scholars of the university, climbed the walls, broke the doors and windows, mounted by ladders into the solars and assaulted the said masters and scholars, imprisoned some, *mutilated others of their members*, and killed Walter de Shelton, parson of the church of Welton; carried away all they could of the books and other goods of all the masters and scholars, so that no person dares to go to the university of the said town to study.

Thirty-four of the clerks lodged individual complaints of assault and robbery, and revealed a further detail: '. . . they trampled in the mud a writ concerning the liberties of the university when it was presented to them, and afterwards the same writ was affixed on behalf of the university to the door of the Tolbooth; they tore it down and again trampled it in the mud.'

That points to the main aim of the riot, or at least of some of the rioters, as being the annihilation of the university and all its privileges. A hint of what sparked it off may be contained in the phrase 'mutilated others of their members'. Cutting off hands, ears and noses was a common form of chastisement, usually reserved for convicted thieves. It may be that the irate townsmen were on the trail of certain students known to be thieves and were determined to inflict on them a punishment which they knew the chancellor's court would not inflict. It is just as likely in my opinion that the 'mutilation' was castration, a penalty frequently imposed, illegally, on clerics guilty of sexual offences (and sometimes self-imposed by monks who found the vow of chastity too difficult to keep). It could be that the expulsion of prostitutes had been effective after all and that the students were providing employment for the town girls in an amateur capacity. The edict concerning the expulsion of the professionals from the town was repeated five years later, slightly amended. The ladies in question were to be 'imprisoned during the pleasure of the chancellor or vice-chancellor'. It could have been better phrased.

Chapter 4

Change of tactics 1323-1380

When that nasty squall had blown over, the university enjoyed a spell of comparatively calm weather lasting more than half a century. The general state of unrest in the country at large continued for a further ten years and erupted again at intervals. There was a serious affray at Oxford in 1333 which resulted in another large-scale exodus of students, this time to Stamford, where some of the Cambridge students joined them, according to some accounts, but none of them were allowed to stay long—and more riots at Oxford in 1355. There were frequent armed robberies in and around Cambridge, frequent commitals to the town gaol and the castle of criminals who almost as frequently escaped. But, as far as I can discover, throughout this period under review, few fatal blows were exchanged between townsmen and gownsmen in Cambridge, no houses were attacked and looted, and no pitched battles took place in the streets. I would not call it peace, rather a sort of armed truce, with both sides watching each other, warily, waiting to see what the next move would be.

The next move by the university was one of great future significance, though at the time so unobtrusive and seemingly innocuous that the townsmen made no attempt to counter it. Ever since the founding of Peterhouse 40 years before, the university authorities must have been increasingly aware of the need for more such institutions, premises independent of the town, where students and masters could live without paying rent to anyone, and not be under constant threat of eviction or attack. The university had the use of St Mary's church and some monastic buildings, but there were no university buildings at this date. It had not the funds necessary to provide any and never would have had sufficient money if external benefactors had not come to the rescue. When they did, it was not with benefactions to 'the university' as such, but to the foundation of individual 'colleges', as they were eventually called. No less than seven were founded in this half-century of comparative peace. Their history is not strictly relevant to my theme, but their existence is, for each one established represented another foothold gained by the university. As yet there can have been no conscious plan in the mind of the chancellor or anyone else for a take-over of the town. What motivated the benefactors was a wish to secure the welfare of the students and the care of souls. The essence of the operation was charity. Its main activating agent was money.

In 1324 Hervey de Stanton, parson of the church of East Dereham in Norfolk, bought for £66 from Roger Butetourt a house in the parish of St Michael, with gardens and a quay adjacent; paid £2 for a licence to infringe the Statute of Mortmain and founded the House of the Scholars of St Michael (soon called *Michaelhouse*) and granted to the master and scholars the advowson of St Michael's church. Four years later the church and one of the manors at Barrington were given to the college; as time passed, more and more land was acquired by gift.

Inspired by this example, the chancellor and masters obtained a licence to found a college and assign to its scholars the two houses which they owned in Milnestrete in the parish of St John's. A year later the master and scholars of this *University Hall* had licence to acquire lands, rents and churches to an annual value of £40. The venture did not at first succeed. No one came forward with pious gifts to save their souls until 12 years later when Lady Elizabeth de Burgh, Countess of Clare, rebuilt the hall which had been destroyed by fire and re-founded the college as *Clare Hall*. A new licence was obtained to acquire lands, etc, 'and to appropriate any churches of which they acquire the advowsons' in 1346. This matter of 'advowson'— the right to appoint to the living of a church—was a valuable asset to both colleges and university; since one of their main functions was to produce parsons, it was a good thing to have control of the posts they would fill.

King Edward II was already maintaining a number of scholars at Cambridge and would no doubt have founded a college if he had lived longer. In 1332 Edward III, after carrying out an inspection of his father's protégées, founded *King's Hall* for a warden and 35 scholars. They received 'wages' at the rate of 4d a day for the warden and 2d a day for each scholar, that is, when the sheriff could find the money to pay them. In 1341 their premises were enlarged by the king's gift of another house, a garden, six plots of land near the river and part of a lane leading from the High Street to one of the hithes, plus the advowson of St Mary's church. The property had been bought by the mayor and the master acting together in the king's name; there was no annexation or requisitioning, or anything that could possibly give rise to a grievance. The university had peaceably acquired, for ever, a considerable site in the heart of the town.

While this was going on, both sides were experiencing some uneasiness as regards the security of their legal backing. In this respect the university had the advantage over its rivals, for its ranks included men more familiar with the law and all its intricacies. In 1327 they were quick off the mark in getting their charters confirmed by the new king and secured two amendments:

1 When a clerk assaulted or was assaulted by a layman, arrest was to be made by the mayor and bailiffs, but commital to prison was to be done by the chancellor or his deputy and

2 The chancellor or his deputy should be present at all assays of bread and ale in order to ensure that, for a third offence, the punishment of pillory or tumbril was used and not fines. Neither provision was really workable; both tended to diminish the power—and the revenue—of the mayor and bailiffs.

Three years later the burgesses got their charters confirmed, for a 'reasonable' fee. At the same time they requested that they be given due notice of any petition by the university which might affect the liberties of the town and this, too, was granted. This marks the beginning of a new aspect of the confict; from now on it became very much of a legal battle. There was money to be made (and spent) if one knew how to manipulate the law. One could even buy and sell writs, as the more astute students had already discovered, but they did not get very rich as the king stepped in with a prohibition which was later revoked.

While getting their charters confirmed, the burgesses put in a plea to parliament about the state of their finances. All they had to subsist on, they said, was 'small tolls and customs from strangers who came to the town with goods on market days'. That cannot have been strictly true, though they did—as did most other towns—frequently have difficulty in paying the £62 annual fee-farm rent. They attributed their plight to the excessive liberties granted to 'great lords'—meaning religious houses, but perhaps with a hint at the university—and their tenants. Yet the only remedy they could suggest was permission to enclose the small lanes and waste places in the town, presumably in order to build more houses for letting. This licence for private speculation was not granted. Three hundred years later the speculation took place, without licence.

The university, evidently anticipating some such move, put in a petition to the same parliament, complaining that the price of wine at Cambridge was too high, that the mayor and bailiffs did not keep the streets clean, scour the King's Ditch or keep the paving of the streets in good repair. The fact that those complaints went unheeded did not deter the chancellor and masters from keeping up a steady barrage of further complaint—negligence in making assays of bread and ale, refusal to take the oath to keep the peace of the university, liberating prisoners sent to gaol by the chancellor, etc. The same complaints were made again and again and some were still being made four centuries later. They were nearly all well founded. They may or may not have been voiced with the object of convincing king and parliament that the town authorities were not fit persons to be entrusted with the management of the town. That was the object they eventually achieved.

In 1335 the townsmen got a bit of their own back in a strange way, having the malicious pleasure of seeing the chancellor caught in the tangled web of legal procedure and being sent to gaol. The fact that he was completely innocent of any crime or offence only added to their enjoyment. It all began when William de Wyvelingham, a student at the time, thrashed Henry Chadde, a townsman supplying the students with provisions. He was arrested, charged with unlawful assault and sent to gaol by the chancellor, Master Henry de Harwedon; his goods and chattels, to the value of £66, being confiscated. William, besides being a 'clerk' and 'noted for divers misdeeds', was also a burgess carrying on a business in the town (another Gogging). Prompted by the mayor and bailiffs, he brought a charge of wrongful arrest and theft of his goods against the chancellor and his colleagues. He won his case and was awarded damages. The chancellor and proctors evidently ignored the court and its finding, for when next heard of they were in Yorkshire, and in prison. In February 1336 the sheriff of Yorkshire was ordered to release them on bail.

They defaulted on their bail and went to London, no doubt to appeal to the king. But the sheriff's officers moved faster than they did. In March the bailiffs of Westminster were ordered to arrest them. Again they fled. William, determined not to let his quarry escape, brought another action against them, on the same charges, at Northampton. By early September their wanderings had evidently caught up with the king at last, for he wrote from Scotland to the sheriff of Cambridgeshire, ordering him not to arrest

Henry de Harwedon who had given security for himself. He also wrote to the three justices who had heard the original charge and told them to conduct a re-trial, because 'there is a great commotion in the university and people of those parts . . . discords begin to arise between the scholars and laity of Cambridge, who encourage and maintain William de Wyvelingham as one of their own against the scholars, and the scholars desert their studies to attend to strife . . .' The letter went on to underline the danger of civil strife everywhere if the law were used maliciously like this. But they were not to do anything more until after Christmas, by which time the king would have considered it further.

On November 10 the king wrote again for full details of the case and issued a writ transferring it to the King's Bench. On December 20 he ordered the justices to delay action as he wanted more time to consider. Something went wrong with the messenger service or the local justices had by this time conceived a grudge against the chancellor, whose conduct had, one must admit, tended to arouse suspicion, for when next heard of Master Henry de Harwedon was in the Marshalsea prison. There he stayed for nearly two years, despite an appeal to the king in May 1337 and finding sureties for his appearance in court and a petition to parliament a year later. He might have got out sooner, but in October 1338 the bedell of the university cited William de Wyvelingham before the judges of the King's Bench to appear before the then chancellor of the university. The action was adjudged to be contempt; the bedell was put in gaol, the ex-chancellor sent back there and fined 40s. When eventually released it was with permission to pursue his case against Wyvelingham. But I imagine he had had enough of the law and no more was heard of the matter. William did not get his money back, but the jubilant burgesses would see to it that he was not out of pocket in the end. They might not be able to afford the town rent; they could find the money to sustain an expensive attack on the chancellor.

Mutual recrimination continued unabated, each side claiming that its privileges were impeded by the other. Inch by inch, clause by clause, the university was slowly winning the legal tug-of-war. With the king's weight on its side, it could not lose. In one year, 1343, these points were won:

1 Cases in which students were involved respecting loans, gifts, lease of houses, hire of horses, purchase of foodstuffs, etc, should be decided by the chancellor's court, whatever might have been said previously.

2 Every townsman should be held responsible for his servants and family as regards buying and selling wine and victuals. For any offence committed by them against a scholar, after one or two warnings, the chancellor should have power to punish the offenders.

3 In future the chancellor or his officers should not be vexed by charges of false imprisonment or in any other manner in the courts in cases involving scholars. (An aftermath of the Wyvelingham affair.)

The enacting of such measures did not, of course, mean that the townsmen accepted or respected them. For practical purposes they were often mere 'scraps of parchment', costly ones at that. Both sides by this time must have collected between them many square yards of parchment. What the university needed was a few more acres of territory.

The fifth college was founded in 1347 by Marie de St Paul, widow of Aymer de Valence, Earl of Pembroke, who was killed at a tournament held to celebrate his wedding. The college, at first called *Marie Valence Hall* (later Pembroke College) was for a warden and 30 scholars. Licence was granted to acquire several houses in Trumpington Street, advowsons of churches and other property to the value of £100 a year.

The next college was founded in 1349 by Edmund de Gunville, king's clerk and parson of the church of Terrington in Norfolk, who bought a house and three gardens in Lurteburghlane in which to establish a warden and 20 scholars in the *Hall of the Annunciation of St Mary*. In 1354 the premises were exchanged for a house belonging to Corpus Christi Guild opposite Michaelhouse, where Bishop Bateman of Norwich, executor of Gunville's will, re-founded the college as *Gunville Hall*.

One would suppose that the indiscriminate ravages of the Black Death virtually closed the university and caused a complete suspension of hostilities. It probably did, though direct evidence is lacking, whereas there is evidence of a further spate of armed robbery and violence all over the country. Indirect evidence is provided by such facts as that the original 20 scholars, for whom Gunville's college was intended, were only four in number when the college was re-founded and that Bishop Bateman made another foundation with the specific aim of ensuring a supply of clergy for his diocese, their ranks having been drastically thinned by the plague. In 1350 licence was granted for the warden, three fellows and three scholars—soon increased to 20—of the *Hall of the Holy Trinity* to acquire three houses and a plot of land in Mylnestreet, plus advowsons, etc, up to the value of £66 a year. Thus began Trinity Hall. The name has survived and it is still on the same site.

The consciences of some of the townsfolk were at last stirred. In 1352 the two guilds, that of St Mary and that of Corpus Christi, 'on account of their poverty', united in one guild with the name of 'The Gild of the Precious Body of Jesus Christ and the Glorious Virgin His Mother'. The aldermen, brethren and sisters of the unified guild were, at the instance of the Duke of Lancaster (a connection which proved most disadvantageous some 30 years later), granted licence to acquire property to the value of £20 a year to found the college or 'hall' of *Corpus Christi* (later called *Benet College* before reverting to its original name) next to St Benet's church. That was the only college to be founded by the townspeople of Cambridge.

'College' and 'university' are often confused, as being one and the same thing. They were, in the sense that, increasingly from now on, the existence of each depended on that of the other although at this stage rather less than a quarter of the students were housed in colleges. The majority were, or were soon to be, housed in 'halls' or 'hostels', which were not colleges, not having endowments, and many were still living in private houses. The colleges, then as now, were independent of the university as regards management and finance. It is an anomaly which almost defies elucidation. The 'masters and scholars of the university' sought and obtained all the privileges granted by the king and objected to by the townsmen. The colleges received all the grants of land and churches made by individuals (including the king) and so became relatively rich while the parent body remained relatively poor.

King Edward made no secret of his determination to uphold the privileged position of the university, however difficult of definition it might be. The local justices were frequently caught up in a legal game which they had not the expertise to referee with impartiality because they were not sure of the rules. The king had to enlighten them even though he, too, was not absolutely sure of these himself but at least he could make it clear to them which side had to win. In 1353 he told them, yet again, to stop accepting for trial, cases involving students, other than those of felony and mayhem (wounding), because 'certain laymen of the town, scheming to infringe the liberties of the university and to disquiet both the regents and the students, have lately procured the indictment of masters and scholars before you, for various offences which ought to have been dealt with by the chancellor . . . and *the king wishes to maintain the liberties and privileges of the university*'.

This was followed by a ruling on a point which had already given rise to a lot of trouble, namely, how wide was the interpretation of the term 'university member'? Was a person who performed some professional service for the masters and scholars automatically 'of the university'? The king and his advisers said he was. The townsmen nevertheless continued to dispute it and only with reluctance accepted that 'from the time of the foundation of the university the chancellors or their deputies have had cognisance of all pleas of trespass except felony and mayhem in the town committed by stationers, writers, binders of books and illuminators there residing, although they may from time to time be employed by others'. This custom had been challenged by 'certain persons who envy the university and its students and scheme to infringe its liberties'. The stationers, etc, had evidently, like the justices, suffered the cross-fire of both sides 'and some have withdrawn from the town, or are trying to do so'.

To ascribe opposition on this point to 'envy' was surely to take too narrow a view of the situation. The book-binders, etc, were men of the town, paying rates and taxes, serving as constables and on juries, living by serving the town and the religious houses as well as the students. If the principle that they were technically 'clerks' was accepted and extended, then before long bakers, brewers, vintners, shoe-makers, chandlers, bedmakers, laundresses—anybody in fact who performed any service for the university— would be under the chancellor's jurisdiction. Which was precisely what the chancellor and masters wanted and eventually got.

Protest from the town was less than might have been expected. The mayor and bailiffs complained to parliament in 1354 that they could not pay the town rent because they had spent so much money in defending their privileges against the university before the king and council. The answer they received was that they should pay up and stop complaining, which they did. Moreover, they duly complied with the demands for men-at-arms and archers for the king's wars and the occasional loan of cash. They did make some effort to resist the increasing take-over of property in the town by colleges, but with little success.

In this they were impeded by some of their own members—Henry de Tangmere, for instance, an eminent burgess and one-time deputy sheriff. In 1359 he was the victim of an attack one night by an armed gang who had sworn to kill him and did, in fact, leave him for dead. He lived long enough to make his will, leaving 18 houses and 85 acres of land to Corpus Christi College. This recent foundation was a target for the hatred of a section of the townsmen, who saw it as a betrayal of their cause. Other gifts of Tangmere to the college—a hermitage and a leper hospital—were later withdrawn by violence. The leader of the attack on him, one Henry de Bungeye, who had been imprisoned for this offence and for rape, as well as breaking out of gaol, was pardoned 'for good service done to the king in the last expedition to France'.

Preparations for war, though it was overseas, affected East Anglia more than the rest of the country. In 1370 orders had been issued that all food-stuffs for sale should be concentrated in the neighbourhood of Ipswich (Orwell), which was to be the assembly-point for the next expedition. The merchants of Cambridge took advantage of the opportunity thus presented to strike at their real enemy. They complied with the order so thoroughly—or said they did—that Cambridge market was bare. 'All the victuals of the town of Cambridge and district are altogether withdrawn thence, so that, unless a speedy remedy be applied, the scholars must depart from their studies for lack of victuals.' The king 'would cherish the study thereof to the utmost of his power', even more than he cherished an attack on his old enemy, France, and the order was hastily countermanded. That was probably not the first, and certainly not the last, time that an attempt was made to get rid of the university by starving it out.

The attempt caused another split in the ranks of the townsmen, as well it might. The mayor, John Gyboun, 'with others of the better men of the town', was at the Guildhall to mete out punishment on all those who had committed offences connected with the sale of foodstuffs when up stormed Stephen Morice and his son, John, (later MP for the borough) with an armed escort. Morice senior addressed to the mayor some 'vile and opprobrious words'. Morice junior reinforced them with blows, and 'would have killed him with his drawn knife if he had not been rescued'. Tension was mounting.

The death of the king did nothing to diminish it; rather the opposite. It was the university's turn to feel the pinch. They had escaped the poll-tax of 4d a head levied on all persons above the age of 14 years (the number of people in the town who paid, or who ought to have paid, the tax was 1,722) but were suddenly required, in 1378, to contribute to the 'tenths' and 'fifteenths' granted by parliament to the king for the defence of the realm. The town's share of this contribution amounted to £71, half the cost of a 'ballinger', a ship of 42 oars built on the Thames. The university did not contribute, just as it declined to pay 'ship-money' two and a half centuries later. That was a bitter enough bone of contention, but worse was to come.

Faced with this extra expense, the mayor and bailiffs asserted their sole right to control the assize of bread and ale and collect the fines for breach of regulations. The chancellor refused to be excluded. This, coupled with the revolt of the Morice clan, caused the mayor and bailiffs to throw in their hand. There was no assize of bread and ale. Bakers, butchers, grocers, brewers and the rest were evidently charging what they liked, adapting weights and measures to suit themselves—or suit the economic circumstances —and likely to get away with it if somebody did not intervene. The chancellor intervened. By petition to parliament he was granted sole control over the sale of foodstuffs for a period of five years which was later extended to seven.

That alone was enough to make an outbreak of hostilities likely. There were other factors affecting not just Cambridge but the whole of the realm which made it inevitable.

Chapter 5

Away with the learning
1380-1381

A combination of circumstances which, on a national scale, included growing discontent among the labouring classes at their semi-servile status, increased bargaining power in their ranks because of their numbers having been depleted by years of pestilence, increasing antagonism towards the higher orders of the Church and violent opposition, in all but the highest ranks of society, to a drastic increase in universal taxation on top of the normal dues and aids—all that, plus political instability, resulted in what is popularly known as the Peasants' Revolt. The area most affected was London, the South-East, the Home Counties and East Anglia. My story deals only with events on a local scale. Although part of the general scene, what happened at Cambridge had more to do with the Town and Gown war than with the aspirations of Wat Tyler or the preaching of John Ball.

Before these two and their adherents came out into the open, there were evident signs that trouble was imminent, especially at Cambridge. On June 2 1380 a special commission was appointed for keeping the peace of the town, consisting of Sir John Cavendish (Chief Justice), John Holt (chancellor of the university), two masters, Edmund Lyster (mayor) and three bailiffs. They were not told what to do. Three months later they were told what not to do, namely interfere in anything that concerned the university. A new commission was appointed, consisting of Sir John Cavendish, John Holt and three masters. They were to make inquiries into larcenies, mayhem, manslaughters, trespasses, forestallings, unlawful assemblies, etc, committed *by the masters and scholars* 'to the disturbance of the people', and to deal with them. Whoever drafted that order had evidently got his wires crossed or had been deliberately misinformed. It was a routine order, applicable to almost any civil disturbance but even the clerk who copied it must have known that, if the masters and scholars were involved, it would be as victims, not as aggressors.

In December an order was sent to the mayor and bailiffs 'on information that there are divers evildoers in the town', to make proclamation and take steps for the observance of statutes dating back over the previous century relating to 'people called roberdesmen, wasters and draghlatches'. In other words, rogues and thieves. I dare say the mayor and bailiffs were well aware of the presence of these undesirables, who existed in every town. They also knew that there was very little they could do about it, apart from giving a pep-talk to the constables and doubling the night-watch. They could not expel every 'suspicious' character from the town; if they had tried, the expelled would have been back in a few days, accompanied by others of like character. They could not round them up and clap them all in gaol; it would not have held a tenth of them, or any of them for long, even if the gaoler had stuck to his post. They could do nothing about the carrying of weapons, for every man, by law as well as by custom, carried a knife which was as adaptable for slitting throats as it was for aiding in the consumption of cheese and onions. They also knew that, in addition to the undesirable outsiders within the town, there were quite a few 'honest' burgesses who, given the opportunity, would gladly use the rabble for their own ends.

Exactly what happened in the town during the next two months is not known. There were evidently a number of 'unlawful assemblies' being held, plots being laid, the details but not the existence of which were kept secret. Identification of the conspirators must have provided some of the students with an exciting diversion from their studies. One after the other their names leaked out and reached the ears of chancellor, proctors and sheriff. On February 2 1381 John Trippelowe, John Berke (draper) and John Herry were called upon to give surety in the sum of £100 that they would obey the justices and commissioners for the peace and make no unlawful assemblies. Two days later John Barber, Henry Brasyer, John de Trumpington, John Ashwell and Nicholas Hede were likewise bound by oath. On February 23 the list was swollen by the names of Edmund Lister (mayor), John Cotton, John Marshall, John Brigham, Thomas Treveth, Peter Lolworth, John Cardemaker (clerk), Robert Baylham, Adam Sergeant, Henry Rande and Alexander Taverner. On the following day John Blancpayn completed the list of 20 names.

Two thousand pounds was at stake. If it were forfeited, half the sum was to go to the king, the other half to the chancellor. The money had not been actually handed over; it never was; if it were forfeited, there would still remain the problem of collecting it, by distraint upon the property of the conspirators and their guarantors. They evidently considered the risk one worth taking and that they were adequately insured. Some of them, in the very act of planning the coup, were already planning their escape-route.

It is no longer possible to determine with certainty who was guilty of what, nor even the exact sequence of events. I will tell the story as it appears to me, reconstructed from the Parliamentary, Assize, Coram Rege, Close and Patent Rolls, knowing that in my version also there must be gaps.

On May 1 a party of townsmen went to the house of the chancellor, taking the chief university officials with them, and compelled them to sign and seal two 'charters'. One purported to be an agreement between the university and the town whereby the former renounced all privileges granted to it 'from the beginning of the world to the present day', which the chancellor and masters, under threat of death to themselves and the destruction of their houses, were compelled to have registered at their own expense on pain of forfeiting the sum of £3,000. The other was an 'agreement' annulling all recognisances and contracts, etc, formerly made between the university and town both as a community and as individuals. The two documents were then deposited in the mayor's office. Something had gone wrong with their timing, for the revolt had not yet started. Something had also gone wrong with their brains if they seriously thought that 'charters' thus extorted could have any legal validity, even if they were registered. (The townsmen at Bury St Edmunds had extorted similar 'charters' from the abbey there 50 years earlier, with disastrous results to themselves, but history was not a strong subject with the Cambridge burgesses.) Secure in that knowledge, the chancellor and his associates did nothing. For five weeks the conspirators watched and waited. At last, on June 5, the revolt began in Essex and Kent and, within a week, it was well under way. The Cambridge uprising was timed to follow closely upon events at Norwich, Bury St Edmunds and St Albans. Saturday, June 15 was their day.

With the looting, burning of manors and destruction of documents that took place in the county we are not really concerned, though it is worthy of note that, when on the first day of the local rising, the manors of Thomas Haselden (JP and steward of the Duke of Lancaster) at Steeple Morden and Guilden Morden were attacked and looted, the rioters were joined by a mob from Cambridge led by John Gibbon and two of the town bailiffs, who then went on to pillage the Preceptory of Shingay. In Cambridge the signal for uprising was the tolling of the bell of St Mary's church near the market-place. A large crowd gathered, townsmen and 'wastours' from outside. Their first target was the house in Bridge Street where lived Roger Blankgreen, whose father was one of the collectors of the hated Poll Tax. They searched the house, looting it in the process, but Roger had fled for sanctuary across the broken-down bridge to the nearby little church of St Giles. There the mob pursued him and would have dragged him from the church and beheaded him in the churchyard but the local parishioners stoutly opposed this sacriligeous act. Violation of sanctuary was one of the things which had caused the universal hatred of the Duke of Lancaster. The mob returned to Blankgreen's house and there threatened his wife. Pleading on her knees, she asked to be allowed to purchase his life and her own. They took her money and left her with life, but little hope.

Later in the day, in response to a proclamation by the mayor, a large crowd gathered in the market-place. With common assent—it is not clear who was leading and who being led—they went to the Tolbooth and elected Jakes de Granchester as their 'captain' and made him swear on pain of death to be their 'loyal captain and governor'. The mayor, bailiffs and council with one accord made Jakes and his brother, Thomas, freemen of the town—presumably waiving the customary fee of £2 or whatever it was at that date. The mode of operating, it would seem, was that the mayor and bailiffs should issue orders and the 'captain' should lead the mob to carry out their orders. (I have no idea who or what this mysterious Jakes was. I would think it likely that he was an ex-soldier who had told some marvellous yarn about his military exploits and made an excellent scapegoat for the principals; apart from his ceremonial installation, he seems to have played no part in the operations.)

That night 'at about 10 de la clokke', the mayor and bailiffs again met at the Tolbooth, held a conference and emerged with a proclamation that every man should go to the house of William Wigmore, bedell of the university, to burn and destroy it and cut off the head of the bedell. They had not far to go, but by the time that the mob, led by Robert Brigham, Simon Hosier, John Russell and Thomas Fourbishour, had broken into the house, William had escaped to safety. The house was ransacked and burnt.

Meanwhile another mob, led by the mayor, Edmund Lister (also known as Edmund Redmedowe) and the bailiffs, advanced upon Corpus Christi College. They broke down the doors and windows and surged inside. In the absence of any detailed description of this episode in the records, imagination conjures up a picture of 30 or 40 terrified students cowering in their beds, while an even more terrified master meekly submitted to the demands of the drunken rioters. It is not until more than two years later that a hint of the true nature of the event is given, when John Kynne, Master of Corpus Christi College, his servant, Nicholas, and ten other scholars (including William Wigmore) sued for and obtained the king's pardon. Pardon for what? There was obviously a fierce fight and by no means a one-sided one. At least one of the attackers was seriously wounded or killed; that is why the scholars needed pardon. Of course the gallant defenders were hopelessly outnumbered. The invaders carried off all the charters, books and muniments they could find. As they left, some of the mob even took away with them the doors and windows. In the darkness and confusion of that night other breakings and robberies occurred, for which no one was ever brought to justice.

On the Sunday morning, while some of the townsmen rode out into the surrounding countryside to bring in more rabble-rousers 'who would not have dared to approach the town except with the assent of the burgesses', another mob surged into Great St Mary's church while mass was being celebrated. They seized and carried off a chest containing jewels and plate, the property of the university, and many charters and documents relating to its privileges. The chest, emptied of its contents, was sold there and then to John Giboun senior for 10s. On examination it was soon discovered that there must be more documents somewhere else. The chancellor was known to have used the house of the Carmelite Friars in Mill Street as an administrative office, so Thomas Fourbissher led the mob there. They broke into the friary church and stole another chest, said to have been full of books and valuables, later valued at £20, also belonging to the university. The books and charters from both chests were then taken into the market-place and burnt. As the flames consumed the precious manuscripts, an old woman called Margaret Starre flung the ashes to the wind and shouted: 'Away with the learning of the clerks, away with it!'

The appetite for looting and destruction was now thoroughly roused. With John Resham and William Draper well to the fore, another visit was paid to Corpus Christi College to complete the looting there, then the house of John Blancpayn (a collector of the pavage tax), on the corner of Petty Cury, was attacked and looted. The house of Roger Harleston (JP and supervisor of the Poll Tax collection) was violently sacked by John Noreys, Hugh Candlesby, Thomas Lister, John Lister and others. It seems that even the house of the mayor, Edmund Redmedowe (alias Lister), did not escape the attentions of the looters, though I must stress once again that in the aftermath there was considerable confusion as to what had actually happened and who was to blame; a lot of the malefactors certainly got off scot free. It seems also that there was on this Sunday yet another rounding-up of university documents—though there is no mention of attacks on the colleges other than Corpus—and every one that could be found, or was handed over under menace of death, was burnt. The royal seals attached to them were 'mercilessly broken with knives, sticks and other weapons'.

On Monday, June 17, came the turn of Barnwell Priory, against which the townsmen had a grudge because the prior had recently enclosed a piece of common land at a place called Estenhall (or the Drove, or 'le Grenecroft') to enlarge the monastery grounds. With the mayor at their head (though in reality led by John Tyteshall, Hugh Candlesby, Robert Barber, Nicholas Wympol and Richard Martin) the mob broke down the monastery walls, cut down all the trees (to the value of £400, the prior said) destroyed the sluices of the fishponds and carried off fish, sedge and peat. The total damage, as assessed by the prior, amounted to £2,000—a figure which nobody believed.

Other than at Corpus, there was no resistance anywhere to the outrages. What the sheriff and the knights of the shire were doing all that week is nowhere stated—most probably staying at home to guard their own property, I imagine. But news of the disorder had reached Henry le Spencer, Bishop of Norwich, at his manor-house near Oakham. This militant Churchman with a small force of men-at-arms and archers, his usual bodyguard, set out for East Anglia, where some of the worst outrages had been committed (including the brutal murder of Sir Robert Salle, Sir John Cavendish and the prior of St Edmund's Abbey). As he passed through Cambridge he encountered a mob of rebels. The official records are silent as to this episode; the chroniclers eloquent and lyrical. The bishop attacked. Several of the rebels were killed, several taken prisoner and the rest dispersed. (Captain Jakes probably perished in this encounter.)

The revolt collapsed. After June 19 there were no more acts of rebellion, apart from odd groups of peasants here and there who had naively believed those who told them that servitude and villeinage were ended and who now looked for further signs of the dawn of freedom. The machinery of the law was set in motion. From July 1 the Assizes were in constant session for almost a month. Surprisingly few people were hanged at Cambridge, and those mostly men of the county. All the identified ringleaders were on trial, including the mayor, Redmedowe. He pleaded not guilty, his defence being that he had been surrounded by a crowd of more than a thousand and had been told: 'You are the mayor of this king's town and governor of our community; if you do not consent to our will and commands in carrying out all that shall be said to you *on behalf of the king* and his faithful commons, you will be at once beheaded'. Asked to name the chief culprits, he could only remember Hosier, Fourbissher, Russell and the Listers. He was detained in prison but, when trustworthy men of the town interceded on his behalf, he was released on bail.

It is quite possible—though not, I think, highly probable—that he *was* innocent and that he acted under duress. It is probable that he, with many others, was duped and bewildered by the frequent assertions that the rebels were acting 'in the name of the king', and that the object of the revolt was to rid the country of 'traitors'. There seem to have been political undertones in the affair which have never been fully understood. One John Shirle was hanged at Cambridge because in a tavern in Bridge Street he was heard to say that the king's officers and ministers deserved to be hanged, drawn and quartered more than did John Ball, who was unjustly condemned to death. Seditious words were more harshly punished than many acts of violence and, once the bulk of the looters and arsonists—those who were not dead or fled—had been dealt with, the king and his council tackled the really serious aspect of the Cambridge disturbance, namely the attack on the university.

On September 22 an order was sent to 'the good men and commonalty' of Cambridge to elect a fit person as mayor in place of John Marshall (smith), lately elected, because the king had learned (from the chancellor?) that the said Marshall was not sufficiently qualified. They substituted forthwith Richard Maysterman. On October 24 a commission of six justices, headed by the Duke of Buckingham, was appointed to inquire solely into 'the excesses, etc, against the chancellor of the university or any scholars thereof committed in this devilish insurrection'. The result was that, on December 6, the present mayor, Maysterman, the bailiffs, Glover, Upware, Calne and William Lister, the late mayor, Edmund Lister, and ex-bailiffs, Herries, Candlesby, Cote and Bluntisham, with three or four other townsmen, were summoned to appear before the council at Westminster 'on Thursday next', or forfeit a penalty of £1,000 if they failed to comply.

It was a very apprehensive party that set out for London on the Wednesday; no stopping on the road for a jolly carouse at a wayside inn, no conversation to speak of, but a violent argument at one stage when the ex-mayor tried, as he had done several times already, to persuade the present mayor to take charge of those two 'charters' which had been wrung from the university seven months earlier and which he was now heartily wishing had been burnt with the others in the market-place. For these two documents were the main reason for those 13 men being in their present uncomfortable situation.

On the Thursday morning they were ushered into the council-chamber. Mayors and bailiffs identified themselves. The three elected representatives of the town were asked if they had authority under the common seal of the town. They replied that the town did not have a common seal (embarrassing, but true; the mayor had a seal, but not the corporation). Where were the extorted charters? Maysterman did not know. Henry Brasyer had tried to get him to accept them the previous evening, but he had refused them; that was the first time he had seen them, and he had had nothing to do with them. It was then Lister's turn. He had never, he said, agreed, abetted or advised in what had been done and never did or said anything against the university except under compulsion from others. The two charters had been brought to his office and secretly left there, by whom he did not know. As soon as he saw them he sent them to London, where they had been ever since, to be surrendered when required. Neither he nor any other person of value had ever assented to the rioting, it was all the work of outsiders with a few local men and they had all been punished; all they had been able to capture were now dead. He and his associates were innocent of all blame.

The king's sergeants-at-law may have believed him. They did not spare him a thorough grilling. At last, with sighs of relief, the illegal charters were handed over. They were read to the assembled parliament and formally annulled.

But that was only the beginning of the proceedings. There followed a bill, presented on behalf of the university, enumerating in detail the outrages to which the mayors and bailiffs, it asserted, had consented and terminating with a demand that they should forfeit all the franchises of their town. This was something for which they had not come prepared. Abjectly they asked for a copy of the bill, time to consider it and counsel to aid them. They were granted the latter only, and only on the criminal charges. On counsel's advice they challenged the competence of the court. (Uniquely idiotic counsel, to question the authority of the second highest court in the land!) Then the miserable men went through their defence all over again. It was not their fault. It was the fault of the traitors and malefactors from Essex, Hertfordshire and Kent, who came to Cambridge in 'vast multitudes'. There was a *small* number of rioters in the town, who have all been captured or killed etc. The pathetic part of it all is—they *might* have been telling the truth.

They might have saved their breath. The king, with the assent of parliament, took the franchise of the town into his own hands, as being forfeit. Then, so that the town should not be without governance, he restored it to them, to hold until the king decided otherwise. There were great sighs of relief from the 13 men of Cambridge. Smiles rapidly changed to frowns as the voice of the Recorder continued (this is recorded in French; it must surely have been spoken in English, or the Cambridge men would not have understood a word of it):

On the advice of parliament, and because it seems some punishment should be made, and because on the other hand the Town of Cambridge is one of the ancient towns of the Realm, and chief town of the county, therefore the king, with the assent of parliament, has granted to the Chancellor and Scholars of the University of Cambridge *a)* the oversight of the assize of bread, wine and ale, and cognisance of all offences against it; *b)* the control of weights and measures in the town and suburbs; *c)* the authority to inquire into and deal with all forestalling and regrating of meat and fish, rotten or otherwise, and punish offences relating thereto and *d)* the governance, correction and punishment of those things, with all fines, profits, etc, accruing from them, as the Chancellor and Scholars of Oxford University have. For this grant the university shall pay the Exchequer £10 per year.

The remnant of the franchise of the town the king gave to the mayor and bailiffs, 'to hold of him for ever', at the customary rent of 101 marks—*plus* another four marks! All this was duly inscribed on charters and in due course presented (on payment) to the university and town. Meanwhile the party had returned to Cambridge. How I wish I could have eavesdropped on the conversation of those men as they rode home! For then, and only then, I believe, would the plain truth have emerged, in *very* plain English. And think of the character-sketches that would have been drawn!

Chapter 6

Fighting a losing battle 1382-1420

The sight of a few shrivelled corpses swinging in the wind or a few grisly heads stuck on the pillory was too commonplace to have any lasting deterrent effect, but the lessons of that resounding victory for the chancellor were not to be forgotten in a hurry. The battle had been won not so much by the chancellor's skill as by the ineptitude of his opponents and the outcome was that the university was henceforth about £100 a year better off (that is the amount which I estimate the university would collect in fines and fees in connection with weights, measures and victualling licences) whilst the town was deficient by the same amount. The moral disgrace of the outrage quickly faded with the passage of time. Many of those still in prison for their part in the riots—Martin, Fourbissher, Brigham, Refham and others—were pardoned within the next three years, mostly at the request of the queen. The general pardon of the town, at first withheld along with that of Bury St Edmunds as being the very worst of the offenders, was granted late in 1382. One battle lost did not mean the end of the war. What that defeat had demonstrated most clearly was that the law could not be coerced by brute force or threats; it had to be manipulated. From now on the burgesses would look for loopholes through which to engage in sniping at the enemy. Unfortunately for them, they were not very expert marksmen and most of the loopholes were stopped up one after the other.

A new battleground was already in the making. The fair held at Steresbrigge in the suburb of Barnwell was rapidly becoming one of the most important in the land. Exploited by outsiders as well as townsmen, it was always difficult to impose strict compliance with regulations regarding fair trading. Now that the university authorities were wholly responsible for weights and measures, etc, whilst the town authorities were still responsible for managing the fair, it was even more difficult. The king had heard that a 'great number of false measures and weights have hitherto been commonly used there, especially at the time of a fair held annually at Steresbrigge, to the deception of the people flocking thither'. He ordered the chancellor to burn and destroy any measures found to be false, seal those which were legal and administer punishment accordingly, with no negligence, otherwise the privilege would be withdrawn. That was almost certainly an attempt on the part of the townsmen to convince the king that the university was not capable of doing the job which he had allotted to it.

In 1383 the university was aggrieved because some of the justices were refusing to acknowledge the chancellor's sole right to deal with cases affecting students on the grounds that the wording of the grants was not specific. Having been repeated and amended a dozen times already, the charters ought to have been clear enough by now, but evidently they were not; perhaps the use of Latin legalese was at the root of the trouble. However, it was all gone over again in great length and the following points made clearer (except to those burgesses and justices who did not *want* to understand):

1 The chancellor and his successors, and his vice-chancellor, should have for ever the sole judicial authority in all cases whatever, except felony and mayhem, involving a member of the university.

2 He could conduct the hearing wherever he chose in Cambridge and its suburbs.

3 This authority was independent of the justices of the King's Bench and all other judges whatever.

4 No judge, sheriff, mayor, bailiff or any other officer should interfere unless [loophole] the chancellor or vice-chancellor should be found defective in administering justice.

5 The chancellor or his deputy could imprison all persons convicted before him in the castle at Cambridge, or anywhere else in the town, as he chose.

6 The sheriff, keeper of the castle, mayor and bailiffs should be bound to receive, keep and deliver all such persons at the command of the chancellor, etc.

In 1384 the mayor and bailiffs thought they had discovered another loophole in the enemy's defences. The town had forfeited all jurisdiction in the market-place, shops, fairs and streets, but nothing had been said in the charters about the boats plying on the river, from the owners of which they had collected 4d a year for every bushel used for measuring corn. They refused to allow the chancellor to collect this sum. I do not know how many boats with how many bushels plied on the river between Cambridge and Lynn, Ely, St Ives, Huntingdon, etc, probably as many as 50; that number could have moored at any one time at the hithes along the river-front from the bridge to the mills. If each boat had one bushel, the total sum involved in the annual checking and stamping of those measures could not have amounted to much more than one pound. But the triviality of the amount mattered less to the burgesses in their present mood than did the principle. The matter was referred to Chancery—at a cost far exceeding the amount that ten years of toll-collecting would bring in—and the mayor and bailiffs lost.

They desperately sought every possible way of augmenting the town's diminished revenues and seemed to have found one in the practice of refusing to grant licences to 'foreigners' to sell food and drink in the town except on payment of a heavy fine, or paying even more to become freemen of the town. At the same time it was, they thought, a blow at the enemy's food-supplies, for the fees and fines could be set so high that the foreign victuallers had to put up their prices—and incur a fine for doing so—or else simply stay away from the town, which some of them did. The blow was quickly parried. The university persuaded the king to order the cessation of the fines on pain of forfeiture of £100 by the town.

Two devastating fires, one the worst ever experienced in the town, and both occurring in the year 1385, destroyed over a hundred houses and their contents. This was a serious blow to the university as well as the town, for the majority of students were still housed in rented accommodation. The burgesses in distress appealed for relief to the king, telling him that from those houses which had been destroyed 'a great part of the fee-farm used to be levied' and that in consequence of the fires many persons had quitted the town and many others were proposing to leave. If they did not receive help they would not be able to pay the rent and they reminded him that he had taken away some of their sources of income and given them to the university. The appeal did not go unheeded. The king granted to the town all the fines and forfeits arising from all cases involving men of Cambridge, wherever imposed, and all goods and chattels of felons, fugitives and outlaws in the town—except, of course, those coming within the jurisdiction of the chancellor. It is difficult to assess the worth of the concession; it could vary from a few shillings to a hundred pounds or more. If half the wealthy men in the town—and they were not all that numerous now—could be persuaded to get themselves convicted of felony every so often, the rent of the town would get paid. But most of the local felons had nothing to forfeit but their lives. Despite its 'poverty', the corporation managed to provide itself with a new Guildhall.

Another loophole in the charters was discovered in 1386. They did not specifically mention chandlers and hostellers selling candles and fuel (mostly peat and sedge) as coming under the chancellor's orders. It was stopped by a royal decree to the effect that chandlers were 'victuallers' for all purposes of the act. The university by now had secured control of about a half of the whole commerce of the town, but they still apparently lacked effective means of enforcing it. The chancellor and scholars petitioned parliament in the following year for a ratification of their privileges with these additional requests:

1 Clarification as to who should impose and collect fines on traders who infringed the regulation about buying and selling in the town and on the way there before the appointed time (forestalling).

2 That wine be sold in Cambridge at the same price as in London, plus an extra halfpenny per gallon for the carriage.

3 That the mayor and bailiffs be prevented from making further charges against offenders whom the chancellor had committed to the town gaol.

4 That the mayor be compelled to attend when forfeited foodstuffs were sent to the Hospital of St John, which he refused to do.

But parliament had other things to attend to and no reply was given.

One of the matters on the parliamentary mind, in view of the fact that the September session was to be held in Cambridge, was the insanitary state of the place where they were to stay for six weeks. In August the king wrote to the chancellor, instructing him (not the mayor and bailiffs!) to remove from the streets and lanes of the town all swine, dirt, dung, filth, tree-trunks, etc, and to cause the streets to be kept clear in future.

Parliament met at Barnwell Priory, where the king was lodged, so at least he had a half-mile of open country between him and the stinking town, but most of the members must have slept and dined in the town. Of the long and varied agenda—liberties of the Church, movement of labourers, control of wages, unlawful games, beggars, provision of justices, parliamentary expenses, size of cloths, etc—the most memorable outcome was the decree relating to urban sanitation. Later referred to as the Statute of Cambridge, its title was doubly apt; for although it related to all towns, it clearly had special application here. I quote a few selected phrases from it: '. . . so much dung and filth of the garbage and entrails, as well of beasts killed as of other corruption, be cast in ditches, rivers and other waters . . . the air is greatly corrupt and infect, and many maladies and other intolerable diseases do daily happen . . .'. And the responsibility for enforcement of the clean-up was placed fairly and squarely on the mayor and bailiffs. Their failure to do anything about it probably contributed to the outbreak in 1389 of a serious malady which affected scholars and townsmen 'so that instantly men ran raving mad' and starved themselves to death.

Less determined men—less pig-headed, the chancellor would have said—than the mayor and bailiffs of Cambridge would have given up the struggle. Not they. What they lost on the economic swings they were confident they would regain on the legal roundabouts; so they kept on trying. In 1390 yet another petition to parliament was sent by the university. The mayor and bailiffs, 'as well of ancient enmity and ill-will as of new', had recently arrested and charged 23 'excellent scholars'. The charges had been quashed by Chancery. The mayor, etc, then charged with trespass and felony the proctors, several scholars and even the chancellor himself, who only escaped imprisonment by leaving the town. Then charges of 'felony' (which was one of the charges to which the chancellor's jurisdiction did not apply and which was clearly in need of definition) were brought against other officers of the university 'for the least offence possible' and for offences which were purely imaginary. The chancellor and scholars 'are so troubled, disquieted and oppressed that they cannot attend to their learning, but will be obliged to leave the said university unless they obtain a remedy'. (That would have been sweet music to the ears of the mayor and bailiffs!) Please, pleaded the petitioners, let us have outside arbitrators to try these cases, not the men of the town.

The king and parliament must have been thoroughly fed up with this quarrel which they were called upon to resolve. There seemed no end to it and no remedy. The mayor and bailiffs were summoned to appear once more before parliament, with authority under the common seal of the town, to give an explanation of their conduct. They went, but 'did not bring sufficient warrant'—they did not *have* a common seal—and were put in contempt. Order was made that no scholars should be arrested or indicted for any offence by the townsmen until after the next parliament. For the next two years the wrangling went on—as a matter of fact it went on for the next *200 years*—and there were wrongful arrests, wrongful releases, threats, indictments, appeals, complaints. The situation from the townsmen's point of view was perfectly clear—if a scholar was suspected or accused of any offence, he was guilty; if a townsman committed an offence, he was innocent. I am surprised that the students did not start to riot—they did, 20 years later, but I am surprised that they were kept in check for so long. Just how farcical the situation could be is illustrated by this episode of 1392:

It happened during Lent, as usual. John Mashrelle had been warned by certain persons that they were out to 'get' him, so he took the precaution of telling the local constable, Robert Cooper. One night as Cooper and two colleagues were patrolling their beat, they saw Richard Sutton come out of

Mashrelle's house and run along the street. Considering him suspect, they gave chase, caught him and took him to the Tolbooth. There they discovered that he was a parson, a university chaplain. 'Out of reverence for the clergy' they released him. The matter should have ended there, with an explanation and apology, but no, Sutton, through the chancellor, charged Cooper and his colleagues with wrongful arrest and Cooper was put in prison. The only way to get him out was by a form of bail known as 'mainprise', ie, by a number of persons ('mainpernors', usually four) depositing or promising a sum of money in Chancery as a guarantee that they would be responsible for the accused appearing in court on a given day. In this case the mainpernors were four London men, a haberdasher, scrivener, cordwainer and a 'mynstralle'. (Acting as mainpernor had become a part-time profession; those four men would be paid for their services). But, despite this, the chancellor had refused to release Cooper and only did so after receiving a special order 'under pain of the king's wrath'.

That was the kind of affair that was taking up the time of those whose job it was to run the country! Of hardly less trivial nature were some of the other matters in the town to which the king's hand, if only to signify assent when a letter was read to him, had to be applied. Such as the confiscation of the boat of John Angold, the ferryman at Chesterton, on the grounds that the ferry belonged to the town, 'which it does not'. Or the levying of taxes by the mayor and bailiffs for the repair of the mill which they ought to have repaired at their own cost, instead of impoverishing the commonalty 'which lives for the most part by handicrafts, offices and services'.

They would not have needed to resort to such methods if they had not squandered so much money on litigation, often out of sheer spite. If they had spent on the amenities of their town one tenth of what they spent in trying to land the chancellor of the university in trouble it would have been a much pleasanter place for all of them to live in. But some of the members of the university were just as bad at fouling their own nest; as witness this order from the king to the chancellor in 1393:

Compel the wardens of St Michael Hall and the Hall of the Annunciation of St Mary to scour and keep clean the open gutters made by them from their halls to a main street of the town along which pass many masters and scholars to the university schools . . . or else stop up and abolish the gutters . . . If the king hears more of it he will have cause to proceed against the chancellor as one who despises his command . . . by report of certain persons [guess who!] it has come to the king's ears that by filth continually cast a long while into those gutters and there remaining . . . so great a stench arises and the air is so poisoned that the passers-by are disgusted . . ..

The overflow of the Michaelhouse and Gonville Hall privies was too much of a bad thing for the noses of even the hardened burgesses and the king ought to have been thankful that it was only his ears which were offended. Still, the burgesses could count that as a point scored to them. Henceforth the academic filth would be drained into the river.

Then, quite unexpectedly, hostilities ceased on all fronts. Trouble was expected by the Prior of Barnwell at his Midsummer fair, to which 'great numbers of the commonalty and the university' usually came; in anticipation he persuaded the king to order the sheriff to be there in person and make proclamation about 'unlawful assemblies' and deal with any that occurred.

Apparently none did. There was no trouble of any kind, as far as I can discover, for the next 20 years. I can only guess at the reason, and my guess is that both town and university were short of money with which to carry on the fight.

It is clear that the fortunes of the town had declined, and continued to decline, to the extent that, had there been no university there, and no Steresbrigge Fair, it would have almost faded into oblivion. There is at least one indication that it had done so. Successive monarchs had kept up the practice of making grants of 25 marks annually to the Friars Minor and Friars Preachers; that of 1413 was made to 'the Friars Minor of the University of Cambridge'. And there are frequent references to the town being 'wasted and impoverished', in a context that excludes the likelihood of it being a tax-dodging device. One reason for this state of affairs was undoubtedly the cost of the constant litigation in which the mayors and bailiffs indulged. It is ironical that an institution on which so many of the townspeople depended for their livelihood should at the same time have contributed indirectly to the impoverishment of the town.

After two centuries of co-existence, the town and university were no nearer to accepting each other as partners than they had ever been. True, there was less bloodshed than there used to be. The wounds now inflicted were mostly on the pocket, but they seemed to engender just as much hatred. Neither side was profiting from the perpetual animosity; both were losers. Why did they not call it a day and settle down to live together in something like harmony? Was it because each side believed that, if the strife continued long enough, the other side would give in eventually or go away? The scholars frequently threatened to leave, or complained that they would have to leave—'purposed to leave the university' is a phrase that occurs again and again. Was it just bluff? Some of the townsmen likewise threatened to go and many of them in fact did.

Just as the war had its slack periods, due to war-weariness, lack of resources, or whatever, so did it have its sudden revivals. These, when they came, were increasingly from now on caused by the appearance upon the scene of one or more individuals of strong character; men who saw themselves as fighters for freedom, leaders and liberators of the people, champions of a just cause. The fact that that just cause happened to coincide with the furtherance of their own interest and ambition was perhaps not entirely lost on the people, yet not resented by them, for it meant that much of the fury of the enemy was concentrated on a few men, or even on one only. We hear of the scholars 'striving day and night with all their might to make riots and unlawful assemblies to the disturbance of the people'. Events soon made it clear that by 'the people' was meant the representative of the people, namely John Bilney, the mayor. What we know of him is mostly as seen through university eyes, and thus biased, but enough of his words and deeds survive to enable a reasonably fair picture to be drawn.

One of Bilney's official duties at Michaelmas 1412 was to attend the 'Great Assembly' in the Tolbooth along with representatives of the town and university and take the oath to keep the peace. The ceremony had been held for the past 140 years. The emphasis initially was on keeping the peace; over the years it had become modified and now the emphasis was on 'observing the statutes, privileges and customs of the university'. Bilney, in the hearing of all, declared that he would not observe any statutes or customs unless he had them under the king's seal. He knew perfectly well that all the privileges of the university had been granted by charters bearing the king's seal. It was a declaration of war.

The plan of campaign was familiar. For a start Bilney persuaded all his fellow corn-dealers to refuse to have their bushel and half-bushel measures checked by the chancellor's men and pay the fourpence due for that privilege. He refused to give aid in carrying out punishments on those convicted in the chancellor's court and prevented the bedells from collecting fines. When Thomas Wering, one of the bedells, distrained on one of the convicted scholars by taking his possessions, Bilney seized them, gave them back to the scholar and threatened to charge Wering with theft. He actively encouraged the scholars to rebel against the chancellor's authority, and soon learnt that this was a way of playing with fire.

Bilney owned a hostel near St Michael's church which was normally rented by students. When the lease came up for renewal he turned the students out, saying that he intended to live there himself, and then let the premises to townsmen, knowing that this was a violation of one of the university statutes, or at any rate a violation of a long-standing agreement.

Whilst making sure that the chancellor did not arrest any townsmen, he arrested scholars on the slightest pretext. One of them was Richard Sutton, the chaplain who had been at the centre of a farcical affair 20 years earlier. The imprisonment and ill-treatment of Sutton caused a disturbance in which Bilney and his associates might well have been killed if the proctors had not intervened to save them. Not that Bilney had any support in the university ranks, but there was still a tendency for the scholars to divide into groups or 'nations' in keen rivalry with each other and, on this occasion, it seems that the Northerners had attacked the Southerners who were attacking Bilney and his colleagues. Thirty of the Northerners were expelled and others heavily fined.

Then there was the affair of Thomas Hierman, one of Bilney's employees. Bilney had sent him to Barnwell Priory to collect 25s owing for six quarters of corn from one Baker, servant of the prior. Hierman was pounced upon by the prior, the proctors and bedells acting in unison and locked up in the Castle. A case of wrongful arrest, protested Bilney later in a petition to parliament. What he omitted to say—and the chancellor took care to explain—was that Hierman had, before this incident, scandalised the university by charging scholars with offences which townsmen had committed, that he was a notorious disturber of the peace, that he had broken into the chancellor's office at Steresbrig Fair, that he kept a brothel in the fair and lived, for two weeks at least, on the immoral earnings of the women. The university had banished Hierman from the town, said Bilney, and broken into his house in order to beat him if they found him. But, said the chancellor, he was permitted to remain in the town, despite the fact that 'he grew from worse to worse, in wandering in the night and jetting'.

'Jetting' is a word that makes its appearance in the annals at about this time. Of uncertain origin, it meant strutting about the streets, usually by night, in gangs of anything up to 40 or 50, looking for trouble and creating it if not readily found. It is still, as apparently it always was, a favourite occupation of mindless youths in urban areas, leaving behind a trail of broken windows, wrecked bus-shelters, obscene scrawls on walls and empty beer-cans on the pavements. In the Middle Ages the activities of the night-jetters had much the same effect on the nerves and tempers of the people in their houses. They, too, preferred to stay indoors behind locked doors and shuttered windows, hoping that the hubbub would recede. Students as well as the town youths indulged in the 'sport', sometimes no doubt as an outlet for high spirits, or as an escape from boredom; sometimes with more sinister motives. Windows were broken (not glass windows—wooden frames with shutters), railings smashed, doors were bombarded with stones and frequently the burgesses cowered helplessly indoors listening to shouts of 'Come out, you villains, whoremongers and scoundrels, or you shall be burnt in your houses'. One who did come out, John Buste, was seriously wounded.

Bilney was an obvious target for such attentions. One night he was roused from slumber by an unholy row in the street outside and through a chink in the shutters saw a crowd of students 'armed in a warlike manner'. It is doubtful whether they were really 'lying in wait to kill him and his officers if they had issued out of their house'; they were more probably intending to scare the life out of him, which they very nearly did. In the morning he found fixed to his gate a doggerel rhyme which, besides various uncomplimentary references to the mayor and his fellows—the bald pate of Bilney, the goat's beard of Bambour, Hierman the harlot with the calf's snout, pot-bellied Attlebridge—threatened them all with rough handling when next encountered. Bilney, wounded in his dignity more than in his person, made much of this episode in his complaint to the Council and accused the chancellor and proctors of being party to it. They insisted that all the scholars had been in their lodgings that night and accused Bilney of encouraging the town youths to go jetting with the intention of putting the blame on the students.

In this it seems that Bilney, or one of his associates, was certainly to blame, for the chancellor cited several instances. In one of them, which occurred in the autumn of 1418, a crowd of youths went jetting, pretending to be students, who were blamed for the disturbance and damage. During Lent of the following year—Bilney was no longer mayor, but still actively pursuing his campaign of malice—another gang of jetters passed themselves off as students until their capture revealed the truth. Two years later, 'at the end of the town' (either Spital End or Castle End), a smith was attacked and robbed by a gang, and so badly beaten that he was left for dead in the street. Again the blame fell on the students, until the smith recovered and was able to identify two of his assailants as townsmen, who were later hanged for the offence.

The students were not altogether blameless. During Bilney's year of office a party of them were persuaded by Nicholas Hauke, one of Bilney's partisans, to embark on a jetting expedition which resulted in the death of a nobleman, whereupon they were arrested by the town officers and handed over to the chancellor, who was bound to administer severe punishment, though not hanging. As the campaign progressed, the chancellor's court was ignored more and more, and offending students, whether in fact guilty or not, were dealt with by the secular judges. Whenever the chancellor arrested a townsman involved in an affray with a student, he was immediately charged with wrongful arrest. The charge did not succeed, of course, but it was a great vexation and hindrance to the maintenance of law and order.

Bilney's behaviour, and that of his cronies, might well have been represented by him as a defence of the liberties of the town, especially when he stoutly maintained that the fee-farm rent could not be paid unless the king restored to the mayor and bailiffs the revenue accruing from the assay of bread, ale and all victuals. But he steadily lost the support of his adherents by his mendacity and the blatant illegality of many of his actions and it became clear that he was lining his own pocket rather than restoring the town's finances. He imprisoned two friars and two of the proctors on groundless charges, but allowed them to be set free on payment of a considerable sum of money. He took 'protection' money from the local fishermen, though by ancient custom all burgesses had common fishing-rights in the river. He extorted money from townsmen who could ill afford it, under threat of forfeiting their status of freemen, declaring that the money was needed to defray the costs of legal proceedings against the university. Those who refused to contribute had their normal taxation increased; those who paid up had their taxes reduced. He compelled the other bakers to have their corn ground at the town mill, but refused to have his own corn ground there because, he said, the millers were fraudulent. He had frequently said in the presence of the university officers that he could not observe the regulations relating to bread (he was a baker as well as a corn-dealer) because of the deceitfulness of the millers; his bread was of poor quality due to the addition of chalk. *He* had not added the chalk, of course. He never accepted the blame for anything. He employed out-and-out swindlers like Attlebridge to do that.

Every representation he made to parliament or the Council was, according to the chancellor, a tissue of lies, and at complete variance with the university charters. Bilney himself made no secret of the fact that he knew that the chancellor had sole jurisdiction over the sale of foodstuffs; he said so publicly in St Mary's church. He may have seriously believed that he could get the law changed by making a nuisance of himself, by setting himself up as a popular leader. On one occasion, when the chancellor, Master John Rikinghale, who was also a justice of the peace, summoned Bilney to the church of the Austin Friars to ask him to moderate his malicious attitude, Bilney offered to fight him. The chancellor's reply to that was that he would send him to the Castle if he did not behave better, whereupon Bilney said that the chancellor had no power to punish him and he had a hundred fighting-men to resist him.

The common fields of Cambridge

The date could have been set two centuries earlier than c 1400 or two centuries later. The map is placed here mainly to illustrate the enormous potential there was for the expansion of the town once agriculture had ceased to be the mainstay of its economy. This expansion did not take place and the reason is not altogether clear. It was partly, no doubt, because the townspeople did not realise the potential, whereas the university did; throughout the latter half of the 15th century and the whole of the 16th the colleges were steadily acquiring, by gift and by purchase, more land in the common fields, particularly in the immediate vicinity of the town. The full signifi-cance of this did not emerge until much later.

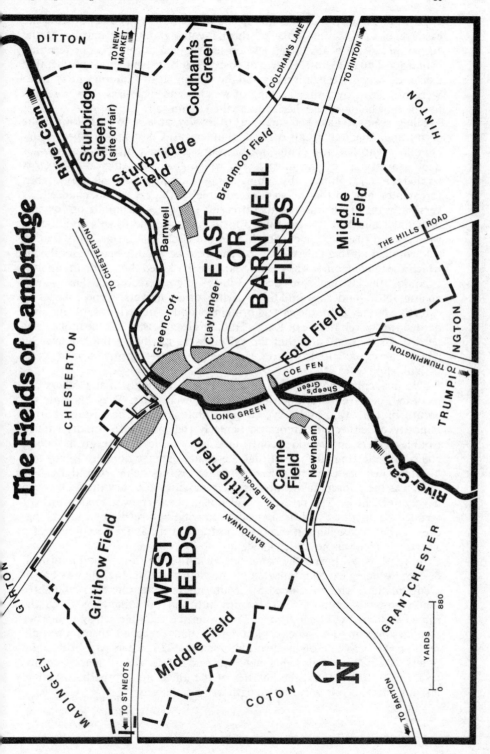

The Fields of Cambridge

DITTON

River Cam

TO NEW-MARKET

Sturbridge Green (site of fair)

Sturbridge Field

Coldham's Green

COLDHAM'S LANE

TO HINTON

HINTON

Bradmoor Field

Barnwell

Clayhanger

Greencroft

EAST OR BARNWELL FIELDS

Middle Field

THE HILLS ROAD

TO CHESTERTON

CHESTERTON

Ford Field

COE FEN

Sheep's Green

LONG GREEN

Newnham

Carme Field

Little Field

Binn Brook

BARTONWAY

River Cam

TRUMPINGTON

TO TRUMPINGTON

Grithow Field

WEST FIELDS

Middle Field

GIRTON

MADINGLEY

TO ST NEOTS

COTON

GRANTCHESTER

TO BARTON

N

YARDS 880 0

To what extent Bilney was implicated in the numerous escapes from the castle gaol at this time—one of them involving the near-murder of the keeper and his wife—or the attacks on several men of quality, one resulting in murder, I do not know. He was almost certainly instrumental in fomenting a dispute, between the university and the merchants of London who came to Steresbrig Fair, over the checking of weights and measures. It was settled for the time being by the sheriff doing the job himself.

Bilney seems to have had some sort of loyalty, at least to his fellows in the corn-trade. One item in his official complaint to Council concerned Henry Dunmow who had prosecuted in the court of King's Bench an action for debt against one of the masters; to which the chancellor and proctors retaliated, said Bilney, by imprisoning Dunmow for 40 days, then threatening him so that he was forced to leave the town. The chancellor's version of the affair was slightly different: Dunmow was in prison for nine days only, and had left the town for his own and the town's good; there were several reasons for putting him in the Castle gaol, one being that he sold rotten malt to an ale-wife, certifying it to be good, when in fact the ale which she made from it was so bad that it nearly killed those who drank it.

Almost the last malicious act of Bilney—the last recorded, that is—was an attempt to hinder the building activities of the university and colleges by extorting money from the carters bringing wood, stone, tiles, sand and lime needed for the rebuilding of King's Hall. His excuse was that the money was needed for 'pavage' and that the carters were infringing the bye-laws by having carts shod with iron tyres. (Imagine trying to transport stone in carts with un-shod wheels!)

The incidents which I have described, and no doubt many others not recorded, occurred over a period of about seven years. They illustrate the nature of the 'war' and serve to show that it could be sustained by a minority on either side; more particularly that a handful of determined trouble-makers on one side, confronted by weak leadership on the other, could cause lasting harm. Not that the actual damage done by Bilney and his associates was very great. In practical terms they achieved nothing. The town was the poorer financially for their activities and they themselves can have gained little. The greatest harm done, however, was to the spirit of reconciliation which had been steadily growing before Bilney came along, even if that reconciliation did take the form of a passive acceptance of a situation which was not much liked.

As for Bilney himself, he came out of it all with stature undiminished, despite his being excommunicated by the chancellor. In 1422 he was one of a commission, which included Sir Walter de la Pole, one clerk and three other burgesses, appointed to inquire into and do something about the ruined state of the Great Bridge. Following the example set by numerous commissions on the same subject which had preceded them, they did nothing. He was one of the two aldermen in 1426, when Attlebridge and others who had been his henchmen also held office. All of them, it seems, took the oath to uphold the liberties of the university. So perhaps he had learnt something—if only that an oath was mere words.

Chapter 7

Resignation 1423-1503

When the town at last acquired a common seal in 1423, a prominent feature depicted on it was the Great Bridge. Since the bridge provided half of the town's name, linked its two halves together and spanned its main commercial artery, this was a piece of apt symbolism. More apt than the burgesses realised. For more than 120 years the bridge was in a dangerous state of decay as a result of malicious damage, misuse, avoidance of responsibility, neglect and sheer apathy. Between 1386 and 1498 no less than 11 commissions were appointed to get it repaired 'speedily'. Such repairs as were done never lasted more than 20 years, yet somehow it survived, somehow people and carts and animals got by—or fell in. The town was not responsible for the bridge—an ordinance of 500 years earlier decreed that it was to be maintained by a levy on certain lands in the county—and so the townspeople did nothing about it, except complain when its condition got too bad. Their attitude towards the bridge seems to sum up their attitude to everything, especially in the 15th century.

In one way it was perhaps a good thing, for their apathy and resignation meant that the Town/Gown war virtually ceased to exist for close on 80 years. There may have been the odd clash between rival gangs of jetters now and then when life became too dull; one instance is recorded in 1452 of a group of students battering a baker to death with 'a staff worth ½d'; on several occasions the local gentry waged private vedettas in the town and several villains made daring escapes from the castle gaol—apart from that, the town remained undisturbed. No one succeeded Bilney as champion of the townsmen's cause. No one attacked the university with weapons or words, pikes or petitions. Most people seem to have been content to let the university get on with its own affairs.

Not only that, some of them were prepared to co-operate actively with it and further its progress. When he died, in 1423, John Herries, ex-mayor and leading burgess for 30 years, left £10 towards the building of the new library and paid for the paving of School Street. He was 'a rare example of a townsman,' said Dr Caius later. In 1424 the town council spent 6s 6d on 'wine given to the chancellor when he came from beyond the sea, in the presence of the mayor and other burgesses'—a gesture, often repeated, which could only make for better relations. In 1424 the corporation allowed Michaelhouse to make a canal from the river to the edge of their garden to facilitate the delivery of fuel. In 1459 Richard Andrew, a wealthy burgess, left money and property to Queens' College—for the benefit of his soul and to provide an annual memorial, admittedly, but the benefit to the college was real enough.

The university during this period, still relying largely on outside benefactors, continued its policy of peaceful expansion and the townsmen, far
from opposing the take-over of their territory, in some cases actually
encouraged it. In 1428 the Abbot of Crowland and the Bishops of Durham
and Norwich founded a college for monks in St Giles' parish; the town gave
them a plot of land called Peads Yard; it later became a secular college
called *Buckingham College* and later still Magdalene. In 1439 William
Byngham, to supply the need for grammar masters, gave his house and
garden and an endowment of £50 a year to found *Godshouse* for 24 scholars.
The site was wanted for a much more ambitious project and the college was
eventually established in 1446 in a house in Preachers Street outside the
Barnwell Gate where, 60 years later, it was refounded as Christ's College.

The ambitious project which ousted Godshouse was the king's foundation,
in 1441, of the new *College of St Nicholas*. Originally intended for a rector
and 12 scholars, the actual building of the college could not keep pace with
the growth of the plan. In the course of eight years it had changed its name
to the College of St Mary and St Nicholas and had swallowed up a church,
nine houses, two cottages, four hostels, three gardens, two inns, a hithe,
sundry pieces of waste ground, two whole streets and part of two others. To
this the town added 4½ acres of their common pasture on the west side of
the river. The land on which King's College—as it came to be called—was
built was all given, some of it by the chancellor; the building was done at the
king's expense, which is why it took 60 years to complete.

There was an element of self-interest in the town's generosity. Before the
building was far advanced the mayor and bailiffs petitioned parliament for
a reduction in their taxes on the grounds that the new college, and the others
which had been built, had reduced their revenues because 'many people have
withdrawn and intend to withdraw'. They were granted a reduction of £26 'for
their kindness in the building of the king's college' and later were given land
on which to construct a lane to replace the lost Salthithelane. The foundation-
stone of the chapel of King's College was laid in September 1447, a ceremony
which King Henry VI had intended to perform himself, but 'for the aier and the
pestilence that hath long regned in our said Universitie, we come not there
at this time' and so the Earl of Suffolk officiated in his stead.

In emulation of her husband, Queen Margaret founded *her* college in
1448, after some delay in getting the king to grant the licence. The *College
of St Margaret and St Bernard* was originally for a 'president' and four
fellows. It did not prosper until re-founded as Queens' College by Elizabeth
Woodville, queen of Edward IV.

The passivity of the townsmen did not result in the gownsmen
abandoning entirely their martial spirit. Incensed at the excessive and
exclusive privileges—to say nothing of the huge endowment—granted to
King's, the students of some other colleges in 1454 attacked the new college
'with guns and habiliments of war' and the mayor had the unusual
experience of being called upon to quell the disturbance and take charge of
the armaments. Fifteen years later the university authorities enacted a
statute forbidding masters and scholars to carry, in the open, bows and
arrows, or crossbows and bolts, by night or day, on pain of perpetual
expúlsion. However, licence could be granted to carry and use these
weapons for 'peaceable' purposes and *in defence of university privileges*.

So, it could be that the lack of hostilities was partly due to the fact that one side was better armed than the other. For the townsmen were under orders that no weapons were to be carried by any man of whatever degree. Security had been tightened up considerably of late, doors were to be kept closed after curfew, harbouring of suspicious persons made householders liable to a fine of £1 and, of course, proclamation was regularly made that 'all mariner of comon women voyde this town within three dayes'.

Another college was founded in 1475; this was the *Hall of St Catherine*, founded by Dr Robert Woodlark, Provost of King's. It did not attract many endowments and long remained one of the poorest of the colleges. Poverty was crippling the town also. By 1481 it was 'so diminished' that the king was obliged to knock £10 off the annual bill. The mayor and bailiffs were still managing to keep up a show of hospitality and dignity by making 'presents' to visiting dignitaries, payments 'to the minstrels' and providing themselves with robes and hoods. I am prompted to wonder how much the town suffered financially over the years from the need—real or imagined—to 'keep up with the university' in the matter of ceremonial trappings and entertainment. The mayors, bailiffs and aldermen were always outwardly very conscious of their 'dignity', however much their conduct might be at variance with it.

The first indication that the long period of inactivity was about to end came in 1492, when the mayor, bailiffs and burgesses sent a petition to King Henry VII, concerning a matter which now seems trivial but was of very real importance then. The university had devised a new weapon, known as 'discommoning'. When a trader in the town persistently refused to comply with the regulations laid down by the chancellor, or supplied commodities below the required standard and refused to pay the fine for so doing, his name was published in all the colleges as one with whom the students were forbidden to have any dealings whatever on pain of a heavy fine. The petition did not specify the faults for which the burgesses had been 'discommoned' nor state how many had been thus punished. Later experience suggests that it may only have been two or three. What alarmed the burgesses was the prospect of the practice reaching a proportion that would affect the pockets of most of them, to their 'Disinheritance and utter undoing, contrary to all right, justice and equity'. If something were not done, they would all be 'utterly undone and destroyed'. The king was not much moved by their hyperbole.

What made the chancellor's new tactics even worse was that they were used in addition to, not as a replacement of, the old methods. William Mascall had been put in gaol for two days, Robert Robinson had been beaten by one of the university officers and John Barber, with several others, had been threatened with imprisonment. It did indeed sound like a rule of tyranny; the actions of law-keepers always do—to law-breakers.

Town money continued to be spent on gifts of wine and sweets, fish, minstrels—not very large amounts as yet. The heaviest item—apart from rents and subsidies—in the town accounts for 1494 was the payment of £2 in fees to Roger Filpot and John Woods, gentlemen and 'lawyers of the counsel of the town'. A legal battle was in the offing and the burgesses had learnt that legal affairs were best handled by professionals.

In 1497 came an event which foreshadowed another of a similar nature, but on a far vaster scale, which was to occur later. The Priory of St Radegund, on the east side of the town, had never really prospered. Now 'by negligence and improvident and dissolute disposition and incontinence *occasioned by the vicinity of the university*', it was utterly decayed. That seems rather a startling accusation on the part of the bishop. What had the nuns been up to? Not much, lately, for there were only two of them; one was 'professed elsewhere' and the other 'but an infant'. The Bishop of Ely was granted licence to suppress the house and found in its place a college (for a master, six fellows and a number of scholars to be instructed in grammar, to pray and celebrate mass daily for the souls of the royal family, etc) to be called the *College of St Mary the Virgin, St John the Evangelist and St Radegund the Virgin*. That title, mercifully, was soon altered to Jesus College. It was endowed with about 70 acres of land in the fields of Cambridge and about 40 houses in the town, and later acquired more property.

The town's reply to this latest territorial gain by the university was to organise the collecting of funds to finance the legal campaign about to begin in defence of their charters and dwindling liberties. A common box was to be provided, complete with lock and key, held by the town treasurer. Into this box would go in future:

6s 8d from the Town Recorder at his election.
20d from any lawyer pleading his first case.
3s 4d each from the mayor, coroner and aldermen.
20d from each bailiff.
12d each from the treasurers.
6d from the head constable.
12d from every freeman hiring a booth at the fair.
4d from every burgess buying his freedom of the borough.
2d from every burgess enrolling an apprentice.
20d from whoever leased the King's Mill.
8d from the lessee of Whittlesford Bridge.

And so on. It looks as though it ought to have brought in a tidy sum each year and probably did. But the money was more easily spent than collected:

£5 for the matter pleaded between university and town.
3s 4d for breakfast at the time of the meeting.
£1 expenses to London with supplication shown to the king.
£2 expenses to London to prosecute the same matter.
Breakfast at the Dolphin; presents to the solicitor of the Lord King; wine at the White Hart; one flagon of red wine; one bottle of sweet wine; two green geese; three lawyers at £1 each, etc.

The box was soon empty. A further source of income was needed. Raffles had not yet been invented. Church-ales were the monopoly of the churches and not very profitable anyway. The idea they came up with was one which they ought to have tried ages ago, for a different reason. They ordered the constables in every parish to do their jobs really thoroughly, without fear or favour. As a result no less than 266 offenders came before the magistrates at the town leet of Easter 1502. Here are just some of the charges on which they were presented:

Overloading the common pastures with grazing animals.
Digging turves of peat on the commons.
Allowing pigs to roam in the streets.
Digging gravel and clunch in the highway.
Leaving blocks of wood in the street.
Failing to repair the 'pavement' in front of houses.

Making dungheaps in the street.

Allowing cess-pits to drain into the street.

Leaving a cart standing in the highway.

Having privies overhanging the river or King's Ditch.

Throwing dead animals, or parts of same, into the river.

Brawling and blood-letting.

Harbouring suspected persons, etc, etc.

A magnificent effort! The constables all deserved medals and even the chancellor himself could scarcely have forborne to cheer—though perhaps with less enthusiasm if he had known what they were raising the money for, more if eight of the colleges and halls of residence had not figured among the culprits, as guilty of some of the most unsavoury offences. Unfortunately, nobody had worked out how they were going to collect all the fines from that number of people.

Further litigation for the present being rendered inadvisable by rising costs and diminished resources, both sides readily agreed to the suggestion of the Countess of Richmond (Lady Margaret Beaufort, mother of the king) that they should submit their disputes to arbitration, an idea never seriously tried before. They agreed to appoint as arbitrators two of the king's sergeants-at-law and John Fisher, then a Justice of Common Pleas, later chancellor of the university, and each party bound itself in the sum of 500 marks to abide by their award. Several meetings and long deliberation resulted in an award a year later, which in May 1503 was finalised in the form of a covenant—later to be referred to, many times, as a 'composition'. This was the substance of it:

1 The university shall not accept as students those who have no intention of studying.

2 Servants of scholars shall only enjoy their privileges during the actual time of their service.

3 University servants—bedells, manciples, cooks, launderers, doctors, scriveners, barbers, bookbinders, etc—shall not follow any other trade or occupation than that in which they are appointed.

4 University servants who dwell in the town shall have university privilege; those dwelling outside shall be subject to the jurisdiction of the mayor and bailiffs.

5 Those claiming university privilege shall support their claim within seven days by a certificate from the chancellor or his deputy; servants shall swear an oath in St Mary's church.

6 As regards the sale of foodstuffs, the mayor and bailiffs shall deal with all cases not affecting scholars or servants.

7 The chancellor or his deputy shall have full jurisdiction over cases of affray involving scholars.

8 In a case of felony or mayhem, scholars shall be dealt with by the common law of the realm.

9 Prisoners committed by the chancellor shall pay to the gaoler 4d for the first day of their imprisonment and not more than 12d for a week or longer.

10 No tolls shall be collected by the mayor and bailiffs from outsiders bringing the following into the town for sale: pigs, geese, rabbits, chickens, butter, cheese, eggs, fruit and fish, carried in their hands, on their backs or by pack-horse without a 'wombtie' (girth-strap). Butchers shall only pay stallage of ½d a day, or 12d a year, for a stall measuring 6 feet by 4 feet.

11 Fishmongers from outside the town shall only pay 3d per quarter for their market stalls or ½d a week.

12 Those bringing oysters, herrings, sprats or any fresh fish shall pay a toll of only ½d for each pack-horse load, and sell without a stall if they wish or 1d for a cart-load of oysters.

13 For every cart-load of wood brought into the town, ½d toll shall be paid, for coal 1d, but if the fuel is intended for a college or religious house no toll shall be paid.

14 Every pack-horse load passing through the town shall pay 1d, every cart-load 2d, droves of cattle or flocks of sheep shall pay passage as of ancient custom.

15 Burgesses bringing in corn and coal by water shall use bushel measures checked and stamped by the university taxors and pay 4d a year only.

16 Brewers and bakers who set up business in the town shall pay 3s 4d to the proctors and taxors. If they change premises, they shall re-apply for a licence, the cost of which shall not exceed 6s 8d.

17 Correction of nuisances shall be done by the mayor and bailiffs at the town leet held twice a year. If they do not amend the nuisance within six weeks, and a scholar is involved, then the university authorities shall deal with it.

18 The 'seges' (loos) built over the river and ditches shall be abolished by the owners. The 'common sege' shall be cleansed before next Easter, and thereafter every third year, at the expense of the town.

19 No butcher shall slaughter animals in the street, or dispose of blood, entrails, etc, in a way that causes annoyance to scholars or townspeople.

20 The inspection of leather shall be done by the town officials, who shall pay 3s 4d annually to the university for this privilege, and inform the university of the names of those appointed to do office.

21 The university shall have no say in the control of sack-cloth.

22 Assessment of liability for taxes, tallage, aids, subsidies, etc, levied by the king shall be done by a committee of eight burgesses and four university members. Amounts due from the university shall be collected by the bedell and handed to the mayor.

23 A list is appended of university servants and officers for the time being. (It contained 64 names; all male.)

24 Any doubt or ambiguity in these agreements shall be settled by the Countess of Richmond and her nominees during her lifetime, thereafter by the Chancellor of the Realm, Chief Justice and Justice of Common Pleas, who shall arbitrate in any subsequent dispute.

I have reduced an unduly wordy document to about one fiftieth of its original length and clarified many of the clauses. It is not difficult to guess which clauses emanated from the burgesses and which from the university, nor does one need to be a legal expert to spot the number of points on which 'ambiguity' would arise sooner or later. The extent to which the chancellor dominated and controlled the commercial life of the town was already alarming. Nevertheless, that document was agreed to by both sides, and the Countess of Richmond must have felt that she had at last succeeded where kings and parliaments had failed. The very fact of acceptance of arbitration was a significant move towards the establishment of lasting peace. Or was it?

Chapter 8

Rebellious townsmen 1503-1534

The method of settling disputes by arbitration as distinct from costly law-suits and petitions to parliament clearly appealed to both sides, particularly the townsmen, who used it to settle a number of issues over the next few years—fishing-rights, the Chesterton ferry, pastures, rights in the fairs, etc. It had disadvantages, however, in that it provided only a temporary *ad hoc* solution and in that it afforded even more scope than did ordinary litigation for the manipulation of the arbitrators. What was really needed at this stage of the war, perhaps, was a clean sweep of all preceding legislation and an entirely fresh start made, taking account of changed circumstances—if either side could have been induced to accept such a measure, which I doubt. Three hundred years of tradition on one side and 500 on the other were not going to be lightly cast aside. The chancellor and masters would not budge one inch from their privileged position. The burgesses had shaken themselves out of the torpor which had enshrouded the town for the best part of a century and for the next hundred years showed a determination to fight as they had never fought before. I do not know for sure the reason for this sudden change. It may have been connected with economic revival, as instanced by the growing importance of Sturbridge Fair, with the under-mining of the Church, the decay of feudalism, the rise of the Common Man, the spread of New Learning—some, or all, or none of those things. Whatever the reason, it happened.

One fault of that 'composition' of 1503, apart from its tortuous verbosity, its obscurity and the triviality of some of it, was precisely that it did not cancel or clarify previous enactments—it could not, for it was not issued by a legal court—especially those relating to powers of arrest and punishment. Nor did it touch on the oath-taking ceremony at the beginning of the academic year. And those were the very points on which feeling ran most high among the town officials. The ordinary run of townsmen were more concerned with tolls and stallage and the like.

Consequently it was not long—less than two years—before the chancellor and masters had cause to write to the Countess of Richmond to tell her of the wickedness of the mayor and bailiffs in continuing to arrest and punish scholars, thus keeping them from their studies. The countess was no doubt touched by the flattery in which their complaint was wrapped, but had more important matters to attend to. In 1505 she founded *Christ's College* for a master, 12 fellows and 47 scholars and endowed it with about 4,000 acres of land in Cambridgeshire and Essex. The former foundation of Godshouse was incorporated in it. Lady Margaret had also intended to do the same with the ancient Hospital of St John, now heavily in debt, but she died in 1509 before her plan could be put into effect. John Fisher, Bishop of Rochester and now chancellor of the university, carried out her wishes, despite opposition from several eminent churchmen, and founded *St John's College* in 1511. The hospital had owned more than 250 acres of land in the Cambridge fields and about two dozen houses in the town (and yet it was 'impoverished'!) all of which, along with other endowments, made it one of the richest of the colleges.

At the same time some of the others, notably Michaelhouse and Gonville Hall, were steadily acquiring more land and property. It seems odd to me that the townsmen never tried to oppose this material enrichment of the colleges; in fact they frequently contributed to it. Investment in real estate as a long-term policy did not apparently mean much to them, they were more concerned with the immediate gains of buying and selling of consumer goods. For many of them, the more student bellies there were to satisfy, the better. What the university population was at this date is not easy to determine. The 14 colleges between them seem to have housed about 400 masters, ministers and scholars, in addition there were perhaps 20 'inns' or hostels housing another two or three hundred, and then there was an unknown number of 'clerks' who belonged to both university and town, so that at any given moment during term time about a quarter of the people in that small town were 'of the university'.

When Bishop Fisher resigned the chancellorship in 1514, it was offered to Cardinal Wolsey, who declined to accept, and Fisher was reappointed for life. From this time on the office of chancellor was always held by an eminent statesman or churchman who acted as 'patron' or protector, and the vice-chancellor became the head of affairs for practical purposes. Previous to 1519 the office of vice-chancellor had been held for an indefinite period, and money paid to obtain the office; now election was made annually from among the heads of colleges, and no payment made or received. This has nothing to do with the fact that, to save space and printer's ink, I shall refer to the vice-chancellor as 'VC' and to the heads of colleges as 'Heads' from now on.

The advantage of having a patron in the very highest ranks of state and society soon became evident. The day was not far distant when the Chancellor of the University (capital letters are, I feel, obligatory from now on) was at the same time Chancellor of the Realm, a source of support which the townsmen could not even begin to match. They did, however, make some effort in that direction by appointing a High Steward of the town (salary £2 per annum) to balance the High Steward of the university (also £2 per annum), although both appointments probably cost more in lavish gifts than the services they rendered were worth.

The university had for a long time wielded a weapon denied to the town, namely the power of excommunication, though just how effective it was depended on the conscience and character of the person excommunicated. When the VC excommunicated Robert Smythe, one of the bailiffs, for violation of the privileges 'granted by the kings of England and confirmed by sundry Popes of Rome', Smythe retaliated by seeking to purchase a writ of *praemunire* against him but changed his mind when he learned what it would cost. The proctors who perambulated the streets were often accompanied by priests, who relied more on worldly armament than on spiritual authority to enforce an order. In 1515 one of the townsmen encountered by the night patrol replied to their challenge by preparing to fight, and was fatally wounded. Another townsman was killed by a junior proctor on night patrol in 1524; the prosecution of the proctor by the town was attributed to 'pure malice' on their part and he was acquitted.

This last incident sparked off the next round of open revolt—that is how the conflict must now be regarded, as a revolt by the townsmen against their masters. George Foyster, mayor, was summoned to appear before Dr Crooke, deputy VC. Being busy with municipal matters, the mayor sent his excuses to that effect and said he would come when he could. When he did later appear, the doctor, 'replete with malice and pride', refused to see him, promptly excommunicated him and caused the sentence of excommunication to be fixed to the market cross. Whereupon the mayor, 'being a very simple man, unlearned and desiring rather to live in peace with his wrong than to seek his remedy', came to the doctor and asked for absolution. This was only granted after the mayor, kneeling in the church of the Austin Friars, had offered a halfpenny candle to the image of St Mary and recited a submission composed and dictated by Dr Crooke, declaring his guilt in having maintained his authority against the liberties of the university.

That such arrogant and humiliating conduct did not immediately provoke retaliation was due solely to the mild character of the mayor. That the spirit of revolt was in the air once more is revealed by the firm conviction of the Duke of Norfolk, when sent to deal with a minor rebellion in Suffolk in 1525, that the 'confederacy of evil-disposed persons' had extended to 'the town and university of Cambridge'.

In 1526 the arbitration committee, which included Cardinal Wolsey, was appealed to by the VC and Heads to amend the Composition of 1503, which by now had been so much breached by both sides as to be made worthless. The committee merely repeated several clauses and amended three others as follows:

1 To the list of university servants was added household servants of scholars.

2 The Chancellor was to have jurisdiction over contracts concerning foodstuffs brought into the town; no victualler should pay money to the mayor 'for opening their windows and selling their victuals'.

3 The mayor was to deal with all common nuisances but the VC was to have power of punishment in respect of them.

Which only made the situation slightly more confused.

In that same year came a hint of a threat hanging over the colleges—possibly no more than wishful thinking on the part of some of the townsmen, though it could have been a deeply laid plot. The occasion was the annual banquet at Corpus Christi, to which the mayor and bailiffs were invited as a matter of custom and courtesy. The mayor, tongue loosened and tact diminished by the circulating flagon, was heard to remark that he was there as of right, not courtesy. A heated discussion arose, in the course of which one of the burgesses blurted out that 'there would come a time when a great part of the houses which the college had received from townsmen would revert to them again'. Later events nearly proved him right. The seizure of monastic property was already much more than a vague threat and the university was as anxious as anybody to be in at the kill—as hunters, not the hunted.

Early in 1529 one of the mayor's officers was sentenced by the VC to be banished from the town. The mayor, Edward Slegge, refused to carry out the order, which he said was made out of sheer spite. So the VC, having charged the mayor with perjury and breach of privilege, excommunicated him. The usual notice was fixed on the market cross and displayed in all the churches. Then, in a series of reports drawn up and presented to the arbitration-committee, the indignation of the townsmen was revealed. This is, briefly, what they accused, at great length, the VC and proctors of doing:

—banishing and exiling townsmen, contrary to the law of the land, at their own will and pleasure;

—excommunicating town officials illegally for refusing to obey illegal orders;

—searching foreign traders coming to Sturbridge fair, illegally, and confiscating goods for their own gain;

—allowing laymen, pretending to be scholars, to escape punishment for dicing and gaming.

The arbitrators, and the university authorities, did nothing. So, three years later, the townsmen again tackled the Lord Chancellor, Lord Treasurer and Lord Chief Justice, reciting at even greater length their grievances and backing their accusations of illegality with greater detail, here summarised:

1 The compulsory oath imposed on the mayor and burgesses in the 'Black Assembly' is an affront to municipal dignity and the cause of many disputes.

2 University personnel do not take the oath which they impose on the townsmen. 'The scholars being nowadays in great number increased in the town, and not being charged by the oath, be many times the bolder to make unlawful assemblies, routs and riots.' They attack the mayor, bailiffs and burgesses 'in the night-time, beating down their doors and windows in the most riotous manner'. (In 1534 a number of the students were summoned to Westminster Hall, charged by the mayor and bailiffs with breaking windows; they were sent back to Cambridge for trial at the request of the VC.)

3 Many so-called scholars dress as laymen, are married, and follow trades in the town such as drapers, mercers, grocers, innkeepers, bakers, etc. They are wealthy. They qualify as burgesses, but refuse to accept any of the duties of burgesses, to sit on juries at the town leet, or pay any of the dues which burgesses pay, thereby depriving the town of income and putting it to the expense of suing them.

4 University officers summon town officials to attend assays of bread and ale, etc, whenever it suits them, without due notice and at inconvenient times, then excommunicate them for not attending. In the old days the colleges and halls relied for their supplies on the inhabitants of the town. 'Now the bulk of the university consists in colleges which, by reason of their great wealth and endowments, be waxen so politic and wise that they have provided brewhouses and bake-houses of their own.' They brew and bake in their own houses, and do not take the trouble to see that the assay of bread and ale is properly made, but take money for conniving at offences. They make money; the town loses money.

5 The VC has usurped the spiritual authority of the bishop and archdeacon in exercising the power of excommunication, which he uses in an arrogant and arbitrary manner. The burgesses are 'daily so sore vexed, troubled and on-quieted that they been purposed rather to forsake the town and inhabit themselves elsewhere than thus to continue in such bondage and thraldom'.

6 Oswald Thompson, cordwainer, brought an action for debt against two 'alien strangers' who, under university privilege, had opened shops in the town. The VC, Dr Watson, summoned Thompson and put him in gaol for three days 'in the most strange manner that could be devised' and obliged him to withdraw his action.

7 The statues make no provision for indemnifying a townsman who suffers serious hurt at the hands of a scholar, who is merely imprisoned, not made to pay damages.

8 The university officers do not hold leets in the town and university twice a year as they ought to do, with a jury of impartial burgesses. Instead, they farm out the leet to an officer called a bedell for a fee of £10 a year. He has to pay the steward of the court £2, the under-steward £1, and provide dinners and banquets for the magistrates, all of which amounts to about £30 a year. In order to recoup this outlay, the bedell makes sure that a large number of townsmen are brought before his court and—by carefully selecting his magistrates—that stiff penalties are imposed. Then the proctors and taxors come along and fine the same townsmen for the same offences all over again, or confiscate their goods, or put them in prison until they pay up a second time. In addition to the £10 which he pays the VC for the privilege of making what he can out of the 'leet', the bedell also has to pay the £10 which the university pays the king for the privilege of overseeing weights and measures and making the assize. Please restore the oversight of the assize to the mayor and bailiffs, or at least the collection of fines, so that it may be done honestly and fairly.

9 Scholars fish illegally in the river, which belongs to the town, and in the private waters which used to be let for about £2 a year and for which the mayor and bailiffs now get no more than £1. Men who hire the fishing are frequently 'driven out of their boats with stones and other like things, to the danger of their bodies and lives'. Their nets and lines are cut and broken.

10 Scholars and pretended servants graze their horses, sheep and cattle on the common pastures of the town. They also damage the pastures by digging and delving.

Please do something about this 'and your said orators shall daily pray to Jesu in preservation of your said most honourable lordships'.

Some of those complaints were exaggerated; some of the charges not strictly true. But there was enough substance in all that to make it clear that the VC and Heads were abusing their authority, neglecting their duties, condoning—perhaps unwittingly—corrupt practices by both scholars and townsmen and revealing themselves as no more capable of running the town efficiently than they had formerly accused the mayor and bailiffs of being. Moreover it would appear that, while trying, not very successfully, to restrain the students in matters which might harm the university, they were not taking any steps to prevent them from harming the legitimate interests of the townsmen. Some of those abuses had apparently been going on for a very long time, which may cast a new light on some of the past disturbances, even as far back as 1381, when the bedell was one of the main targets of the violence.

The reply of the arbitrators is not on record, but they evidently did reply to some effect, for in 1533 the VC renounced his power of excommunication in personal cases. This was partly no doubt because it was now dangerous to wield a weapon received direct from the hands of the Pope and partly because it was realised that the new weapon of 'discommoning' was far more effective. Moreover, on July 11 of that year, representatives of both parties met together in St Mary's church for a recital of complaints by the town and the answers thereto by the university. It is a long list—23 items— which included some old grievances, some new, some important, some very trivial, and the majority of them were concerned with cash. I have selected a few of the complaints and answers (all simplified) to give an idea of the tone of the meeting:

Complaint: The proctors and other officers hear suits relating to contracts and offences in the fair and outside it.

Answer: We do the same as the mayor and bailiffs, as agreed in the composition.

Complaint: They usurp the authority to examine all fish, pheasants, hares, girth-webbing, silks, furs, bedding, upholstery, spices, rape-seed, mustard-seed, fustians, worsted, bays, honey, soap, sold in the fair, and often confiscate the merchandise although no offence is committed.

Answer: We have royal warrant for this. Tell us the names of those from whom goods have been wrongly taken, and we will restore them, and punish the proctors concerned.

Complaint: The proctors imposed a fine of £1 on three lasts of good Scotch salmon, 6s 8d on a barrel of salmon that was perfectly sound and, having taken the fine, then allowed the owner to sell the fish in the fair.

Answer: We doubt that. Prove it and we will see that restitution is made.

Complaint: They demand 4d for every load of oats, 12d for stamping a bushel measure (sometimes 16d) and a bushel stamped one year is disallowed the next and a further fee demanded.

Answer: The fee is in accord with statute and the composition. From one year to the next a bushel loses capacity by a pint or two: if correct, it is allowed.

Complaint: They take 1d for checking a yardstick every year, even though it has already been checked and sealed.

Answer: Prove that and it will be amended.

Complaint: For every 40 barrels of beer brought for sale in the fair, the taxors take one barrel of beer and 8d in cash.

Answer: Only by amicable agreement with the owner.

Complaint: A fine of 15s was taken by one proctor and 12s 4d by another from Thomas Clark of Wisbech for certain barrels of rape-seed oil which was perfectly good, because the barrels were not marked with the merchant's mark and the cooper's mark.

Answer: It was sold ungauged and therefore forfeit.

Complaint: The VC sent for John Howes, one of the bailiffs, to know how much tallow he had sold to men of Lynn and for how much. Howes said he had sold 100 stones for £5. He was ordered to pay the £5 to the proctor. When he refused, they imprisoned him in the Tolbooth for 14 days, until he paid a fine of 13s 4d.

Answer: There was so much tallow being exported out of Cambridge that people had no candles. A ban was therefore imposed, which Howes secretly contravened. That is why we fined him.

Complaint: One Saturday last mid-Lent, John Vause, apprentice, stood with Mr Howes in the market, selling herrings and other goods and shouted 'Away with it', as did many others in the said market. The VC had him put in the stocks on Market Hill and kept there from three o'clock, to the shame of his master, Howes, and causing him a loss of £1.

Answer: It was done to avoid further trouble likely to arise from the use of lewd words seditiously and openly uttered in the market.

That last incident is confirmed by an item in the university accounts—'Paid for a pair of stocks to punish a servant of Howes the Bailiff'. So evidently the proctor was refused the key of the town stocks and had to provide his own. I would like to know just what young Vause did say; something more lewd than 'Away with it', I imagine.

The mayor and bailiffs had wanted the answers in writing, so that they might make comment on any which did not suit them, but the VC would not agree to this. However, the whole exercise in good relations—which is what it must be considered—passed off with a remarkable absence of animosity. When the session was ended both sides adjourned to the Pump Tavern, where the proctors stood treat. Before they parted company the mayor-elect, Mr Chapman, invited the VC to dine with him on Michaelmas Day. Alas, before that day came, the disputes had broken out all over again, and the Black Assembly that year was as stormy as ever. One good thing did emerge from the meeting—the VC and Heads were made aware that, whether they knew it or not, they had been employing unscrupulous men in the service of the university. A number of them were dismissed soon afterwards.

During Lent the next year, despite all that had been promised and agreed, writs were served on various university members at the suit of the mayor. The sergeant who served one on Mr Peynell in St Michael's church received a clout on the head with a heavy book. Evidently anticipating another, he kept his cap on his head when summoned before Dr Buckmaster, deputy VC, and was severely rebuked. That night there was a pitched battle up at Castle End when a party of townsmen, led by one of the bailiffs, armed with bill-hooks, cudgels and flails, encountered the proctors and their escort searching for a prostitute. There were casualties on both sides. On the night of Shrove Tuesday a gang of about 30 'jetters' on Market Hill espied Dr Buckmaster and chased him to King's Hall, where the slamming of the gates saved him from injury, but not from a prolonged shower of threats and insults.

Complaints and recriminations were resumed. The VC asserted that the townsmen 'be wunderfull malicious and do prosequte ther sayd suts with uncharitable lyes'. Having secured from the Privy Council a stern reproof for the townsmen which, he thought, had 'made a final ende of all matters late in contencion betwixt the universitie and the town', he somewhat optimistically expressed the view that 'we shall hereafter live more quietly among them'. Little did he know!

In the university accounts for 1534 appeared these items:

To Mr Cromwell his stipend 40s
Expenses when we brought to him our Letters about our privileges at Sturbridge Fair; expenses of the VC at Court to preserve our liberties in danger on account of the suit of the Townsmen and in hopes of obtaining that the VC for the time being should be a justice of the peace that he might *mulct the rebellious townsmen* and to have our privileges confirmed by the King £54

So much for arbitration!

Chapter 9

A near thing 1534-1546

By some strange alchemy of circumstance the 16th century produced a new breed of 'common' men. Yeomen and merchants for the most part, their main preoccupation was with money and the status conferred by it. Their faith in God was not diminished, merely overshadowed by their faith in themselves and their own capabilities. Self-assured, ambitious, independent, not over fastidious as to the strict legality or morality of their methods so long as they succeeded, they were the type of men who were least likely to accept with complacency the domination of learned doctors of divinity whose authority rested mainly on privilege granted by royal favour in a bygone age.

One such was Thomas Brakyn, burgess of Cambridge, mayor on several occasions, MP for the borough for some 15 years and eventually self-styled 'gentleman'. He began life as the son of a fishmonger and continued it as a fishmonger. By means best known to himself he secured appointment as official purveyor of pikes to HM King Henry VIII. This enabled him to buy 'for the king's use' large quantities of fish offered for sale and dispose of them, at his own price, regardless of what the university officers might say, to the visiting fish-merchants from London. In one single day he bought 96 fish at 7½d each, (one penny in the shilling discount because bought 'for the king') and sent them to London priced at 14d each, plus carriage. In 13 years it was reckoned, by one of his less successful rivals, that he had defrauded the king of nearly £400. He ought, surely, to have lost his head for that? No, heads did not roll for that; only for seditious words uttered indiscreetly. Anyway, the king never got to hear about it. Cardinal Wolsey did, but he had other fish to fry.

While deploring, therefore, the purse-lining tendencies of the minor university officials, we should do well to remember that they did not hold the monopoly in that respect; also that neither side held the monopoly of currying favour with those in high places who might sway the course of the battle. Brakyn showed characteristic astuteness and foresight when, on December 20 1532, he went as the bearer of a letter from the mayor to Thomas Cromwell thanking him for 'the serrvice they owe him and for his favour in their causes'. Flattery and fawning were part of Cromwell's daily diet. So, evidently thought Brakyn, was fish—for the letter was accompanied by a gift of 20 pikes and ten tenches.

The main objective of the manoeuvring at this time was to secure complete control of Sturbridge Fair, which had now reached such proportions that in the two weeks of its duration more business was done than in the market throughout the whole year. In July 1534 Messrs Brakyn, Slegge and Chapman and four doctors of the university were summoned to Lambeth to state their respective claims before the Privy Council. The outcome was a declaration that the VC had the right to hold a court at the fair and had the oversight of all weights and measures there. The burgesses had to accept defeat, for the moment, and look around for some way of getting their own back.

One seemed to have been presented to them when, a few months later, parliament granted to the king one tenth of the annual income of all religious and collegiate bodies. It was known by now that the official axe was about to fall on the monasteries and some of the Cambridge townsmen hoped that the colleges would be similarly felled, for there would be rich pickings to be made if they were. The commissioners sent to assess the 14 colleges found that their total annual value was nearly £3,000. If they were mulcted of £300 in tax, they would not be able to spend so much in litigation and bribery and the town would find it easier to compete with them. The townsmen's hopes were dashed by the very man on whose 'friendship' they had counted for the furtherance of their aims. Thomas Cromwell, already High Steward, was appointed Chancellor of the university in June 1535 in succession to Bishop Fisher. Letters addressed to the king and to Queen Anne Boleyn requesting that the payment of tenths and first-fruits be remitted 'on account of the poverty of the persons who will have to pay them, and of the colleges' apparently went unheeded. But a letter to Cromwell, making the same request on the same grounds, met with success and the colleges did not pay the tax.

Meanwhile, knowing that they could not match the university in the matter of 'presents' to a man of Cromwell's appetite—except as regards fish—the burgesses tried ingratiation of a cheaper kind. In order to demonstrate their staunch loyalty to the king, they sent Cromwell a detailed report of a conversation between one of the townsmen and the vicar of St Clement's. The vicar invited his neighbour, William Richardson, to drink a pint of wine with him at the Pump Tavern, and soon the talk progressed from the subject of the vicar's poverty to its prime cause.

'Rather than that the king should have the money paid to him and his successors, it were better that the king had no head above his shoulders, nor none that should succeed him,' said the vicar, his tongue loosened by the wine.

'Are there any more of that opinion?' asked Richardson.

'Twenty thousand in England,' replied the vicar—or the wine.

'Those be seditious words, Parson Bassett,' warned Richardson.

'Neighbour Richardson,' said the vicar in alarm, 'there be no one here but you and I.'

The vicar was arrested by the mayor and sent under escort to London to be examined by the Council. Thus did those wily men, under the guise of loyalty, seek to further their own interests by trading the unguarded outburst of an impoverished priest for the favour of a man who, if the truth were known, probably felt in his heart the same sentiments.

Cromwell was not in the least swayed by the subtelties of the mayor and bailiffs. Whilst in duty bound to favour the university, he did all he could to maintain peace, or at least a state of non-belligerence between the contending parties. He and Lord Audley, Lord Chancellor, wrote to the townsmen in July 1535 regretting their lack of time (how did they *ever* find time, and patience, to deal with these petty affairs?) to settle the argument over Sturbridge Fair and urging compliance with the last edict of the Council, as trouble was to be expected at the forthcoming fair if they did not.

Trouble had already started. The VC dared not deliver in person the letters from himself and the Heads 'for fear of a riot of the townsmen in our absence. They vex us now more than ever'. The vexation took the form of a declaration by the mayor and bailiffs that the university officers would not be allowed to meddle with anything but food-stuffs sold to be eaten at the fair, all merchandise being under their own jurisdiction, and a threat that the university would not be allowed the use of the Tolbooth as a prison.

Cromwell wrote at once a long and courteous letter to the town, stressing his determination to secure peace and again urging compliance with previous orders. This was followed by an even more conciliatory epistle to 'my loving friends the Mayre and his Brethren of the towne' beseeching them, for himself, but commanding them, for the king, to allow the university the use of the Tolbooth, to make due appearance at the VC's court and not to interfere with his control of weights and measures. On December 15 he wrote again—his fourth long letter to the town in six months—still to 'my loveinge freendes' but with more than a touch of asperity this time. He pointed out that the town gaol belonged to the king, not to them, and listed various offences which they had committed in recent weeks; then added a warning that he would see justice done and severely punish those who tried to impede its course.

His words evidently did have some effect, for the next letter he received from the mayor and bailiffs explained that the ex-mayor had been negligent about the oath-taking and assured him that they were willing to conform with custom. What they did not tell him—he already knew—was that there had been an awful rumpus at Sturbridge Fair in 1536. The townsmen had invaded the VC's office, in pursuit of a swindler who had taken refuge there, and put the man in gaol; in the tumult a bedell had been killed. This had been followed by the familiar situation of refusal to present offenders at the VC's court, charging students in the mayor's court and wholesale ignoring of offences regarding weights and measures.

Once again it was a case of local unrest being aggravated and to some extent obscured by general unrest in the country at large. When the general disturbances had died down, and the VC had had an opportunity to bring the Chancellor up to date with matters at Cambridge, the mayor and bailiffs wrote to Cromwell with the usual expressions of loyalty and a further protest of their earnest desire for peace. They really were not, they said, as keen on making charges against the scholars as he had been led to believe. The recent trouble had been caused by one of the proctor's servants acting without his master's knowledge. Once again they demonstrated their loyalty by reporting 'certeyn words' uttered by 'a certeyn Felew' of the town, for which they arrested him. Cromwell replied immediately to the effect that he was thoroughly tired of their 'contentious foly'; they must either stop their deliberate vexation of the university and contempt of its privileges, or he would tell the king.

They did not, and he did tell the king. On August 14 Cromwell, still addressing them as his 'loveing friends', slated them well and truly, and transmitted these express orders from the king:

—the university was to have full control of weights and measures and all victuals and merchandise at Sturbridge Fair;

—the VC was to have sole jurisdiction in cases involving scholars;

—the mayor should take the oath before the VC;

—the Composition of 1503 should be observed in all respects. Coming from Henry VIII, that ought to have settled the matter. It did not.

I must confess to a sneaking admiration of the dogged perseverance of those Tudor townsmen and I suspect that there were some at Court who admired (secretly, of course) their audacity in standing up to the highest power in the realm. The king was furious at being disobeyed. What seems to have angered him most was that one of the bailiffs had said that taking the oath was 'but a feete matter' (meaning 'trivial'). He repeated his commands that previous orders should be obeyed. But Brakyn, Slegge, Chapman and associates were determined to pursue the matter further, whatever the risk and whatever the cost—and heaven only knows what it was costing! They must have had friends at Court, and they must have been enjoying the battle as much for its own sake as for any gains they might win. That autumn they spent a fortnight in London, bringing bills of complaint before parliament and the Star Chamber, with at least one visit to Hampton Court. The net result of all their effort and expenditure was nil—'all was lost, as it fortuned'.

They still kept up their self-appointed role as watchdogs against seditious speech, probably in the vain hope of catching out some of the university. One Towson was heard to say in Rous' shop that, 'Since this six yeares there never was a good man in England, and if there was, he was burnt'. Asked if the king was not a good man, he replied, 'No, all was nought till within this six years'. Later that day, primed with ale, he said, 'I truste within two yeres to see never an abey, monkes, chanouns ner fryers stondyng within this realme to be worshipped'. Confronted by the mayor and aldermen, Towson said he would abide by his words and be burnt for them.

He was not burnt, merely gaoled. When he came out he had the satisfaction of knowing that his prophecy regarding the monasteries was fulfilled. In 1538 the Austin, Black and Grey friars all surrendered their possessions. The university promptly begged the king to give them the Franciscan site on which to found a college as a perpetual monument to his name. The town wanted the site for a hospital. Neither side won, for the present. The possibility that the colleges might suffer the same fate as the monasteries was secretly being worked for, though not much talked about openly. Over the past three years there had been four meetings of commissioners in the town, entertained by the corporation at their expense, to inquire whether the lands held by the colleges had been acquired by licence in accord with the Statues of Mortmain. Of course they had. The inquiry was wholly superfluous. It can only have been intended to frighten the colleges or raise the hopes of the town.

Early in 1539 the old dispute was resumed as though Cromwell and the king had never existed. The points at issue were still the same—taking the oath, charges against scholars and control of the fair. The townsmen were quickly made to realise that they still had a lot to learn as regards manipulation of the law. The Attorney General filed a suit in the Court of King's Bench, charging the mayor and bailiffs with having held a fair at Sturbridge for four years and more (a lot more!), held a court there, and taken fines, all of which they had usurped from the Crown. The suit was upheld and the mayor and bailiffs were required to show by what authority they had exercised these rights. This they could not do; no one knew by what authority they claimed the fair—they probably *had* usurped it. Judgement naturally went against them and the fair, with all its rights and profits, was delcared forfeit to the Crown. The only way to get it back, legally, was to obtain a charter granting it to them. One was drawn up, the main point of which was that the town should have the fair on payment of 1,000 marks; it also granted pardon to the mayor, etc, for having held the fair illegally. This charter was never signed or sealed for it contained a proviso that nothing in it should prejudice university privilege. So it was back to square one! The fair continued to be held as usual, the town paying an annual rent for it to the Exchequer, and the VC continued to exercise his partial control over it. The bone of contention remained, but both sides played safe for a few years, avoiding open conflict which would have brought the matter to the notice of the courts.

A new point of quarrel was soon to hand. In 1541 the commissioners appointed to muster the militia in Cambridge and the county included Thomas Brakyn and Simon Trew, aldermen. They persuaded their fellow commissioners that it would be a good idea if those young men in the colleges did a spell of military service ('give them a taste of discipline') and proceeded to muster them. Howls of protest from the university! The VC, Dr Standish, sent an urgent appeal to the Privy Council, who promptly ordered that the scholars should be exempt from muster and marvelled that such an unprecedented step should have been taken. This particular trick was attempted frequently during the next century. It never succeeded and might have proved dangerous to the townsmen if it had, for many of the students would have welcomed the opportunity to get hold of some real weapons with which to play their part in the campaign.

Brakyn scored one notable point—not, incidentally, against the university, but in co-operation with it—when in 1544 he successfully and cheaply put forward a bill for the paving of the town ('for putting forth a booke into the parliament' only cost £6). By its terms all householders were to repair the streets in front of their tenements, or forfeit 12d per square yard of surface. Supervision was to be done by the VC or his deputy, the mayor and bailiffs and four assistants, two from the university, two from the town. Negligence on the part of the overseers was to be punishable by a fine of £5. Payment to roadmenders was not to exceed one penny per square yard. That act was a minor historic event in its way; it remained in force for nearly 250 years.

Brakyn was a pillar of strength to the town and remained active to his dying day. In 1543 he supplied five pounds worth of swans, pikes eels and tench to be given to the Lord Chancellor at Walden. In 1544 he combined with others to send four ships to Newcastle for sea-coals, having first obtained a guarantee of indemnity from the corporation in case the Lynn merchants brought an action against him. For years he had striven to secure the promotion of what would have been considered by many his greatest act, an Act of Parliament for the Dissolution of Colleges, Chantries, etc.

By this act, passed in the autumn of 1545, parliament empowered the king to appoint commissioners to examine all colleges, chantries, hospitals, fraternities and guilds and take possession of their property if the king so wished. There can be little doubt that the act was promoted and passed by those who hoped to gain eventual possession of the lands and property of the colleges as they had already done with those of the monasteries. Little doubt also that the king had no intention of abolishing the universities of Oxford and Cambridge. But how to reconcile those two considerations—

abolition of the colleges, preservation of the universities—I do not think anybody had seriously thought out, least of all the king.

Initial reaction in the university was one of near-panic, followed by level-headed thought and resourceful action. 'Certen frendes of the unyversity', persuaded the king not to appoint any of his 'costly officers' as commissioners to inquire into the state of the colleges, as that would cost too much (ie, cost the colleges too much; they bore the cost of the inquiry). The king agreed and appointed the VC, Matthew Parker, two chaplains of the university, along with clerks of the Court of Augmentations (which dealt with the ex-monastic property) and no townsmen, of course. In a letter to them on January 16 1546 he made it perfectly clear that he wanted to preserve the colleges, 'where most of the youth of the realm is nourished in good literature'. There was no hint of dissolution in the letter.

But many of his subjects knew only too well that the king could change his mind. Many of the masters and fellows knew that 'reform' might not be to their advantage, that the university was by no means solely concerned with 'good lytterature' and other studies and not wholly innocent of some of the excesses which had justified the seizure of the monasteries. Tact, diplomacy and speed were called for.

Three letters were sent off at once. The first was to the king, declaring their loyalty and obligation to him and their readiness to put all their possessions at his service. The second to Secretary Paget, extolling his virtues, reminding him of the importance of the university to the State, asking for his protection and begging that the dissemination of learning be not handed over to those who only understood the dissemination of money. The third was to Queen Catherine (Parr) beseeching her intervention on their behalf. This tipped the balance in their favour. The queen would have preferred that they had written in English rather than in Latin, but she gave them the answer they wanted, namely that she had 'attempted' the king and that he had promised to safeguard their interests.

The commissioners had finished their task by the end of the month and had done a very thorough job. The survey which they presented to the king was very detailed; that part of it which interested him most is summarised overleaf (shillings and pence omitted). It will be evident at a glance that some of the colleges were very small and, with three exceptions, catering for an absurdly small number of students. It will also be evident, as it was to the king, that with one exception they were all spending more than their income according to the survey. When asked how this could be, Dr Parker replied that the deficit was made up by fees for the renewal of leases of property and by the sale of timber from the estates. He did not say why those items were left out of the accounts. I would not say that the accounts were 'cooked' but obviously they were tailored to fit the requirements of the situation, and it was a good fit.

The king turned to the lords about him and remarked that it would be a pity to alter those estates for the worse—'which disappointed some of his hearers, who were hoping to secure the said lands'—according to Dr Parker. When directly asked to leave the colleges in possession of what they had, the king smiled and finally, 'bade us hold our own'. 'With which wordes we were wel armyd and so departed.' The storm-clouds had blown over. The colleges were safe.

College	Annual income £	Expen- diture £	Inmates Students	Servants	Total
St Peter's College	138	187	13	8	37
Michaelhouse	141	143	4	4	20
Clare Hall	132	163	5	5	29
King's Hall	214	263	8	15	48
Pembroke Hall	171	185	4	7	29
Gunville Hall	119	155	5	6	22
Trinity Hall	119	139	7	7	25
Corpus Christi College	171	190	3	2	15
King's College	1,010	1,058	24	17	123
Queens' College	272	273	6	5	33
St Catherine's Hall	55	59	1	3	11
Jesus College	130	140	7	6	27
Christ's College	287	297	47	6	69
St John's College	536	607	63	13	138
Magdalene College	43	33	1	1	7

More than that, within the year, and from the very hand which might have delivered the death-blow, they received an addition to their number which was to rival King's for wealth and spendour. In December 1546 King Henry VIII founded *Trinity College*, being an amalgam of Michaelhouse, King's Hall and seven adjacent hostels, to house a master and 60 fellows and scholars. It was endowed with 55 churches, ten manors, lands in 40 villages and towns, to a total annual value of £1,678; much of it the former property of dissolved monasteries, including the Grey Friars at Cambridge.

Thomas Brakyn did not live to share the disappointment of the leading townsmen, whose reaction to the university's success was just what one would expect. They refused to take the oath at the Black Assembly in St Mary's church on October 22. In response to the VC's complaint, the Privy Council wrote to the townsmen urging them to comply with custom. So in November they attended the ceremony and took the oath with such 'unseamly and uncharitable facinge and crakinge' as to make a mockery of it. The proctors who entered Mr Rust's shop to seize candles considered below standard were driven out to shouts of 'pollers and pillerers'. Any attempt to arrest a trader of the town was vigorously opposed by a howling mob. Summonses to the VC's presence were ignored. One Dickenson, sentenced by the VC to the stocks, was saved from disgrace by the removal of the stocks. The mayor and bailiffs, faced with complaints about all this, made no attempt to deny anything and no promise to do anything about it.

There is an interesting postscript to that affair. Thirty-four years later, one of the six prisoners detained in the castle gaol was Thomas Brakin, Gent, the son of Thomas Brakyn, MP and fishmonger. He was detained because he was in debt to the tune of nearly £1,000. I have no proof, but neither have I any doubt that the debt (the equivalent of £100,000 in modern value) was inherited from his father and that it had been incurred in the promotion of the Bill to abolish the colleges. Brakin got out of debt, and out of gaol, by selling the manor of Chesterton, one of the ex-monastic properties which his father had acquired.

Chapter 10

Licensed jetting 1547-1560

If an excuse had been needed for the outbreak of trouble, Sturbridge Fair could be counted on to provide it. Given the vast numbers of outsiders who came to it, the drinking that went on and the dubious nature of some of the business transacted, this was inevitable. Even if everybody who went to the fair had been law-abiding and reasonably honest, the regulations and restrictions were so complicated and numerous—no card-playing, no dice, bowls or any other games, no taking away butter until its weight had been checked, no selling of more than the regulation amount of cheese to any one person, no suspected persons to be employed on the stalls, no hawking, no sale of tallow to any but approved chandlers, etc—that disputes and complaints were bound to arise every few minutes and most of them involved the proctors, taxors and their staff. They probably enjoyed their work. Pouncing on traders playing tricks with weights or yardsticks gave them a sense of power and checking the quality of beer had its compensations. They might even have derived some pleasure—spiritually at any rate—from ferreting out whores and rounding up the brothel-keepers, though I doubt it. Like the townsmen, they often turned a blind eye to the 'houses of sin'. On one occasion at least, in 1542, they delegated the punishment of the delinquents in what seems an incredible way: 'to two boys for whipping lewd women, 3d'.

One night in September 1547 these houses of sin were the scene of a row in which the proctors were summoned to intervene. They arrested 'various persons' and marched them off to the Tolbooth to be locked up for the night. The door was locked and the keys were with the mayor, James Fletcher. Whether he had recognised one of his friends or relatives among the 'naughty and corrupt' captives is not certain, but he refused to hand over the keys. The proctors had no choice—apart from the unthinkable one of letting their prisoners go free—but to escort them up to Castle End. Rousing the keeper from his bed, they had them locked in the gaol of the castle.

An hour later the under-sheriff, Thomas Harrison, arrived, having been urgently summoned by his father-in-law, James Fletcher. Dragging the keeper once more from his bed, he ordered the release of the prisoners, who then presumably staggered home to theirs. Complaints to Archbishop Cranmer and Sir William Paget resulted in Fletcher and Harrison being summoned to appear before the Privy Council, severely admonished and obliged to make public admission of their fault.

Encouraged by this success, the VC and Heads decided to petition the king to grant them extra privileges relating to items not already covered by their charters. These were permanent exemption from musters for military service; exemption from requisitioning of horses for postal service; a ban on purveyors to the royal household taking any foodstuffs, except fish, within five miles of Cambridge; a request that the VC and certain masters be made Justices of the Peace (they had been trying for that for the past 50 years) in order to try all cases involving students, even those of murder and felony normally referred to Justices of Assize; and full control over the sale of all merchandise in the town, without having to render account to the Crown; also full powers of search, arrest and punishment of suspected persons, prostitutes and vagabonds, with power to demand the assistance of the town officials.

This was really going too far, a bid for absolute power which the Privy Council was not prepared to grant. The petition was not rejected, however, before the town had been asked for its views. Surprisingly, the town agreed to the proposals concerning musters and post-horses (almost), they wanted a clearer definition as to what was meant by 'scholar's servant' and insisted that the university should pay its share of the cost of equipping the 'should-yeares'. They insisted also that a layman who killed or wounded a scholar should be dealt with, after trial at the Assizes, by the mayor and bailiffs, who should dispose of his goods and chattels and that the keeper of the town gaol should have the usual fees in respect of a scholar committed by the VC, as he had in the case of a townsman. They had no objection to the proctors and their deputies dealing with prostitutes—they never did take kindly to that task, partly because there was no money in it, partly, I believe, because they saw nothing very wrong in prostitution. But they objected strongly to servants of the proctors (who were mostly townsmen) interfering in the trade and insisted that vagabonds and suspected persons were solely the concern of the mayor, bailiffs and constables.

Amongst their objections was one constructive proposal (one at least which they thought was constructive, though its chance of acceptance by the university was slight) namely that all authority, jurisdiction and liberties formerly enjoyed by the VC at the Midsummer and Sturbridge fairs be transferred to the mayor and bailiffs in return for an annual payment of £10. They supported their suggestion with a list of the reductions in tolls and other charges they would make. Neither the Privy Council nor the university was at all impressed.

Whilst realising that their own attempt at securing further privileges was not well-timed, the VC and Heads decided at the same time to have all their existing charters confirmed; routine procedure, not obligatory, but advisable on the accession of a new sovereign; its omission might encourage the enemy to steal a march on them. Two learned doctors set out on horseback, with three servants, spending three days and two nights on the road via Barkway and Waltham Cross to London. Travelling along rough roads on hard-backed hired hacks was bad enough, sleeping in flea-infested beds and eating indifferent fare at high prices was worse, but worst of all was the waiting, first at Westminster, then at Kingston, then again at Westminster. Fifteen weeks elapsed before they returned, weary, disappointed and £92 18s the poorer. They had spent £44 on food and lodging, £14 on horses, and £35 on the materials and labour of copying (several times because of mistakes) and registering the charters.

The amount of time and money spent on such a venture is significant in itself. The university did not have a lot of money at its disposal—unlike the colleges, with their endowments. How could it afford to spend nearly a hundred pounds (the sum sounds trivial enough now, but you need to add a couple of noughts and then multiply by about one and a half to arrive at the modern equivalent) on a vain effort to secure more privileges? In this particular instance almost the whole amount was raised by selling a large silver cross weighing 21 lb—probably ex-monastic property rescued from the royal grasp—which the doctors took down to London with them, dismantled and strapped on the back of a horse. Imagine their trepidation as they trotted along those lonely roads through Hertfordshire, where every copse could have concealed a band of robbers!

It becomes increasingly evident that this conflict between town and university was basically an economic war, certainly as far as the upper ranks were concerned. True, civic dignity and academic prestige played their part, true, the university wanted a more civilised environment, a more moral atmosphere and neither side really liked dishonest dealers. But, in the last analysis, what the incessant strife between them boiled down to was pounds, shillings and pence. The money they spent was spent in the hope of ultimate gain. There is no way of knowing just how much they did spend over the centuries in litigation, bribes, fees, favours and the costs of defending their 'liberties'. I believe it would be no exaggeration to say that, if it had all been saved, kept safe and wisely invested, it would suffice to build a whole new university today—or a whole new town. Cantabs will say that it *was* wisely invested!

Another half-hearted attempt at compromise was made even while those transactions were in progress, with Sir William Paget and Sir Thomas Smith as umpires. The same points were raised—musters, post-horses, royal purveyors, search for 'hores'—along with further points on which obviously no agreement could be reached. The university would not give up its right to control the sale of silks and pewter. The town increased its bid for control of the fairs to a ludicrous £13 6s 8d. The university wanted £20, almost as ludicrous, except that it was conditional upon total freedom from toll for all members of the university and their servants. The result was stale-mate and 'nothing ended'.

The morale of both sides was at a low ebb. Cambridge students had an unenviable reputation for mean trickery of the unsuspecting and simple-minded peasantry. The eminent scholar, Roger Ascham, wrote to Arch-bishop Cranmer, speaking of the university, that 'it was then in so depressed and drooping a condition that very few had hope of coming thither at all and fewer had any comfort to make long tarrying when they were there, that abroad it retained not so much a shadow of its ancient dignity'. Bishop Latimer took up the theme in a sermon preached before the king: 'It would pity a man's heart to hear what I hear of the state of Cambridge'. By 'Cambridge' he meant the university, not the town. Every-body did from now on. The town was becoming something of a non-entity, situated vaguely between the university and Sturbridge Fair.

Estrangement was not total, never had been, and never could be, in view of the degree of interdependence between them. But when they did join forces, as happened every now and then, it was to face a common danger, or the result of one section of the town being at variance with another. Such as the trouble over enclosures in the summer of 1549. The mayor and bailiffs, VC and Heads combined to quell a riot of about a hundred people, angry at the loss of common pastures; they also shared the cost of obtaining a general pardon for the rioters. When the royal commissioners came to inquire into the extent of the illegal enclosure which had taken place in the town, the reason for the joint action became clear. They found some 30 cases of enclosure, overcommoning, misuse of commons, etc. In 19 cases the offenders were bailiffs, ex-bailiffs and aldermen; in seven cases they were colleges. Trinity, King's and Queens' had all encroached on the common land west of the river.

For several years the disputes were overshadowed by national events, in particular the abortive attempt to place Lady Jane Grey on the throne in July 1553. Then there were the religious fluctuations, troubling the university much more than the town, which was less concerned with heresy and martyrdom than with interference in its commercial dealings. The distraction of the university did, however, furnish an excuse to re-open a few old sores. In May 1554 the mayor and bailiffs invited the VC and his officers to a parley on 'certain matters'. His reply was that 'he could not come, nor would not'. So they met without the opposition—that was one sure way of reaching agreement—and set down in writing, for the 20th time, 'the wrongs committed and doon by the Vyce Chancelor, Masters and Scholers'. It was much the same old story as before (weights and measures, courts, privileges of university servants, misuse of commons, etc) with two new complaints which reveal developments strongly reminiscent of a return to the Middle Ages.

One of these complaints probably stemmed from a shortage of pocket-money on the part of the students. Since time immemorial, when a theft or other offence was committed in daylight, it was obligatory on all bystanders to raise the hue-and-cry and make pursuit of the offender. Lately the raising of the hue-and-cry had become the signal for all students in the vicinity to set off in pursuit, outstrip the townsfolk, capture the thief—or some other unfortunate person who happened to be running in the same direction—and strip him of everything he had, stolen or otherwise, before handing him over near-naked to the constables. Far from being grateful for this assistance, the mayor and bailiffs were most aggrieved, for the criminal's possessions were by law their own perquisites. Moreover, they might find themselves charged by the thief's victim with not making pursuit as the law required, to say nothing of being charged with unlawful arrest and spoilation of an entirely innocent bystander. There was no answer to that. It was one of those things which earned 'the Cambridge scholars' their evil reputation. No doubt the Oxford scholars had the same reputation.

The other complaint arose as a result of a foolish mistake on the part of both university and town officials or, to be more charitable, as a result of an attempt at co-operation which turned out to be farcical and dangerous. They ought to have foreseen, though, what would have happened if students were allowed to play at being policemen.

The war had always been a two-tier conflict. At the higher level the officials of both sides waged what was mainly a legal battle, involving charters, liberties, customs and, above all, money. At the lower level the rank and file—students on one side, town youths on the other—indulged in more-or-less constant fighting with a variety of weapons and mainly for the sheer fun of it. In the early days the two levels of combat had often merged; town and university officials alike had often led or incited the mob, the latter usually in a defensive role. Now, when students and townsmen clashed, it was usually in defiance of orders from above. Actual bloodshed was far less common, largely because the lower ranks had adopted cudgels or 'clubs' as their normal weapons (thereby possibly originating one of the everyday words of our language; the 'club', which began as a weapon, eventually being used to denote an association of people with a common interest).

The special combined 'police-force', or 'watch' was first set up to keep order at the time of the fair. This was a body of 20 students, with another 24 in reserve, and a similar number of townsmen, all on a rota basis. The system seems to have worked quite well for a time, that is, until the students realised that it provided them with just the opportunity they needed for a bit of excitement and activity as a relief from study. The vagrants and suspects for whom they were watching made themselves scarce and there was simply nobody left on the streets except the watchmen of the town. So the student watch attacked them! The official complaint gave no details, only 'them do oftentymes Beatt, Stryke and wounde'.

Then this new sport—which is what the students clearly considered it—caught on in a big way. Those who were not on the official rota saw no reason why they should be debarred from participation on that account, or that the watch should be restricted to fair-time. 'A great multitude of people take upon them a certen kind of watche called a Jettinge' which resulted in 'sundry misdemeanours and hurts'. One can well imagine that it would!

But something had to be done, or tried, so long as no agreement could be reached as to who really owned or managed the fair. The device suggested was that student-watch and town-watch should do duty on alternate nights and Lord North, High Steward of the town, gave special instructions to the VC to that effect. Orders from any town official did not come very high on the VC's list of priorities, if they figured there at all. In 1559 he failed to provide his contingent of watchmen, so the mayor's men had to do duty for two nights. On the third night the proctor turned up between 11 pm and midnight with an escort of 70 young stalwarts, who promptly beat up the town watch, took away their weapons and sent them home. The VC next day denied all knowledge of the matter and agreed to the alternation of the watches.

The next night at ten o'clock the town watchmen were going along Jesus Lane towards the fair when they met three students, armed with daggers, leading a poor wretch off to prison. Questioned, they replied with insults. One, brandishing his dagger, said he intended to 'paunch the villains of the town' with it. The watchmen arrested all three and had them locked up in the Dolphin Inn, then went on their round. Returning at midnight past Christ's College gate they were showered with stones hurled from above by a crowd of some 40 students.

The intervention of Lord North on the morrow restored peace and for a whole week the two parties kept their respective watches, nothing more hurtful than insults being hurled at the townsmen. Then, on the Wednesday night, one of the members of the town watch on his way to the assembly-point met with a group of students armed with clubs and was felled, his bill and sallet being stolen from him. The proctor's watch, briefed to say that they had all behaved with propriety, did duty with the town watch until 4 am. On the way home another of the town watch was knocked down in All Saints Lane, his weapons stolen and 'he would have been killed' if one of the scholars had not stood over him and then taken him home.

The next night the VC said he would send no watch and ordered the town watch to go home, which they did, thankfully, and for the rest of the fair-time the drunks and disorderly were given a free hand. As a consequence of this, two years later the freelance activity of the students was checked—in theory, that is. It was ordered by the Senate that no scholar should be out of his college at night, or go jetting, except in the company of the proctors and that the proctors should not go jetting without the licence of the VC. It was easy to issue such orders. Getting them observed was a different matter.

Chapter 11

Patronage and perversity
1561-1591

The university today acknowledges its indebtedness to a long list of bene-factors, patrons and protectors, mostly men and women of renown. High on that list ought to be—I do not know that he is—Sir William Cecil (later Lord Burghley), Secretary of State, chief adviser and most loyal servant to Queen Elizabeth, and Chancellor of the University from 1559 until his death 40 years later. During that time, with infinite patience, tact and that blend of courtesy and firmness which characterised both the age and the man, he strove to reconcile the contending parties at Cambridge, whilst making certain that the privileged position of the university should not be impaired. Perhaps he was too patient, too tactful, too courteous with the townsmen. Only once, however, did he lose patience with the university. In 1562 he accused the heads of colleges of being incapable of the 'ruling of unordinate youth and the observation of good order' and tendered his resignation as Chancellor, but he was persuaded to stay on and, having accepted the thankless task, determined to make the best of it. The town likewise had its champion, first the Duke of Norfolk, then Lord North, and rivalry between these eminent champions added a third tier to the conflict and also added to its cost, for patronage was not to be had merely for the asking.

It was largely due to Cecil's influence that the university, in 1561, was granted a new charter which represented the very peak of privilege, never to be surpassed. It confirmed all privileges previously granted, gave specific ruling on various issues long in dispute and added several points not before mentioned. Summarised and simplified, this is what university privilege now consisted of:

1 Full use of the town gaol and county gaol (castle), with full co-operation of the sheriff, mayor and bailiffs, who were responsible for the safe custody of all persons placed therein by the university officers.

2 Sole jurisdiction over all offences (except mayhem and felony) involving scholars and university servants.

3 Total exemption from military service or payment towards it.

4 Total exemption from requisitioning of horses for postal or other State purposes.

5 Power to forbid purveyors of the Crown to take any provisions within five miles of the town.

6 Total control of the market and fairs. (NB *not* ownership.)

7 Total control over forestalling, regrating and profiteering in the town and suburbs.

8 Authority to seize and destroy rotten meat, fish and other foodstuffs.

9 Possession of all foodstuffs forfeited for infringement of regulations in the town and fairs.

10 Powers of search for, and punishment of, all suspects, vagabonds and prostitutes in the town and fairs and authority to demand the assistance of the mayor and bailiffs in performing that office.

11 Authority to licence 12 of its members to preach anywhere in the realm, independently of any bishop's authority.

12 Power to claim the person of any scholar or servant of the university convicted by any other court in the realm.

13 Exemption from all forms of taxation, rates, subsidies, reliefs, etc, except the £10 which was paid annually to the Exchequer for the assize of bread and ale.

14 A definition of the 'suburbs or precincts of the university' as being one English mile around the town in every direction.

There was only one other corporate body in the kingdom possessing such absolute power, namely Oxford University. Absolute power—in theory. In practice, it did not quite work out like that. For one thing, those Cambridge burgesses took an awful long time to be convinced that acts of parliament, royal edicts and charters really meant what they said. For another, it was always possible to find, or to believe that one had found, points on which the charters, etc, had not said anything, or not said it clearly enough, despite the fact that lawyers and clerks had by this time perfected the art of never using ten words to say what could be more expensively said in a hundred.

Within three months the Senate had to write to Cecil soliciting his protection and that of the queen against the town, and repeated the request a year later. Two years later the queen herself had to write to the town officials forbidding them to grant licences to any victuallers or 'tipplers' in the town, reminding them that this was the sole prerogative of the university. Several victuallers, licensed by the mayor, were sent to prison by the VC, at the town's expense. The mayor and bailiffs did not flinch at the trifling outlay of 22s 8d to maintain the victuallers in prison for a few days in reasonable comfort. It was put down to campaign expenses; like the £25 spent in one year on 'presents' to the Duke of Norfolk and other 'honourables of the realm to secure favour in the suits of the town'.

The strife receded into the background once more, temporarily, with the visit of Queen Elizabeth to Cambridge (more exactly, to 'her university of Cambridge') in August 1564. Elaborate preparations had been made. The streets were strewn with sand, the mace was re-gilded, the town-waits fitted out with new collars and the market-cross repaired and re-painted. That, plus the gift of a silver cup costing £16 and containing £20 worth of 'angels', was the limit of the town's capability as regards hospitality, although the mayor and bailiffs did greet the queen on her arrival at Newnham and escort her for a mile on her departure. The university entertained her lavishly for four days—it would have been five days if the supply of beer had not run out—with speeches, banquets, orations, plays and flattery, all of which she enjoyed, and gifts including a silver cup worth £26 with 40 'angels' in it. The townsmen were excluded from all the academic treats, no doubt to their relief.

As soon as the pomp and ceremony were over, the VC was free to deal with two prominent burgesses who had been a thorn in his flesh for some time, namely Henry Serle and his son-in-law, Roger Slegge. Both were ex-mayors and aldermen, and Slegge had been MP for eight years. Serle had been involved in a case in the VC's court, where the verdict had gone against him. He had appealed, then abandoned his appeal and sued for a writ of error—a costly business, but Serle was not paying—which was thrown out by the Lord Keeper as being in violation of university privilege. The VC, now a Justice of the Peace, issued a warrant for Serle's arrest.

Two accounts of the arrest of Serle exist. They are worth quoting as an illustration of how different the same episode could be when viewed from two different angles. This is how Serle and Slegge saw the affair, and wanted the Duke of Norfolk and the Privy Council to see it:

Vice-Chancellor Hawford, in extreme hate and malice against one Mr Seerle . . . raysed a companye of scholers to the number of 60 and above, with swords, bucklers and clubbes and animated the sayd unlawful assembly of scholers with force of arms to enter in to a yard at Cambridge . . . as savage people and with forcible words regarding nor fearing any lawes . . . to the great terror, fear and damages of the life of the said Seerle, haling him in threatening manner . . . increasing in fury and malice and number of malefactors to the number of 100 . . . extremely hayled and pulled one Roger Slegge . . . in such violent sort that his clothes were torn . . . Thus we live in dangerous case and unseeable state, assured neither of life nor goodes neither day time, tossed and pulled as aforesaid in the night time, feared with breaking of our windows, gates and houses, etc.

At the request of the Privy Council, the VC held an inquiry, calling numerous witnesses, mostly townsmen, and this is the account which he was then able to give:

On St Bartholomew's Day last, at about 10 am, the proctor, having heard that Serle and Slegge had left St Clement's church before the sermon began, and were playing bowls in Pedes Yard, went there with a party of about six students to arrest Serle. Three of the students were armed with swords, two had bucklers and three had clubs. On entering the yard the proctor, Mr Riby, remarked that the burgesses might have been better occupied in sermon-time. Slegge replied that he had been to a sermon. Serle, as soon as he saw the proctor's party, and knowing that they had come to arrest him, ran to the back of the yard, seized a ladder and placed it against the wall. He was dragged down before he could escape, but not before he had called loudly for help. Slegge meanwhile told his companions to lock the yard-gate; then, turning to the proctor, said: 'What, are ye come to take Christ?'

Serle snatched a dagger from the belt of one of the bystanders, the students released their hold on him, one drew a sword, Serle held his assailants at bay, brandishing the dagger as he walked up and down. The following dialogue, or something very like it, took place:

Proctor: 'We are come to arrest this man in the Queen's name.'

Slegge: 'Ye shall not take him except ye drag him.'

Proctor: 'I charge you in the Queen's name, sir, to keep the peace and to assist me in the arrest of this man.'

Slegge: 'Peace! Peace, is it? I am a justice of the peace, and I'll see you damned ere I'll keep the peace for you.'

Proctor: 'Sir, I beg you to take that dagger from this man, lest harm ensue.'

Slegge: 'I'll be damned if I do. I fear not you, ye slaves, ye boys! Do what ye dare, rascals. Do your worst, ye ruffians!'

The students overpowered Serle, disarmed him and led him, unprotesting, to the gate, where they were halted until two of their party had broken it down with their clubs, one of which was broken in the process. Slegge sent one of his companions over the wall to summon help. When the gate was opened, the yard began to fill with townsmen and students. Seeing an audience, Slegge put on a dramatic act. 'The scholars are trying to steal our gowns,' he cried. 'Murder! Murder! Strike! Strike, an ye be men!' The proctor, fearing a worse disturbance, ordered Slegge to go with him. At first Slegge agreed to go, then changed his mind and said he would only go if dragged. So they took him by the shoulders and dragged him. Again he raised the cry of 'Murder!' As the crowd swelled he called 'Strike, an ye be men. Will ye suffer us to be carried with these rascals, slaves and knaves?' He kept up his shouting, to no effect, all the way through the town to Christ's College, railing against the VC, the preachers, proctors and scholars. The mayor arrived on the scene and lent support to the proctor. There was no disturbance except that created by Slegge. Not a single townsman came to their assistance.

Serle, but not Slegge, was locked up in the Tolbooth. The town gaoler, Christopher Russell, encouraged and abetted by Slegge, released him. All three, with one of the bailiffs who had been in the bowls party, were summoned before the Privy Council. There the characters and misdeeds of both ex-mayors were revealed and recorded for posterity. Serle—according to the VC and his deputy Dr Perne—was a habitual drunkard, a gambler, hopelessly in debt, a defrauder of the poor, having defaced the town records in an attempt to conceal his misdeeds and had been excommunicated for sleeping with his servant-girl. Slegge was considered by the whole university and town, 'a few light persons excepted', as a man of little honesty or truth and 'not worthy to bear authority'. As mayor, he had spent more than £200 of the town's money in law-suits, quarrels and bribes; he had borrowed money from the town chest and failed to repay it, sold municipal property and kept the money, and now lived at the town's expense. For 30 years he had been a notorious trouble-maker, a role he inherited from his father, doing everything possible to foment hatred between town and university. Worst of all, he kept a common gaming-house, to which the young gentlemen of the colleges were attracted, to their undoing.

Of course the VC would contrive to present the case of these men in the worst possible light, but he said nothing that he could not substantiate, and one is left wondering how such men could possibly have risen to the positions of responsibility which they had occupied in the town—until one looks back a couple of centuries, and then forward the same distance. Then it becomes clear that the system of election to municipal office made it all too easy for men like that to rule the roost, rob it and foul it as well. Their contribution to the subservience of the town was greater than they knew.

All four of the miscreants were committed to prison from which, after a few weeks, they were released, having acknowledged their offences and given pledges of good behaviour in future. On their return, the Town Council authorised the payment of all their expenses out of common funds. That could only mean that the Council and some of the townsmen approved of what Serle and Slegge did and what they were. The next year they were both elected as members of parliament for the borough, a gesture of defiance which Cecil countered by declaring them disqualified. It cannot be known just what proportion of the townsmen supported the leadership of such men, for the Town Council was itself a self-creating, self-perpetuating body, almost a 'closed shop', which generally put its own interests before those of the town. Cecil must have known this, but he still believed that there must be *some* way of restoring and maintaining peace. The Privy Council wrote to both parties early in 1565, urging the formation of a joint committee of eight, four from each side, to meet and consider 'what order they thought most meet to be decreed for avoiding all quarrels between the two bodies, and by what means there might be established a perpetual concord of peace between them'. Nothing came of it.

Part of the trouble lay in the fact that the university, for all its superiority in prestige and privilege, was so very vulnerable on various fronts. One such vulnerability it shared with the rest of humanity was that its members had to eat and drink. They might bake their own bread and brew their own beer, but they still had to rely on the town and district for the supply of the raw materials. One of the priorities governing the licensing of movement of corn was the need to guarantee an adequate supply for the citizens of London. Bitter experience over the centuries had taught successive governments that shortage of bread and beer in London was a sure recipe for riot. Large quantities of grain were sent from the Cambridge area, via Lynn, to the capital (a distance of 240 miles by water, but cheaper than the 50 miles by road). In times of relative scarcity the price of corn in Cambridge market rose to as much as £1 a quarter, from an average price of around 5s. It did so in 1565. The VC saw in this the malicious design of the local corn-merchants to starve out the university. He was probably mistaken, the corn-merchants were simply cashing in on the scarcity as usual, though attempts had been made in the past to exploit the situation to the university's discomfiture. The VC wrote plaintively to Cecil of 'the pinching of poore scholars' bellies' and requested a total ban on the export of corn within five miles of the university. The answer he received was non-committal, but left him in no doubt that his 'poore scholers' would have to take second place to the hungry hordes of London.

Another chink in the university's armour was, as always, the lack of any really effective means of supervising and controlling the activities of students *all* the time, especially those students, and they were apparently becoming more numerous, who were not at the university to study, but to enjoy themselves. Slegge and his dice-house had emphasised this, and it was with him in mind that Cecil drafted a letter to the university in 1565. He was concerned about 'light actions that might draw the students from their learning' or 'bring infection of popular diseases to the same'—a reference to the plague, which made an alarming re-appearance at this time. There had been attempts by 'light persons, for filthy lucre, to set up places of shows for unlawful games near the university, whereby a great number of the youth may be enticed to be beholders and practisers of lewdness and unlawful acts'. The remedy he suggested was that the university and town officials should unite to prohibit all 'open shows' and assemblies—except for preaching, exercises of learning, fairs, markets, law-courts and executions—in the town or within a five-mile circuit of it. (There was some strange irresistible appeal about that 'five-mile' limit.)

However well-intentioned, the suggestion had no hope of success. No amount of legislation or preaching could abolish gaming-houses, brothels, 'lewd' shows, low taverns and high jinks; it could make them illegal, but that was not abolition. No amount of prohibition could keep youth away from them or prevent non-youth from exploiting them. Hence a permanent headache for the VC and Heads.

Cecil's exhortations for harmonious relations did not go wholly unheeded, however, for in 1568 he received a letter from the VC and Heads *and the principal inhabitants of Cambridge*, relating the differences existing between them and declaring that 'a perpetual concord and agreement might have been settled, but for the factious conduct of Mr Kymball, mayor, and his adviser, Roger Slegge'. It did not quite tally with the facts of the past few years, but at least it offered some hope for future negotiations. For a few months, that is.

The very next year brought to light further machinations of Mr Slegge, once again mayor. This time the attack was on the subject of mustering for military service. The commissioners, Lord North and three county gentlemen, were obeying orders in not mustering the scholars or their servants but, to the indignation of the VC, they proposed to muster *the servants of the servants*, about whom no mention had been made in the latest charter. This was a deliberate affront, he said, on the part of the commissioners, who were all freemen of the town and had been incited by Roger Slegge who, he supposed, 'had been elected to that office on account of his having, by crafty counsels and deceitful frauds, opposed the university for the last ten years'. The Privy Council wrote to the commissioners to reinforce the exemption of scholars and their servants, but evidently thought that the extension of university privilege to the servants of servants was carrying things a bit too far. The implications were alarming. If the barber who trimmed a master's beard was a servant of the university— which he was—then the man who trimmed the barber's beard, the baker who sold him bread, the brewer who sold him beer, etc, were *his* servants. At that rate there would be very few men in the town who were *not* exempt from military duty.

It may have been this prospect that prompted the Duke of Norfolk to weary of his office as High Steward of the town and talk of relinquishing it. On hearing of this, the VC wrote to Cecil asking him to persuade the duke to stick to his resolution to abandon the townsmen, lest the latter should try to regain his favour, not that it had been of much advantage to them, except perhaps to boost forlorn hopes. The townsmen in fact appear to have already abandoned the duke. During the year 1569 they spent more than £17 on dinners and 'making merrie' with Lord North and Baron Freville, nothing at all on the Duke of Norfolk, and in that same year Lord North became their patron.

He quickly proved himself the kind of patron they needed. Soon after his appointment as Lord Lieutenant of the county, one of the students addressed 'evil and fowlle wordes' to the mayor. Lord North, without reference to the VC, sentenced the young man to spend three hours in the pillory, with one of his ears nailed to it, and to give surety for his good behaviour in the sum of £100 or else, within nine days, have both his ears cut off. North told the VC of this and that 'for their sakes' he had abated the punishment to three hours of pillory only, without any ear-nailing. If the culprit had been a townsman, he said, he would have lost both his ears. 'The Mayor shall forgive, so as you shall see the Town loveth your favor and quyetness. The rest I pray you see done and make the Varlet to ask the Mayor on hys knees openly foregeveness.' Whether the VC did so or not is not recorded, but Lord North had made his own attitude clear. A little while later he ordered the release from goal of a townsman committed by the VC. The money invested in dinners was therefore paying some dividend and, whilst not bringing peace any nearer, the support of his lordship did at least cause a temporary cessation of hostilities. Two years later he provided the town with a new court-house.

In June 1570 a really novel suggestion for ending the conflict was put forward, almost certainly at the instigation of Cecil. This was that the university and town should be united into one corporation with the title of 'Chancellors, Governors, Scholars and Burgesses of the University of Cambridge'. A conference in the Star Chamber seriously considered the proposal and the views of both parties were evidently sounded, for the town assembly immediately made an order that the mayor should swear to oppose the union and should give warning of the matter being raised again, on pain of instant dismissal and the loss of freeman status. What the university authorities thought is not recorded though, since the plan, if implemented, would obviously result in the total disappearance of the municipal status of the town, it would no doubt be considered a good thing from their point of view. No one could have seriously believed that such a proposal would have been accepted by the townsmen, or that it could have worked satisfactorily in practice. Quite apart from the emotional aspects of the matter, it would have placed on the 'governors' an administrative burden which they were wholly unfitted to bear. The plan was quickly abandoned, like that other impracticable suggestion, the amalgamation of the two universities.

An interesting glimpse of the situation at this date is provided in a letter by William Soone, one-time Professor of Civil Law, written from abroad where he was exiled as a papist: 'None of them [students] live out of the colleges in the townsmen's houses, they are perpetually quarelling and fighting with them, and this is more remarkable in the mock fights which they practise in the streets in summer with shields and clubs. They go out in the night to show their valour, armed with monstrous great clubs furnished with a cross piece of iron to keep off the blows, and frequently beat the watch. When they walk the streets they take the wall, not only of the inhabitants, but even of strangers, unless persons of rank. Hence the proverb that a Royston horse and a Cambridge Master of Arts are a couple of creatures that will give way to nobody'. (A Royston horse was a pack-horse that carried malt to London.)

Another is provided by a letter from the VC, Dr Andrew Perne, to Lord Burghley in 1574, prompted by another outbreak of the plague, of which he gave some details. In four months 115 people had died, mainly in the very congested area of the town centre. The university had suspended operations for the whole of the autumn term and only two scholars had caught the plague. As a result the townsmen had 'well lerned in this tyme of the absence of the Schollers what great benefit theie received by the university withoute whome the most part of them do nowe confesse that theie should not be able to live'. The cause of the plague, according to Dr Perne, was not the corrupt air, as the physicians asserted, but 'our synnes is the principall cause of this'. He also blamed it on infection brought to Barnwell by a Londoner visiting Midsummer Fair and on the foul state of the King's Ditch. His suggested remedy for this was to cleanse it by diverting a stream (from Shelford) through the town and the Ditch—a plan which was eventually adopted more than 40 years later. While in the mood, he added a postscript to the effect that Sturbridge Fair, instead of being leased to the town, should be given to the university, which should then rent the booths to the townsmen.

There was little hope of his last suggestion being adopted, but the persuasive Dr Perne (whose initials on a weathervane, and his ability to stay in office despite the shift of the religious winds, gave rise to the quip that they denoted A Papist, A Protestant and A Puritan in turn) did succeed in getting Roger Slegge and the leading burgesses to sit amicably at a meeting with him and reach agreement on measures to be taken to clean up the town. This, too, provides an interesting glimpse of the town, as well as demonstrating that the two sides could work together, when they had to. Moreover it shows, even with the college buildings already erected, how very *rustic* was this university town. This is what they agreed:

1 All householders, inhabitants, scholars and churchwardens should sweep and cleanse the streets on Wednesdays and Saturdays and have all the muck carted to the common dumps [of which there were five—near Newnham Mills, Spital End, the Fair Yard, end of Jesus Lane and Pudding Pits beyond Castle Hill] or into the fields by common carters. Innkeepers and horsekeepers were not allowed to dump manure in the streets, except just before removal time. Two overseers were appointed in each parish and they were to have one half of the fines imposed. The carters were to be paid by levying a special tax to be assessed by a joint committee of two of the university and two of the town.

2 Butchers were to slaughter animals only in the common slaughter-houses and no blood was to be allowed to run in the streets.

3 No carts with iron-shod wheels were to be allowed in the town except when harvest-carting. The dung-carts were to have 'bare' wheels.

4 No pigs of any kind were to be allowed in the streets, college precincts or churchyards unless accompanied by a drover, on pain of a 4d fine. Runaway pigs would incur a fine of 4d on the drover.

5 No ducks or geese were to be allowed in the streets, on pain of 2d.

6 Any house where plague is known to be shall have, in large letters over the door, 'Lord have mercy upon us'. No one in that house shall go abroad on pain of a fine of 20s for the first offence, 40s for the second and perpetual

Cambridge in 1574
This is based on the map by Richard Lyne. What it shows most clearly is the takeover by the university of virtually the whole of the western half of the town, with important acquisitions outside the original town limits. The town itself was becoming more and more cramped and compressed, yet still practically no expansion was attempted, except to some extent at Chesterton and Barnwell, just off the map to the north and east respectively.

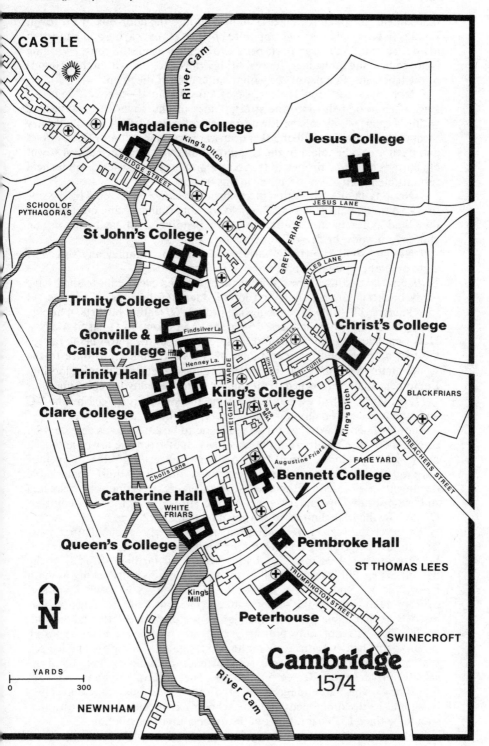

CASTLE

River Cam

SCHOOL OF
PYTHAGORAS

Magdalene College

King's Ditch

BRIDGE STREET

Jesus College

JESUS LANE

St John's College

GREY FRIARS

WALES LANE

Trinity College

Findsilver La.

Gonville &
Caius College

Henney La.

Trinity Hall

HENNEY

WARDE

SHOEMAKER LS

Christ's College

PETI-CURIE

King's College

BLACKFRIARS

Clare College

King's Ditch

PREACHERS STREET

Augustine Friars

Cholis Lane

Bennett College

FARE YARD

Catherine Hall

WHITE
FRIARS

Queen's College

Pembroke Hall

ST THOMAS LEES

N

King's
Mill

TRUMPINGTON STREET

YARDS
0   300

Peterhouse

SWINECROFT

Cambridge
1574

NEWNHAM

River Cam

banishment for the third. Fines shall be paid into the poor-box of the town. Food is to be supplied by one appointed by the VC or mayor, and handed in at a door or window. Straw or rushes are to be burnt inside the house. Washing is not to be hung on hedges, fences, bridge-rails, etc, but within the grounds of the tenement. Penalty of 20s within half a mile of the town.

7 Nobody must throw the carcase of a dead animal—pig, cat, dog, rat, fowl, vermin or fish—into the streets, lanes or churchyards, or anywhere within a quarter-mile of the town, on pain of a 3s 4d fine; but shall bury them on their own ground or 3 feet deep at the common dump. Dead horses and oxen are to be taken to the common dunghill, or further out of town. No corpses are to be thrown in the river. Parents and guardians will be held responsible for children offending in this respect.

8 Nobody shall wash clothes in any brooks in any streets, only by the side of the river, on pain of a 3s 4d fine. No washing shall be hung out to dry on lines and poles in any churchyard. No bedding shall be hung out on churchyard walls, bridge-rails or fish-shambles.

9 Nobody shall knowingly burn in his house or chimney any shreds of cloth or leather, bones or horns of beasts.

10 Firefighting measures. Within three months every college shall have ready buckets, scoops, short and long ladders (66 buckets, 17 scoops, 14 long ladders, 14 short). The town shall provide 60 leather buckets, 4 hooks, 4 long ladders, 4 short ladders, 16 scoops—to be kept in Great St Mary's, Holy Sepulchre, St Andrew's and St Botolph's. On the alarm being raised, the two proctors and two constables of the ward shall go at once to the scene, summon scholars and townsmen, organise rescue and prevent looting. Equipment shall be returned to the market-place next day for checking.

11 Provision is to be made for lighting the streets as agreed by the VC and mayor, except on moonlit nights, from November to Lady Day.

The agreement was to last for 20 years and to be amended as necessary by a committee of 12, half from the university, half from the town, and each party was bound in the sum of £100 to observe the terms of the agreement. I have quoted it at some length because I find it a most remarkable document. It seems as though a sweet breeze of common-sense had suddenly sprung up and swept away the stupid squabbles of centuries. Could it be the first glimmer of the dawn of a new age?

Whatever the reason, reconciliation was definitely in the air that year. The annual oath-taking had for a long time been a source of trouble and, because of that, the university had of late been inclined to let it go by default. They still insisted on all members of the university taking an oath before the VC and masters and the town insisted on all councillors and officers taking an oath before the mayor and bailiffs. Then it was discovered that some people, 'not fearing perjury', had lately taken both oaths. This was not only putting their souls in danger, it was causing offence, for the two oaths were mutually repugnant. So the Senate decreed that any member of the university thus offending should be deprived of the society, privilege and degree of scholars. They added, for good measure, that if any townsman impugned the privileges or customs of the university, he should be discommoned, and any scholar having any dealings with him should be fined £5. That rather put the damper on reconciliation.

Both sides continued their manoeuvring to get control of Sturbridge Fair.

The town repeated its offer of 1,000 marks for outright purchase. Lord Burghley sugggested a joint conference to discuss the matter, making it clear that he did not favour the town's hopes. Lord North made it equally clear that he did and in 1577 approached the queen on the subject. She said that she would not take away any of the university's privileges, 'rather add to them'. North warned the townsmen to be careful and to seek agreement with the university as to the 'book' which was about to be presented to the queen ('book' meant 'charter'). For this advice the town showed its gratitude in the usual costly way.

One topic on which town and university saw eye to eye, and later co-operated with commendable goodwill, was the provision for the poor, now beginning to assume distressing proportions, though at the first opportunity that arose for co-operation the university was strangely obstructive. The town wanted to enclose and let a part of Jesus Green for part of the year and devote the proceeds to the provision of a hospital, the relief of the poor and facilities for setting the idle poor to work. The university objected and the Privy Council vetoed the project. Alderman Slegge, evidently a reformed character now, made a special journey to London to explain, and the Council's consent was obtained, subject to the agreement of the university, which was also obtained. Both sides were playing their hands carefully because of the prize each was hoping to win in the exclusive grant of Sturbridge Fair. Burghley and the queen knew this perfectly well and were deliberately withholding a decision. It was the best peace-keeping device that had ever been found.

It kept the peace at the high level of the conflict but, unfortunately, the lads were getting restive. A new outlet for surplus energy was needed. As it happened, one had lately come into vogue. It was called 'foot ball'. The very thing, you might suppose—or you might have supposed if your knowledge of football was confined to the game as it used to be played when we were young—to work all that 'jetting' nonsense out of their systems. But the game as it was played 400 years ago made even today's game look quite refined.

The match was one arranged between the town youths of Chesterton and a team of scholars. A 'team' consisted of all those who cared to attend; the pitch was a grass field alongside the river, which was one of the 'goals'. The referee—if that is the right word—was Thomas Parish, head constable. Perhaps 'organiser' would be a more appropriate term, for he certainly had things organised. The local 'team', on his instructions, had all come equipped with cudgels, 'divers staves', which they secreted in the church porch before the visitors arrived. The scholars had gone without any such equipment, not even the odd knife tucked up their jumpers, not even a club or two. I suppose they *did* have a ball of sorts—probably a pig's bladder stuffed with wool—though there is no mention of one. Anyway, it would not have mattered. Within minutes of the 'kick-off', the home team began to pick quarrels with the visitors and suddenly rushed to the church-porch, grabbed their cudgels and belaboured their opponents over the head with them. Those students who were not prostrate on the pitch ran to the river, jumped in and sought safety on the far bank. From there they called out to Parish, who was now acting as striker for the home team, to keep the queen's peace. He, reverting to his role as constable, turned to such members of the university team as were still on the pitch and ordered *them* to keep the peace, then told his team-mates to 'beat them down'.

The score? Parish was hauled before the magistrates and put in the castle gaol. Later that year the Senate placed a total ban on scholars playing football anywhere but in the precincts of their own college. No strangers, visitors, even visiting scholars, were allowed to join them. Those minors who infringed the rule would be 'openly corrected with the rod'. Adults doing so would be fined 5s for a first offence, 10s for a second and 40s for a third. Refusal to pay the fine would result in being sent to prison. The little green between Trinity and the river was to be used only by Trinity scholars for the playing of 'fote ball'.

Chesterton seems to have been something of a sporting Mecca. On Sunday, April 22 1581 a bear-baiting had been arranged and widely advertised. The VC sent a proctor, Mr Neville, with three others and a bedell to stop it. They found the bear tied to a stake and learned that the baiting had already taken place between 1 pm and 2 pm, 'during sermon time', which aggravated the offence. Asked by what authority he presumed to be there, the bear-ward said he was Lord Vaux's man and had a licence from the magistrates. The proctor told him he was acting against the privilege of the university, ordered him to cease that disorderly pastime and go with the bedell to appear before the VC. He agreed to do so. But then Richard Parish and a few other bystanders had a word with him, so that he flatly refused to go. Parish, brother of Thomas, the head constable, whose deputy he claimed to be, came between the bedell and the bear-ward and ordered the former not to interfere. The bear-ward, he said, was *his* prisoner, and if he had done any wrong they would take him to a magistrate not to the VC. This declaration was emphasised by a tap on the bedell's chest which sent him reeling backwards into the arms of the bear, to his intense alarm, though he suffered no physical hurt. Then they led the bear-ward away, knowing that the bear would not be impounded in his absence.

Parish informed the crowd of spectators that, when evensong was over, and the university officials had gone, they would bait the bear again. One Jackson, with whom the bear-ward lodged, refused to hand him over, saying that the VC had no authority over him. The proctor's party had retired in discomfiture to the vicarage, where Jackson joined them. He told them that he had heard Thomas Parish give permission for the show to be staged, having said: 'It is very likely that there will be a resort of scholars, and the proctor will come to stop it, but take no notice of him, I will bear you out'. Jackson promised to appear before the VC the next day, if the constable did not advise him differently. Needless to say, Parish did advise him differently. When the proctor's party confronted Parish, he told them to mind their own business (he knew what the university privileges were, he had a copy of them in his house). The crowd, considerably swollen by now, began to laugh and jeer. The proctor cited the five-mile rule. Parish said he knew of a justice not far off before whose door he might bait the bear, with the VC looking on. This was undoubtedly a reference to Lord North, who made a practice of granting licences for 'illicit shows', knowing that it would incense the university officials.

Lord Burghley, with all the cares of State on his shoulders, was obliged to add this ludicrous episode to them. He summoned the Parish brothers to appear before him in London, and delayed their return to Cambridge by ten days spent in the Gatehouse prison, whence they were released on making a submission of their 'wilful contempt' and an abject apology for it. They were 'very sorrie'—to be in prison. Once out, they carried on their vendetta against all ranks of the university.

The individual pitting his strength against the might of the university had little hope of success but, every so often, by dint of perseverance, even more by dint of patronage, it could be done. John Keymer was one who did succeed. He was a vintner and had been granted a licence to sell wine by none other than Sir Walter Raleigh who held the royal patent for licensing wine-sellers throughout the kingdom. When Keymer opened his wine-shop in Cambridge in 1584, the VC naturally objected to this violation of his privilege and wrote to the Earl of Leicester to ask him to tell Raleigh that he had exceeded the terms of his patent. Raleigh said the matter should be referred to his counsel, who would discuss it with the university counsel. Meanwhile a band of students, incited, it was said, by the other vintners, gave Keymer a rough handling. He informed Raleigh, who sent him personally to the VC with a letter protesting at the students' 'riotous demeanour', accusing the VC of acting in contempt of the queen's authority and containing veiled threats of 'some other course' being taken if Keymer was further molested.

Keymer was summoned before the VC and Heads and ordered to close his shop. Raleigh wrote to them on February 10 1585 to this effect: 'You said you were sorry about the unseemly outrages committed by young and unbridled heads, so I did not tell Lord Burghley of this matter. I dealt fairly with the other four taverners, but now I see that I was too tolerant. You are trying to stop Keymer from doing his lawful dealing authorised under the Great Seal. Be just and lawful, as I am sure you will be'. They committed Keymer to prison. Raleigh wrote again, saying that he was amazed at their 'peremptory and proud maner of dealinge' and that he would vindicate his patent. 'I was courteous—you are unsufferable. You have sent a poor man to prison unwarranted. I will not take any disgrace from you. I will do my uttermost. Your Frind as you shall give cause'.

The VC, Dr Norgate, decided that, with an adversary of this calibre ranged against him, he had better make sure that the Chancellor was acquainted with the facts, which were these:

The proctor had gone to Keymer's shop to order him to close it and take down the sign. If he thought he was being wronged, Keymer could have a hearing in a court of law. Keymer said he was in the right, and would not be prevented from keeping his shop. Next day the proctors and bedell arrived and again ordered him to take down his sign. He refused. The bedell tried to take it down. Keymer resisted violently and there was the likelihood of someone getting hurt, so the proctors left. On the following day the proctors, bedell and their assistants arrived at the shop, threw a rope over the sign and pulled it down. A day later it had been set up again. The next day Keymer was sent for by the officer of the proctor, who brought back word that he was not at home. The VC told the proctor's party to pull the sign down again. When they tried to do so they were drenched with a cascade of boiling water mixed with lime and ashes and had to dodge a shower of brickbats and stones. Reinforced by three or four Masters of

Arts, they did manage to get the sign down, then retreated, licking their wounds. Next day, the sign was again triumphantly swinging in the wind, and there it stayed.

Dr Norgate told Burghley of Raleigh's threats and accused Keymer of telling lies. A few days later he wrote again, begging him to continue his protection and asking for his advice, for there was a danger, he said, that others might follow Keymer's example. There was a greater danger even than that. Sir Walter Raleigh was not a man to be worsted by a handful of scholars. Tudor yeomen were not the only ones who could be pig-headed and Raleigh had the resources, and the know-how, to fight back. In the course of the next 12 months this petty dispute over one man's right to sell wine in a little shop in a Cambridge street had swollen to dimensions that embraced the Secretary of State, the Justices of Queen's Bench, Justices of Common Pleas, Parliament, Lord North, The Lord Chancellor, The Chief Attorney, The Master of the Rolls, The Archbishop of Canterbury, the Earl of Leicester, the four other vintners of Cambridge, the butchers of Cambridge and, of course, John Keymer. The only person of importance not in the picture, as far as I know, was the queen, and Raleigh kept well in the background, acting through his agent, a Mr Browne.

Keymer was sent to prison again, having been tried in his absence, but was released as a result of a kind of legal blackmail. In February 1587 his sign was still displayed defiantly above his shop. The High Steward of the university, the Earl of Leicester, urged the VC to pull it down and 'put down' Keymer. But it stayed there, and so did he.

Then there was the case of the mayor, the brewer and the pigs. It all began, like so many other teacup storms, with the mayor, John Edmunds, making a mockery of the oath-taking at the Black Assembly by contriving that only he and the town-clerk should be present. Dr Perne wrote to Lord Burghley about it, quite rightly, university privilege had taken a few hard knocks recently. In this case Dr Perne wrote with more feeling than usual; he was sorely hurt by the ingratitude of this wretched man, Edmunds, and explained at great length why. Edmunds was the son of Dr Edmunds, DD, once Master of Peterhouse, often VC, who had kept his marriage secret and had handed young John over to the bedell, Mr John Mere, to be brought up. Thanks to Mere, John Edmunds (alias Mere) obtained service with Archbishop Parker, until sacked for ingratitude and stubbornness. Then he was employed by Dr Perne, became his butler, then butler at Peterhouse, was provided with a house, was appointed as an appraiser of the university, then appointed as one of the vintners of the university, an office which he sold for £80. All this thanks to Dr Perne. Or rather, Dr Perne ought to have been thanked, but he wasn't. He had been responsible for Edmunds being elected as mayor, and was not even invited to the mayor's inaugural banquet. As a university official, Edmunds had refused a wine-licence to another vintner because that man would not admit that he was beholden to the university. Yet here he was, displaying the same lack of gratitude! When reprimanded by Dr Perne at the Black Assembly, Edmunds said he didn't know the custom, yet the town-clerk, Ball, had attended the ceremony for 20 years.

Burghley was very sorry for the aggrieved doctor, but there was nothing he could do about it—and he *was* rather busy. So was the VC. The spite and ingratitude of the mayor increased week by week. Keymer and his bush (the traditional vintner's sign) were being openly sustained. University personnel were being prevented from having booths at the fair. Supplies of corn and malt were being deliberately withheld from the colleges and the county magistrates were supporting the actions of the corn-merchants. The only way to hit back at this insidious enemy, John Edmunds, was to discommon him, which the Senate did on May 27 1587. The reason given for the prohibition of all dealings with him, on pain of a fine of £5, was his 'ingratitude to the university, the scholars and their servants'. What really caused it, however, was William Hammond's pigs.

Hammond was a brewer, also bailiff of Jesus College at a salary of £58 a year, and thus a 'privileged person'—although not according to Edmunds. He had no land in the common fields, and therefore no common rights, but he had 35 pigs and he drove them on to the 'common' to graze. No pigs were allowed on the commons, said Edmunds. The pigs were not on the common, said the VC, they were on freehold land belonging to St John's College, *'the colleges are in effect the owners of all the land in the fields of Cambridge'*, and the farmer of the land had given Hammond permission to put the pigs there. Be that as it may, the mayor took three of his men with him, rounded up the pigs and drove them into the pound, on Pound Hill. Presently up rushed an irate Hammond, demanding his pigs. He could have them, said the mayor, on payment of 2s per pig (as the dispute progressed, the figure was advanced to 3s, the legitimate charge, agreed in 1575, was 4d per pig) or, he might accept a choice piece of silver plate in lieu. Hammond refused, and the pigs stayed where they were. Hammond went straight to the VC's office.

That night the pound was attacked by 'a great multitude of riotous persons' armed with clubs and other weapons. The railings were 'saune a sunder' and the pigs released. None of the liberators was identified. The VC said they could have been, and most probably were, townsmen instructed to do the pound-breaking to aggravate the matter against the university. Edmunds said they threatened 'with clubs to beate into ther dores all such persons as offered to come out to see who they were'. Next day the VC arrested one of the pounders (two them, said the mayor). The mayor released him, having obtained a writ of habeas corpus which he served on the VC as he was leaving the Schools, in full view of the public. Since when, said the VC, the mayor had been paying the 'lewde person' 8d a day for his 'lewde service'. So the mayor was discommoned, an action which he considered 'infamous and baffling'. Not so baffling as his own conduct, though; he spent more than £20 on another trip to London to get another writ for the release of a man whom he had already released!

And so the dispute raged on round poor old Burghley's head. What patience that man must have had! It would be something of a relief when the Armada came. Hammond got his pigs back, but lost half his customers. Two of them were discommoned for refusing to buy his beer; one repented and was forgiven. Several aldermen had promised Hammond that, if he would become a townsman, and stop being a servant of the university, he 'should have all favour and toleration in this and in all else freely'. He must have brewed exceptionally good beer. The university petitioned for a revision of the statutes relating to commons, pound, etc, and once again it was stressed that they now owned virtually all the land in the common fields; a fact of enormous significance, yet one which had almost passed unnoticed in the turmoil of the last half-century.

All else, including the coming and going of the Armada, was forgotten when at long last, on August 15 1589, the charter relating to Sturbridge Fair was sealed, signed and delivered. Town and university had waited, worked, schemed and spent for 50 years. As the preamble stated, the fair had been 'the mainstay of the town financially' for a long time. The queen granted it out of her hands and confirmed to the mayor, bailiffs, burgesses and their successors the fair with all profits, commodities, courts, jurisdictions, booths, etc. She gave it to them *a)* out of a sense of pity, *b)* out of sense of the utility of the fair to the town and to the merchants of the kingdom, *c)* from a desire to provide for the continuance of the fee-farm—trust Queen Elizabeth for that! and *d)* from a desire that the town be lightened in its burdens, increased and honoured under her prosperous and peaceful government. *But*—all privileges, customs, franchises and profits granted to the university within the last 20 years were to be maintained! Trust Queen Elizabeth for *that*!

The charter contained certain regulations relating to the location in the fairground of mercers, grocers, wool-merchants, goldsmiths, pewterers and braziers. To obviate, it was hoped, any ambiguity, the university was granted a new charter on August 30 1589, which stipulated clearly its rights and privileges in the fair as regards trading, courts, proclamation, etc, and giving precise definition as to who was and who was not a 'privileged person'. There could be no excuse for further quarrelling; or so the queen and Lord Burghley must have thought.

Little did they know those obstinate townsmen, if that is what they thought! Nicholas Gaunt, mayor and MP, instead of being hailed as a hero or victor when he got back from London, was considered by his fellow-townsmen as a traitor. At the foot of their brand-new charter—which, incidentally had cost them £133 in four months, and five times that sum over the past 50 years—someone wrote later: 'One Gaunt was Maior of Cambridge who att London assented to these newe Jurisdictions of the Universitie, and therin betrayed the Towne, who shortlie after was putt out of his Aldermanshipp, and lived the remainder of his life in great want and miserie, and hatefull to all the townesmen'. Poor Gaunt!

He wanted peace. He got a 'settlement', but no peace. In less than two years the war had flared up again. On Wednesday, September 15 1591 a party of students were crossing by the ferry from Chesterton to the fair. In the boat with them was Richard Parish, whom we last met nine years earlier at the bear-baiting incident. His spell in prison, and several more since, had done nothing to change his attitude towards students. Two years after the bear-baiting affair he was involved in a brawl in which he seriously wounded two of them. Five years after that, when arrested by a proctor's officer, he used such diabolical threats of violence towards him that the officer flatly refused ever to try to arrest him again. The latest arrest of Parish, only a few months earlier, was performed by one of the town officers, who for his pains received a wound which nearly proved fatal. In the same affray a fellow servant of Parish was so badly injured by him that he sought safety in an alliance with him. The party of students on their way to the fair did not know what kind of man was their fellow-passenger. They would not have spoken to him in any case, being engrossed in their own light-hearted chatter.

Next to Parish in the boat sat Walter Hawksworth, a scholar of Trinity. Half-way across the river Parish suddenly grasped him by the front of his tunic and tried to push him over the side of the boat. Failing in this, Parish drew his dagger and stabbed the student in the breast. Hawksworth cried out that he had been murdered, as he must have been had the dagger not lodged in a rib. His nearest companions tried to lay hands on Parish, who lashed out indiscriminately with his dagger, striking one of them in the head and hand, and almost scalping the other. They managed to secure him, however, and decided to take him to the Sturbridge bank of the river. Parish's shouts for help brought a crowd running to the Chesterton bank, where a number of students were waiting to be ferried across. At the sight of the armed oncomers, the students fled, some of them seeking refuge on a barge moored a short distance downstream, others wading and swimming across the river.

Parish shouted to the nearest stall-holders in the fair that these students were coming to wreck their booths, so that the saturated youths found themselves attacked with sticks and driven back into the river. Other university men were there, including a fellow of Trinity, who seized Parish and led him through the fairground towards the court-house. They ought to have taken the precaution of gagging him, for on the way, seeing a crowd of apprentices, he called out to them that he had once been an apprentice and that the scholars had arrested him to do him wrong and he appealed to them to rescue him. This they did with characteristically violent camaraderie and, while the scholars were warding off a rain of blows, Parish disappeared into the crowd.

He was not seen again by the various people who most wanted to see him, including a magistrate in Chesterton, until a fortnight later, though a warrant for his arrest had been made out as soon as the affair was reported to the VC. At about 2 pm on Thursday, September 30, word came that Parish was in Cambridge, in Castle Yard, where he was in attendance upon his master, Lord North, who, with other justices, was engaged at the county sessions. The proctor's officer to whom the warrant for Parish's arrest was committed declined the honour, partly on account of his own weakness, partly because he knew from previous experience the kind of man he would be dealing with. So the task was committed with due legal formality to two very able-bodied students of Trinity, Nicholas Gifford, BA, and Thomas Atkins, singing man. These two, gowned and armed, waited in Bridge Street for Parish to put in an appearance on his way to the Dolphin Inn, which they had reason to suppose would be his destination once the sessions were over, some time in the evening. They took up a position near the door of Mr Slegge's house, for that, they thought, was another possible destination of the wanted man. Anticipating the likely need for reinforcements, several large groups of students, all armed, were posted in neighbouring courtyards and alley-ways. Gifford and Atkins were told to make their own plans, even to allow their quarry to escape if arrest proved too difficult, in the belief that Parish would not dare to appear in the town again.

But the students had no intention of letting Parish escape. They were in

no way disconcerted when Lord North appeared on horse-back, followed
by a crowd of retainers, amongst whom was Parish. Gifford accosted the
latter, showed him the warrant and explained briefly the charge on which he
was arrested. Brief though the charge was, it had not been fully stated
before Parish drew his weapons, as did all the retainers of Lord North and
Sir John Cutts. Gifford stepped back a pace, threw off his gown and drew
his own sword and dagger. Shouts for help were raised by the two intrepid
scholars, augmented by the cry of 'Clubs!' from a barber of Trinity who was
on his way with a companion, both unarmed, from the Castle to the college.
The effect of this cry, long familiar in Cambridge streets, was dramatic.

From the house of one Charleton nearby issued John Shaxton, MA,
deputy proctor, followed by nine or ten students, all armed. Shaxton called
on the retainers to keep the peace and hand over Parish, then surrounded by
friendly swords. The answer, if any, was inaudible in the tumult. The
swords were not lowered. From St John's college, just round the corner,
came running Mr Nowell at the head of a band of students at least 30 strong
and all armed, some with swords, others with clubs. Within seconds other
groups of scholars were on the scene, so many so quickly that Lord North
swore afterwards that they had been lying in wait in every house and shop in
the street. He was no doubt right.

Lord North turned to his followers and those of Sir John Cutts and
ordered them to keep the peace. Then he faced the threatening mass of
students, demanding to know the reason for this affray. His horse was as
frightened at the confrontation as he was and he dismounted while he still
had the choice. When informed of the reason for the students' presence,
North denied the legality of it and the ensuing argument at times assumed
the character of a brawl, though no hurt was intended against his lordship.
When, after assuring the assembled crowd that he would uphold the cause
of justice, he announced his intention of proceeding to his lodgings, the
students made way for him, but did not leave the streets. Turning into High
Street, the press passed the Dolphin Inn; a few yards further on they were
halted outside the Bear Inn by the Earl of Cumberland, who had a brief
word with Lord North, then addressed the students. They told him how
Parish had resisted arrest by the officers of the 'Eunyvercety', Lord North
added more placatory remarks and the earl accompanied many of them
back to their colleges. Meanwhile, Parish had disappeared.

On the way towards the Falcon in Petty Cury, Lord North encountered
another band of about 50 students, armed with swords and clubs, but they
made no attempt to molest him. As he crossed the market-place a large
party of 200 students was advancing along Shoemaker Lane but he did not
see them, or they him. That night at the Falcon he and his fellow justices ate
their supper to the sound of a rowdy gathering of students outside the main
gate which, prudently, was bolted and barred.

Parish, everybody knew, could not have got far away and could not be
kept hidden for long, even in the rabbit-warren which was the Cambridge of
those days. It was Mr Nowell, fellow of King's, who found him hiding at
the back of a house near the Round Church. This Nowell, like his colleagues
Gifford and Atkins, was a huge man built for this kind of task (three
centuries later he would have been a tower of strength in the rugger XV). He
disarmed Parish, picked him up, slung him over his shoulder and, with a

little help from Mr Tomson of Trinity and a large crowd of students, carried him to the VC's lodging. He was committed to the care of Mr Shaxton, who took him first to Trinity then to the Tolbooth. Parish offered no more resistance. I should think he was rather relieved to hear the Tolbooth door slam behind him.

Next day, Friday, Parish was brought before the consistory court of the university. The VC first demanded security of £200 for his good behaviour, then charges were brought by each of the three students whom Parish had wounded at Chesterton. Hawksworth claimed damages of £500, the two others £100 and £20. They never got them, of course. Parish could offer no security, either for his good behaviour or for his appearance to answer the charges, so he was committed to prison and stayed there for some time.

There must have been, over the centuries, hundreds of such incidents, the vast majority of them unrecorded except for the bare facts stated in the court records and soon forgotten even by those who had participated in them. This one would have been, but for the strange conduct of Lord North. He alleged that an elaborately planned attempt had been made on his life by the university authorities. When the charge was well and truly shown to be ill-founded, Lord North revealed his malice by besmirching the characters of Gifford and Nowell and accusing the VC of tyrannical conduct towards Parish because he demanded so much as security and because of 'the strict and rigorous usage since he was committed'.

The usage of Parish was so 'strict' that, by the collusion of the town gaoler, who was also one of Lord North's retainers, he was allowed to walk up and down the streets of the town by day, and go into the fields with his fowling-piece as often as he liked. Hoping to bag a brace of students, no doubt.

Amidst all those goings-on, two more colleges had been unobtrusively founded. In 1584 Sir Walter Mildmay founded *Emmanuel College* on a corner of the site formerly occupied by the Black Friars, with moderate endowments which were increased later. From the outset it was markedly Puritan in character. It may be said to have been the 'parent' of Harvard University in America, for John Harvard was one of its scholars in 1627. *Sidney Sussex College* was founded in 1589 by the executors of the will of Frances Sidney, Countess of Sussex, who had bought the site, once the home of the Grey Friars, from Trinity College in 1576, and bequeathed £5,000 to establish a college for a master, ten fellows and 20 scholars. Thus the territorial takeover of the town was advanced, though no further gains were to be made for 200 years.

As a short postscript to a long chapter, and in case you are wondering whether the VC ever managed to get his own back on Lord North for that display of spite, here is a quote from a document of 50 years later, relating to the precedence of the VC: 'I have often heard Mr Stringer, an ancient Bedell of the university, say that the Lord North did once offer to take the wall of Dr Soame, Vice-Chancellor, but he and Mr Smith goeing before the said Vice-Chancellor put his Bailiffs to the Channel and my Lord also, telling him they knew the Vice-Chancellor's place.'

Chapter 12

Poor town 1591-1605

Candles must always have been a vitally important item on the university shopping list. It is surprising that they have not cropped up earlier as a subject for complaint. In 1595 they did. The chandlers, it was complained, made unreasonable application to the magistrates to increase the price of candles, then sold at a price above the rate allowed. Their candles were 'exceeding badd and much worser than in other places'. Instead of being made of pure tallow, they were made partly of 'kitchin stuffe' which made them burn quickly and give off 'filthye smooke'. Worst of all, the chandlers made their own rules for the trade, as though they were a guild, they wanted 'to be their own carvers' and secretly derided the authority of the VC. That had to be stopped. The method suggested was that one chandler only should supply the needs of the whole university; he should be allocated one third of all the tallow available in the town, at a price fixed by the VC, ie, 2s 6d per stone, and sell candles at between 3d and 4d a pound. A fund was to be set up to purchase tallow in the summer to provide a stock for the making of candles in the winter, when most needed. The price fixed by the VC was to apply equally to all the other chandlers, who were forbidden to trade without licence.

That meant a niggardly profit of just over a penny per pound; when labour, transport and other materials were taken into account, the profit was almost nil. Needless to say, there sprang up a brisk trade in smuggling candles made without licence out of the town. The attempted suppression of it led to some bitter clashes.

John Barber, having made a hundred pounds of candles, surplus to local requirements in his opinion, loaded them into the panniers of his pack-horse and set out before daylight to go into Essex. It was still dark when he and his horse plodded up the slope of the Gogmagog Hills and both stopped at the top for a breather. John then heard a most unwelcome sound—the thud of galloping horses' hooves. To have attempted flight would have served only to proclaim his guilt, so he waited. It was, as he feared, two of the proctor's men, who had learnt of his early departure from an informer, probably from one of the other chandlers who even now was on another road with a similar load. The two officers dismounted and did their business quickly—that is, seized horse, candles and chandler and took them back to Cambridge, where Barber, after a brief appearance before the VC later that morning, was imprisoned until he paid a fine of £6.

Richard Robinson was stopped on the London road; his horse, which he valued at £40, was killed by a musket-shot when he tried to outstrip the pursuing officers. Its load of 240 lb of candles was confiscated. Robinson was taken before the VC and fined £12, remaining in gaol until his wife secured his release by paying £8 of it. Christopher Ray spent 18 days in gaol before he could raise the £6 fine imposed on him for carrying 120 candles out of the town. Steven Newman paid 6s for a licence to carry candles out of the town; soon afterwards he was stopped by the officers at Barnwell when on his way to Newmarket, before daybreak. In his hampers he had £23 in money and £40 worth of goods—but no candles. The proctor, Mr Lylesse, emptied the contents of the hampers into the mud and compelled Newman to return with him to the town. That same proctor took James Robson's horse as he was going to market, kept it for four days, then demanded 3s 4d from Robson for the horse's feed, confiscated 13 dozen candles which a man had bought from Robson and was carrying to Bedford, so terrifying the owner that he did not dare to claim restitution, and fined Robson for carrying five dozen candles out of town, with the alternative of going to gaol.

'And all this,' asserted the mayor and bailiffs, 'at a time when neither the town nor the university lacked candles'. The university officers disagreed: 'The chandlers are to blame. They are well and cheaply supplied with tallow, thanks to us. We insist on our needs being met first, but they refuse the reasonable terms we offer. If they take candles out of the town to sell, we and the artisans of the town will go short'. The university officers managed with surprising frequency to construe their actions as protecting some of the townsmen as much as the university's interest—and they were often right, of course. But they did not stop candle-smuggling, or prevent chandlers from making what they considered a fair profit.

They were equally unrepentant about having broken into Martin Wharton's house by night in search of a student who had secretly married Wharton's sister-in-law, a match which Wharton was suspected of having arranged for his own advantage, the student being very well-connected. In fact they had a low opinion of Wharton and frankly disbelieved his story that, as constable, he had been told by the proctor to 'gett him home, or else he would have a sword thrust in him'. He was, they said, in league with Keymer, 'our new vintner, and makes wager that he will continue in that trade'. He was 'a common scorner, a depraver of our officers and authority'. He had been summoned before the VC because of the condition of certain herrings which he sold and had asked the proctor whether he sued him as promoter, an 'insolent' question which cost him a fine of £4.

Likewise Thomas Harrison, for calling Dr Leedes a 'papist', was fined £10 and kept in gaol until he paid it. 'See how malicious they are,' said the officers, 'they are not ashamed to reckon it no discredit to be called papist.' Proctorial authority must be upheld, even if it meant entering forcibly into a man's house when he was asleep in bed with his wife, on the grounds that he had sold meat during Lent, with licence from the mayor. The latter, Henry Clark, who lived next door to the butcher, came out to see what the trouble was, and was ordered to 'gett him indoors', or be arrested. Even justices of the peace, said the townsmen, were ordered by the proctors not to interfere when trouble broke out, as when John Goodwyn's house was entered by night in a search for his step-daughter. She was suspected of being a prostitute—perhaps rightly, for she was pregnant then, and had had another child since, being unmarried. Young John Goldsborough, son of an alderman, nearly got killed on that occasion but, said the proctor, it was entirely the fault of his brother for leading an armed rabble against the proctor's party on Market Hill.

Determination to enforce the law—university law—and the manner of its enforcement were giving rise to the most bitter resentment felt in the town for many years. Some of the town's complaints were no doubt exaggerated, some biased in their presentation and some of them inspired by malice. But not all of them, as the university officers asserted. In particular they denied the charges of extortion and malpractice, especially at the fair. Yet if only half the details cited by the townsmen were true, it is evident that there had been the same kind of malpractice that had bedevilled relations some 50 years earlier. The university authorities put most of the blame for the 'frivolous' complaints on Messrs Slegge and Serle, 'that ancient knowne enemy to the general estate of the university, with the help of his handy instrument'.

Nevertheless, they did shortly afterwards issue an order dismissing a number of officers 'expert for their own commodity but negligent in faithful service' because they had brought the university into disrepute by their 'lewd behaviour' and were 'not meet to serve any honest man'. Needless to say, some of the dismissed officials were then admitted as freemen of the town and elected as town officials. They were very soon figuring in complaints from the other side.

Another cause of resentment was the punishment meted out by the VC in his role as guardian of morals—meaning mainly sexual activity and religious observance. It was not so much the severity and nature of the punishments—the townspeople, as spectators, derived a good deal of entertainment from them—as the mere fact that they were imposed by the VC. Many people considered that he had usurped the office of archdeacon. The archdeacon certainly did. Here is a selection from the scores of cases which were heard in the VC's consistory court in the latter part of the 16th century:

Rowland Smith, beer brewer, having done penance for adultery with Jane Fanne, at the second offence was whipped and banished from the town for ever.
Marmaduke Middleton for going to bed with Trabers his wife was censured by the VC to be imprisoned and then carted about the Towne with basons ringinge and then to be banished.
Barnes, a privileged person, was disprivileged for receiving Jane Fanne, being banished.
Robert Walker, John Blanks and his wife censured to be carted and sett at the bullringe for incontinence by the VC. [That is what it says.]
The churchwardens detected and presented Bullock for not repayering to his church and John Dennis for not receaving the Sacrament, both censured by the VC; and Bullock, being privileged, for saying the VC was not his competent judge in his cause, was imprisoned.
Wilson convicted for a whoremaster and banished the towne and Elizabeth Newman, his whore, carted and her banishment excused because of her husband.
Elizabeth Greene and Wilson carted for suspicion of incontinency after being often warned not to keep company and yet keeping company, they were carted with this proclamation in six verses made before them in several places:

'All men and all women behold and see
What judgement befall such as contemne authority.
They that their own wife most filthily forsake,
The Devill to himselfe most willingly doe take.
True repentance therefore god to them send,
That they be not damned world without end.'

Apart from the banishments, those punishments for those 'crimes' were quite normal—as was the use of the ducking-stool for scolds and the pillory for dishonest bakers—but here are three which smack of petty tyranny:

—Brisell, Schoolkeeper, in the crying of the price of Ale and beer, for adding the price of Hostle Ale (*vilissima cervisia*—the very worst type of ale) without the consent of the VC and Taxors was imprisoned;

—outdwellers were fined for buying chickens, capons and ducks in the market;

—poulterers were punished for buying 18 dozen Larks within 5 miles of Cambridge.

That cannot have inspired much respect for university authority, though perhaps more lenient treatment would have produced no better results. The townsmen knew that they had lost the war and most of them admitted it. Others from now on devoted all their energy and ingenuity, though far less cash than formerly, to making life as difficult as possible for the victors and derived a certain malicious satisfaction from doing so. In 1596 the mayor, Robert Wallis, refused to take the oath at the Great Assembly. Despite the efforts of Lord Burghley and the town recorder, two complaints by the VC, Dr Jegon, and two postponements of the ceremony, he adamantly persisted in his refusal on the grounds that it was 'illegal', and got away with it.

Meanwhile, having scored some success with their earlier list of complaints, and realising that this was a cheaper weapon than law-suits, the townsmen drew up another list of complaints, this one addressed to the Lord Keeper and the Lord Treasurer in accord with the 'Composition' of 1503, although that had long been superseded. The list is too long, and some of it too trivial, to be given in full. Here are some extracts of interest:

—the Consistory Court of the university is called by the scholars *the Townsmen's Scourge;*

—the mayor went out to keep order among the students and was assaulted by several of them, his gown rent and spoiled, and lewd words addressed to him, so that he was 'in danger of his life'. On complaint being made to the officers of the university, they said they could not amend it, *for so it always was and always would be*;

—University privilege was granted to about 220 graduates and others in the town who practised trades as their sole means of livelihood, also to various widows, thus depriving the Crown of subsidies and other dues;

—the number of privileged persons exceeds the number of townsmen who pay subsidy. Scholars' lands are not rated for subsidy, though by statute they ought to be.

The rest of the list consists of yet more accusations of malpractice on the part of the university officials. As Archbishop Whitgift said to Burghley, 'some of them are very frivolous and like enough to proceed from the wisdom of that Towne', but he still thought they should be answered. So Burghley, making yet another plea for unity, gave the university a friendly warning: 'Do not abuse your privileges or you may lose them' and asked for specific answers to some of the charges. The VC and Heads denied *all* the charges of 'our unkind neighbours the Townsmen'. But, 'to remove all justification for the calumnious aspersions of the townsmen', the Senate did pass a 'grace' forbidding, on pain of loss of office, the acceptance of any money or promise of money in the execution of official duties, other than the accustomed fees, and fines imposed by a judicial sentence. That could be considered as a sort of victory for the townsmen.

They evidently thought so, and kept up the pressure. In January 1597 the mayor and bailiffs intervened in the university's implementation of the regulations governing the corn-supply, a very sensitive issue, almost a 'rationing' system. From the inquiry instituted emerged statistics of the university population: 1,950 students, 657 graduates, 122 preachers 'unprovided for', 269 poor students 'likely to be forced to abandon their studies'—but those figures may well be suspect as having a propaganda element. Two maltsters were charged with profiteering, both refused to pay the fine imposed, one was gaoled and brought an action for wrongful imprisonment (which he won) with damages. Too much corn was being used for making beer, not enough for bread. As a temporary remedy the number of alehouses in the town was reduced from 80 to 30, a move as unpopular with the students as it was with the townsmen, for, although Trinity alone consumed over 2,000 barrels (36 gallons to the barrel) of beer in one year, it was of such poor quality that the students had to go to a pub if they wanted a real drink.

A dispute at the town sessions after Easter led to another list of complaints against the university being sent to Lord Burghley. It dealt only with legal matters and was an attempt to undermine the authority of the VC and impugn the justice of his court. Once again the complaint was vitiated by the intrusion of malice. Robert Laurence brought a charge against John Cragge, Fellow of St Catherine's, of raping a nine-year-old girl, which ought to have been heard in the Consistory Court. The VC wisely transferred it to the County Court and Cragge was acquitted. Dr Jegon wrote to Burghley: 'The accusations are foule and odious' and attributed them to 'the quarrelous disposition and insolent behaviour of our neighbours of the Town, who are more factious and stirringe now of late than in former years'. He added a list of deliberate offences committed by the mayor and bailiffs—disfranchising townsmen who served on university juries, charging privileged persons in the town courts, taking scholars' horses for post-duty, etc.

One of the proctors, Mr Bolton, gave an account of an episode, typical of many which occurred in 1597 and the next few years and illustrative of the attitude confronting the university officials:

Between 8 and 9 am, coming from the VC, Mr Wallis, mayor, wished to speak to me. He said he was greatly grieved and abused that some in the watch the night before had threatened to break open his gates, and added: 'Before God, if any man be so sawcy as to break open my doore, he shall not come out again alive'. I asked him to have more patience. My deputy, who kept watch the night before, was standing by. I said he might hear what he had to say. He answered he would hear no such varlet. I told him I did not employ varlets, but MAs and Fellows, and asked him to use good words, and send me his informant.

Mr Greaves, junior proctor, had a rather more obnoxious encounter in the course of his duty. He had been informed that there were unreported 'guests' lodging at the house of Leonard Whaley beyond the Great Bridge. He saw lights in the house, but got no answer to his knock. Seeing a light in the chandler's shop next door, he knocked there, a window was partly opened, and he was told that there were guests next door. More knocking at Whaley's still produced no answer, so the proctor and his party went on up to Castle End. When they returned, between 11 pm and midnight, a candle was still burning at Whaley's; by its light they saw a woman in her smock lean out of an upstairs window. When they knocked on the door, the candle was extinguished. The company stood below in the street. Then, 'as it were a rotten egge, or some pissepott or some other like unsavourie thinge was cast or throwne out at the same window uppon the saide company'. More knocking at the door; still nobody came to answer. The door at last fell off its hinges and Mr Greaves went inside.

In the entry he met Whaley and told him that he would go up and search the bedrooms.

'That you shall not', said Whaley, 'this is no alehouse. You are over-stepping your rights.'

'Indeed I am not,' said the proctor, 'and your behaviour is such that it were well done if you were committed to the Tolbooth.'

'Take me there, then, if you dare.'

So they took him, not to the Tolbooth, but along Jesus Lane, in the direction of Barnwell. Opposite the Dolphin, Whaley, who had kept up a running fire of abuse and jeers, with occasional references to the nasty smell hanging round his captors, turned to Mr Greaves and said:

'Why, Mr Proctor, this is not the way to the Tolbooth.'

'No, but you shall go along now with me.'

'I shall then go a-jetting with you and your company, Mr Proctor. I have gone a-jetting with the proctors ere this, before you knew Cambridge.'

By the time the party had finished their round, about 2 am, they had had enough of Whaley's company and gave him the choice of going to the Tolbooth or going home. He went home, and next morning was haled before the VC. All he would say in his own defence was that he would make sure that he had a stronger door next time the proctor came. He was committed to gaol, where he spent the next two weeks, more or less, that is. The mayor and the gaoler saw to it that he was allowed out all day and every day if it suited him.

Mayor Wallis' attitude became so objectionable that Dr Jegon felt obliged to write to Lord Burghley (who had urged him to be 'temperate') in a despairing tone: 'I have refrained from provocation, but, whatever we do, the mayor still with violence does so cross my proceedings and abet the offenders . . . if you do not look into this, I shall not be able to govern, nor the poor town reap those benefits and relief by scholars that it hath always received. I must maintain the privileges of the university . . . but for the common peace of both bodies, and the good of *the poor town*, I submit to arbitration by anybody you care to name . . .'. He then listed 11 specific complaints against the mayor, including the use of the word 'varlett'. Other than that, they were all deliberate infractions of university privilege.

As the good doctor saw it, things were rather alarming, giving rise to the fear that the bad old days of the 14th century were here again. But it was not quite as bad as it seemed. What had happened was that a mild-mannered, nervous, scholarly gentleman had clashed with a tough, ill-mannered, outspoken yet not wholly hard-hearted Tudor 'yeoman'. Jegon and Wallis soon afterwards got together over a flagon of wine and composed a *joint* letter to Burghley asking for authority to remove one Wilkinson from the house which had been granted to him to set up a weaving business to provide work for the poor; he had not done the job properly, so the mayor and VC had sold the house to buy materials for the business.

Nevertheless Dr Jegon wrote again to the Chancellor in September again reciting the faults of Wallis and cunningly added that Wallis had 'slandered *you* with injustice'. Burghley got the Attorney General to rectify two minor injustices arising from the mayor's indiscretion. Wallis was re-elected mayor—in breach of municipal regulations—and on September 29 actually took the oath at the Black Assembly. But his manner of doing so was the cause of yet another letter to Burghley. The ceremony was held in the Town Hall, not in Great St Mary's church; since Wallis would not go to them, the VC and Heads decided to go to him. The mayor kept his hat on his head throughout the ceremony; instead of a Bible, an old parchment-book of the town was used, and Wallis 'not so much as offering to put hand unto head when he heard the name of Jesus Christ', made various uncivil gestures. 'This was endured by us,' wrote Dr Jegon, 'we had agreed before we came to tolerate whatever was done, because they stood among a crowd of townspeople.'

Lord Burghley must have smiled wearily as he read that. But he was not prepared to let Wallis get away with the 'slander' on himself, and wrote demanding an explanation. Wallis replied promptly in terms of the most unctuous flattery—I cannot believe that he actually composed the letter— saying nothing in fact, but saying it very well and at great length. He particularly stressed the importance of his office to which 'great wrongs have been offered'. By the next post Burghley got an even more unctuous letter from the VC telling him, amongst other things, how Wallis had received his lordship's letter. 'He is so moved that he threatened to *make those smoke* that informed your honour thereof.'

The VC and Heads could count on the staunch support of their Chancellor while he lived. They were on less sure ground when it came to defending their actions in higher courts of law, such as the Queen's Bench, whose judges perhaps, like those of the Star Chamber, regarded with some jealousy the excessive privileges granted to the university. That was made apparent when four corn-profiteers, gaoled by the VC, took their case to a higher court. It was not that they were innocent of the offences of which they had been convicted, simply that they had the resources and knowledge— the latter supplied by Francis Brakyn, the Town Recorder—to ply the law with cunning. The VC was fined £20 for making 'bad' writs, and £20 for wrongful imprisonment of the corn-dealers, all of whom remained at large and continued to flout the VC's authority. On their own admission, Dr Jegon and his colleagues were 'not learned in the law'.

Alarm spread through both universities when Parliament took up the attack. It was asserted that masters of colleges were converting the revenues of their colleges to their own benefit and that of their wives and children;

that fellowships were bought and sold; that poor scholars, deserving of preferment, were kept back while rich men's sons bought preferment. A Bill to remedy these abuses was prepared by one Mr Davies of the Inner Temple. The universities in alarm appealed to their respective Chancellors. An Act was passed appointing a commission to inquire into the misapplication of funds given for charitable purposes but a clause was inserted in it exempting the colleges of Oxford and Cambridge and their lands from its attentions. That was a near miss, the second scored by a member of the Brakyn family.

The VC and Heads took the precaution of writing to Lord Chief Justice Popham, humbly stating their willingness to submit to his authority. They wrote two more letters to Lord Burghley, begging his support once more, not just in the legal tangles which were too much for them, but also in the matter of the 'personal misdemeanours' of the mayor and townsmen. Lord Burghley could help them no more. On August 4 1598 he was freed at last from the vexations of the townsmen and the importuning of the scholars— for ever. They elected in his place Robert Devereux, Earl of Essex, Earl Marshal, Knight of the Garter—an unfortunate choice, for he was beheaded for treason less than two years later.

Had they but realised it, the VC and Heads had at their disposal a cheap and potent weapon in the wits of the young men whom they strove to control. It was used for the first time in 1599. A group of students of Clare Hall got together and wrote a play—still something of a novelty—a comedy which they called *Club Law*. They enlisted the aid of Miles Goldsborough (brother of the boy who was injured in a brawl a few years earlier) who contrived somehow to get hold of the costumes which were needed. The mayor, bailiffs, aldermen and their wives were invited to the performance and allocated a block of seats in the centre of the hall, with students all round them. Imagine their discomfiture when they saw themselves impersonated on the stage by young actors wearing *their* clothes, imitating their speech and gestures, portraying the worst of their characters! The municipal dignitaries were not amused—everybody else was, immensely— but they could not leave their seats because of the human wall hemming them in and were obliged to sit out the comedy to the bitter end.

It is a pity that the script of the play was not preserved, for this was a truly historic event—the first time, in 400 years of strife, that a sense of fun had entered into the fray. The mayor and bailiffs complained of this 'libellous' comedy to the Privy Council, unreasonably magnifying the offence and making special play of the 'insult' afforded to the civic mace. The Council saw the humorous side of the affair and sent only a mild reproof, which failed to satisfy the townsmen. They pressed for more severe punishment, so the lords of the Council promised to come to Cambridge and see the play performed again, in the presence of the offended townsmen. The offer was not accepted.

Wounded feelings did not prevent town and university from acting together in the matter of relieving poverty—real poverty, not the pretended poverty which both sides made play of from time to time—now becoming an increasingly urgent concern almost month by month, especially in the parishes of St Giles, St Andrew's and Holy Trinity, to which parishes the other ten were asked to contribute. On all other matters the rift between them was widened, impossible as it might seem. In April 1601 Dr Jegon wrote to Sir Robert Cecil (elected Chancellor, before the execution of Essex) in the expectation that he would give the same support as his father had done: '. . . the disposition of our town adversaries, the hard issue of our forebearance, and your loving direction . . . embolden us to tell you of the wrongs offered against our charters by a few principal authors here . . . find how to deliver us from their insolent vexations . . . show how great benefit we receive by your means in being delivered from so many violences as have not in the memory of man before been offered to this poor university'.

It is a fact that, during the years 1597-1602, there was a spate of charge and counter-charge of an intensity and volume never before or since known in the whole of this long conflict. It is true, as Dr Jegon said, that the inspiration on the town side came mainly from two men—Robert Wallis and John Yaxley. These two, along with the bailiff, William Nicholson, and the gaoler, Benjamin Payne, were described by the VC as 'verie factious, troblesome and insolent persons of verie furious and violent dispositions, wholly malicious and envious of the state of government of the university, men of evil conversation and of verie ill name and report'. Whether they were really quite as black as painted by the VC is open to question, though he must have had grounds for his assertion that Wallis and Yaxley had got themselves appointed as justices of the peace and MPs by bribery, had embezzled and misused public funds, had erased their names from the Subsidy list to avoid paying taxes, had robbed the poor and opposed the mayor when not in office themselves. It is also clear that both sides exaggerated and overstated their case—for instance by using the general term 'they' as if large numbers were involved when in fact only two or three were guilty; a feature which only emerges from perusal of the mass of original documents in the university archives.

Appended to Dr Jegon's letter was a long list of accusations made by the town against the university and the answers which the latter made to some of them. Cecil may have had the time and patience to peruse them all. You may not, so I will be brief and selective:

Town: The university magistrates will not allow scholars or servants to be charged by the town magistrates in matters concerning breach of the peace, bastard children or ale-houses.

Answer: Quite right, our charters justify it.

Town: They license 100 alehouses and take money for licensing food-stalls in the fair.

Answer: We only license 30 and we don't take money for food-stalls.

Town: Burgesses should only be tried by fellow burgesses.

Answer: The town has no charter entitling that claim.

Town: They tolerate the killing, eating and dressing of meat on fish days, killing flesh during Lent and take money for such toleration. They tolerate bakers and brewers breaking the assize of bread and ale at the fair. They license 'badgers' and 'kidders' to carry corn out of the town, but won't allow the townsmen to do so. They take fees for licensing the sale of poultry and oysters, thus putting up the price.

Answer: We license one butcher to kill during Lent, to supply the sick and infirm, as the law allows. Name the officers who take illegal fees and we will deal with them.

Town: Some of the privileged persons keep dicing houses, bowling alleys, etc, but are not allowed to be charged in civic courts.

Answer: No civic court has any jurisdiction over privileged persons except in cases of felony.

Town: Many substantial freemen of the town, and others of the richer sort, in order to escape subsidies, musters, jury-service, etc, obtain university privilege for small payment, as laundresses performing little or no service, retainers giving little or no attendance, so that there are more privileged persons than free burgesses, and the subsidy is abated to near half the former sum, although the wealth of the town is as great as it has been within memory.

Answer: We only bestow privilege in accord with the charter of 1589. The rest of what they say is untrue.

Town: Their officers, on pretext of searching by night for suspected persons, break open the doors of honest people giving no cause for suspicion. They do the same when searching for flesh on prohibited days. They keep all the meat which they confiscate, instead of giving one third of it to the poor, as the law requires.

Answer: Our officers only search as authorised, and only keep such meat as is allowed, for which privilege we pay £10 to the Crown.

Town: In the time of Edward VI the colleges contributed 26s a week to poor relief. Before 1589 they contributed £5 6s 8d a month. Now there are 16 colleges, all richer than in times past, yet for a year and more they did not contribute at all, and then only 8s 4d a week, being 6d a college, though the number of the poor by their means are much increased.

Answer: We have always helped to relieve the poor, though not bound to by law. Since 1589 we have joined with the town in contribution to the poorer parishes. The townsmen have withdrawn their weekly contributions from the poorest parishes for nearly a year, but we have continued ours.

Town: The scholars in taverns, alehouses etc, are abusive to the townsmen, especially the magistrates, and also at plays and sermons.

Answer: Not true. Except that on April 23 last certain scholars in a tavern spoke ill of the mayor and his brethren when passing, for which they were all punished and censured.

Town: They send people to prison without written order of committal.

Answer: Our word is good enough.

How anybody could determine the rights and wrongs of that, I do not know. It was a good deal easier in the case of Thomas Crayford. He was an innkeeper and baker. Some years before the case now under review, he had been charged in the university court with breaking the regulations concerning bread, faggots, hay and other commodities, and fined 5s, which he refused to pay. After the usual demands formally made, the proctor's officer came to Crayford's house to make distraint of some object of value equivalent to the fine, in this case a brass pot. Crayford's version of the incident was that his house was entered by force, his goods taken and his wife beaten and wounded so that she languished a long time and then died. The truth was that Crayford, his wife and son, John, attacked the officer, beat him, pulled off half his beard, wrenched his staff out of his hand and threw it in the gutter, and snatched back the brass pot. No one was beaten except the officer and Mrs Crayford lived for more than three years after the incident.

Crayford said he was arrested and gaoled for rescuing his wife. In fact, he, his wife and son were sued for rescuing the distrained brass pot and the matter settled by arbitration. Then, said Crayford, Dr Jegon tried to terminate the lease of the house which Crayford rented from Corpus Christi; Dr Jegon owed him money; the college owed him £12; Dr Jegon refused to let him have certain panelling which he had bought and paid for; Dr Jegon would not let him sell his property. All of which was a twisted version of the true facts. To cap it all, Crayford asserted that one day Dr Jegon, standing at his window, saw his man crush Crayford's daughter behind a door, so that she shortly afterwards had a miscarriage, and refused to do anything to obtain justice for her; a charge which the VC stoutly denied.

Fortunately Dr Jegon was able to produce testimony other than his own word. The overseer of the poor, two churchwardens and four parishioners of St Benet's testified that Thomas Crayford, alias Crowfoot, was 'very contentious; getting goods from other men and not paying his debts; disobedient to government in the university and town, and intractable in the parish; and that for six months, being at home, he comes not to church, but lives a very unChristian and bad life'.

To his dossier were soon added others. Stephen Payne, keeper of the Tolbooth (an office held by the same family over many generations) when ordered to release a prisoner gaoled for debt, refused to do so without a written order. James Robson, alderman (in trouble over candles ten years earlier) had confiscated a bedell's horse for, he said, trespass in the fields, had refused to accept the offer of 2s compensation and refused also to take the case to the VC's court, preferring to keep the horse. The bedell, Benjamin Pryme, sent his lad to rescue the horse from Robson's back yard. Young Robson, already with a number of fines to his discredit for breach of the peace, came out to dispute the removal of the horse. The bedell's lad lashed out at him 'and soe they twoe fell together by the eares and Pryme's servant had a broken head'. Thomas Robson was fined 3s 4d which, of course, he refused to pay and was committed to the Tolbooth. The mayor and other justice stood surety for him, paid the fine (to the gaoler) and released him. Payne, the gaoler's son, had been committed to the castle gaol earlier for contempt and had released himself; now he was committed there again for one night for contempt in releasing Robson, but refused to be released without an order from the VC in writing.

William Andrews, alias Orton, late bailiff, was charged with selling sea-coals in a faulty bushel; in his struggle with the officer the bushel was broken, but he still continued to use it. That case provides an interesting example of how some of the 'wrongs' done by the university were in fact the righting of long-standing wrongs done by the tradesmen of the town. Sellers of sea-coal claimed the right by ancient custom of selling by the 'narrow' bushel, one which was taller than the normal bushel and tapered towards the top like a milk-churn (for greater ease of handling, no doubt). It held the same amount of grain, salt, rape-seed or mustard-seed (normally used for checking) as did the wide bushel. But, as the VC pointed out (after experiment at the coal heaps in Andrews' presence) its shape, and the size of the lumps, prevented it from holding the same quantity of coal; the difference was a shovelful and a half. Why they sold by measure rather than by weight I do not know. Just as I do not know why there was such objection to the planting of willows in the swampy areas of the common meadows; a charge made by each side against the other—the only instance, I believe, of accusation and counter-accusation coinciding.

With few exceptions, the accusations were all part of a deliberate campaign of vexation and vilification. Then Robson, Payne, Andrews and Crayford were all summoned to London in October in the custody of a pursuivant, on orders from Cecil to the mayor; and all were committed to the Gatehouse prison until they should admit their offences. Crayford did so after seven weeks, persuaded by Cecil's chaplain, and admitted that all the accusations which he had made against Dr Jegon were false. The others were also released in December on writs obtained and paid for by the town.

Meanwhile Sir Robert Cecil had written to Sir John Cutts, Sir John Cotton and Mr Wendy, local justices of the peace, expressing his determination, with their help, to put an end once and for all to this stupid conflict. It is a long letter, revealing Sir Robert as a true son of his father in his fairness and integrity. In it he refers to 'some oversight on the part of rash-headed scholars, and on the town likewise very many injuries' and seeks first and foremost the truth. He knew that there were faults on both sides. So did Dr Jegon and the masters. They followed up Cecil's letter, which the justices must have shown to them, with a list of positive suggestions for improvement:

1 Reduction in the number of alehouses as agreed with the town.

2 Written statements of committal to gaol and delivery by an officer known to the gaoler.

3 Only MAs of three years standing to be appointed as deputy proctors, and they in all searches to carry the proctor's staff.

4 The university to make regular contributions to poor-relief, to the inhabitants of the town, if they will accept it as an act of charity, not compelled by law. Or, if the town prefers, the university will relieve their own poor and the town theirs.

5 University officers shall not bring suits against townsmen except as regards victuals and victuallers.

Then, as a postscript, a few more suggestions concerning the procedure for complaining, penalties for bringing charges without proof, arrangements for meetings and a request for another commission of inquiry as soon as possible—so long as it did not include Mr Wallis or Mr Yaxley, 'the chief disturbers'.

Having brought the town to heel, Cecil in the following year gave the university a taste of the whip. What, he asked, were they doing about lecturers who were supposed to give four lectures a week and only gave four in a year? About monitors to ensure that students attended lectures? About students who did not wear caps, gowns and hoods and did not speak Latin or did not dine in hall? About the negligence, dissoluteness and 'boyishness' of many tutors, 'which is the undoing of many youths'? About the negligence of many heads of colleges?

The university authorities, as they no doubt told him, had already banned curled locks, great ruffs, velvet pantables, velvet breeches, coloured nether stocks, football, dogs, walking on market hill, sitting on stalls, going to pubs on Fridays, bull-baiting, bear-baiting, bowling, nine-holes, 'Dagges, Gunnes, Crossbowes and Stonbows', plays, public shows, interludes, comedies, loggets. What else could they do? Keep every young student on a lead and lock him up at dusk? It did not help matters when the town authorities deliberately built a new bull-ring in 1604, and bear-baiting was regular, if illegal, entertainment at Chesterton, and 'shows' were now part of the annual Sturbridge scene.

The new charter which was granted to the university in March 1605, on the face of it, put the final seal on the VC's authority as guardian of the morals, controller of the commerce, overseer of entertainment and chief keeper of the peace in Cambridge. It confirmed all privileges previously granted, enlarged upon them and brought them up-to-date, stressing in particular:

1 The right of university officers to search in the town, suburbs and fairs for all common and public women, harlots, bawds, night walkers, scholars wandering by night out of their colleges without just cause, or frequenting the houses of townsmen, taverns or alehouses, vagabonds, suspects, those who used dice or other illicit games, those who had not honest means of livelihood, or those without lawful cause dwelt there or came to the town, suburbs, fairs and markets; and to punish them by imprisonment or banishment. In this the mayor, bailiffs and constables were firmly commanded not to impede the VC and heads or their deputies, but to assist them when required to do so, under pain of facing a charge of contempt and incurring the king's wrath.

2 The prohibition of all actors, wrestlers, exhibitions of fights of bears or bulls, jugglers, puppets, fools, jesters and all idle games in the town and within a radius of five miles of it; on pain of expulsion or prison. The VC and Heads were forbidden to license or tolerate such trifles.

3 Authorisation for scholars, servants and all privileged persons to buy and sell all commodities and to exercise all manual arts in the town and suburbs, quietly and freely with all the liberties enjoyed by the burgesses and be exempt from all contributions or payment for any agreement or licence to the mayor and bailiffs.

4 The precincts of the university, previously too vaguely defined as regards the point from which 'one mile' was to be measured, were re-defined as one mile beginning at the outermost building of the town in every direction, and thence in a straight line.

5 Authority for the VC, Heads and scholars to hold in Mortmain any manors, messuages, lands, rectories, tithes, rents, etc, not held of the Crown in chief, or by knight's service, and not exceeding in all the value of £200 in a year.

If there is a time of which it can be truly said that then was hammered home the last nail in the lid of the municipal coffin, then that was it— March 9 1605. There might have been still a few transactions, a few people, in which or with whom the university authority could not meddle either directly or indirectly. I cannot think of any. The VC's authority was now at last virtually absolute. Not quite as wide in some respects as that of the feudal lord—he could not, for instance, choose whom a man should marry—but in most respects far wider.

That being so, I wonder what prompted the town 'authorities' to apply for a renewal of their charter at the same time and spend £90 on getting it? In 1600 they had elected as their High Steward Sir Thomas Egerton, Lord Keeper of the Great Seal (later Lord Ellesmere), and as Recorder Sir John Fortescue, Chancellor of the Exchequer. It was these gentlemen who prompted them and petitioned the king to grant the charter. This is what it granted:

1 That the borough was and should be henceforth a free borough and have all the liberties of a free borough for ever.

2 That the mayor, bailiffs and burgesses, whether before lawfully incorporated or not, should be a body corporate and politic, by the name of The Mayor Bailiffs and Burgesses of the Borough of Cambridge.

3 That the burgesses should have freedom to acquire, possess and enjoy property and dispose of it.

4 That they might be impleaded by that name in all courts.

5 That they should have a common seal and change or renew it at pleasure.

6 That they should be empowered to make laws and regulations and punishments for infringement subject to the laws of the realm and the reasonable ancient customs of the town.

7 That they should have power to acquire property in Mortmain not exceeding the value of £60 per year.

8 That all their previous liberties, grants and customs be confirmed.

I have extracted the substance of the verbiage in which those clauses were phrased. It is not difficult to work out what it all amounts to. Now balance it against the final clause:

9 That nothing in this charter shall prejudice or impede the privileges, liberties and profits of the Chancellor, Masters and Scholars of the University.

And what is left? A very expensive sheet of parchment. Not so much a charter as a pretty consolation prize. Poor town, indeed!

Chapter 13

If you cannot beat them
1605-1660

The fact that the university had no more privileges to win, and the town nothing to lose, did not, of course, end the war, for the university still had all its privileges to defend against an enemy that had not yet abandoned hope of winning some of them back. Besides, the war had become such an integral part of Cambridge life that mere 'settlements' could not bring it to an end. People were fed up with it, as Dr Jegon had said 'they seeke peace, having digested what is past without any resolution to complaine again thereof'. But there were more complaints to come and they did not all seek peace. Some did not want peace. Some actually needed war. Various town officials from time to time needed it to display their mettle, so did some academic gentlemen. The students and town youths needed it, to provide them with a bit of fun and excitement—the term 'for kicks' had not yet been invented. The VC could well have done without it; so could the shop-keepers and stall-holders. The VC could well have done without the constant vigilance which the war entailed.

That vigilance was not always maintained. They slipped up, for instance, on the matter of the town gaol. The university had secured a 40-year lease on it in 1601 at an annual rent of 13s 4d or more if someone else came up with a better offer. How such an improper transaction came to be made I do not know—probably part of the Wallis campaign to ensnare the university in a legal tangle. How the town authorities intended to carry out their judicial duties when the gaol was in the hands of the enemy I do not know—unless it was that they had totally abandoned their judicial duties. Anyway, in 1607, the gaoler, Benjamin Payne, was encouraged to take possession of the building (not difficult, since he held the keys) and sue the university for its return to the town, which was at once granted. The university apparently never considered building its own prison on its own ground, although it had just as much need for a safe lock-up as the town had. Greater use of such an amenity might have resulted in effectively curbing many of the students' activities against which the Senate continued to pronounce graces for the next two centuries and more.

Night-jetting, despite the bans, was still a favourite pastime, all the more so now that it involved acrobatic feats in breaking out of colleges designed to resemble medieval fortresses and breaking in again when the forays were finished. 'The students go forth in the town pretending and abusing the proctor's authority, to the disquiet of the inhabitants and the discredit of the university.' Armed with guns, crossbows and catapults, and accompanied by greyhounds, they went into the town fields and neighbouring villages, shooting, coursing, destroying game and 'misspending their time'. The threat of fines and imprisonment had little effect. The proctors would have needed greyhounds to catch those nimble sportsmen. The less energetic filled in their evenings, and a good part of the night, with 'excessive drinkings, foul drunkenness and taking tobacco in taverns and shops too commonly and immodestly frequented'. For that the penalty was banishment and de-grading for a whole year, and a fine of 4s on any householder or taverner caught entertaining students after the curfew bell had rung. Any student found smoking in Great St Mary's church in commencement time, in the Schools during Lent, in college dining-halls, at plays, etc, was fined 6s 8d for the first offence, double that for the second, and a year's suspension for the third. The punishment for 'non-adults' was still a whipping in the Schools.

A near-riot ensued when the proctors, searching for disorderly persons at Chesterton, found some of 'lewd conversation' and put them in gaol. John Battisford, local resident and magistrate, considered along with many others—quite wrongly—that Chesterton was not within the sphere of university jurisdiction. He charged the proctors with wrongful arrest and the case was found proved against them—not surprisingly, with Battisford on the bench. This resulted in the first appeal to the Privy Council for 12 years. The Council inevitably ruled that the proctors had acted within their rights. Despite that rebuff, Battisford persisted in licensing and punishing victuallers at Chesterton and initiated another charge against the proctors, but quickly withdrew it when the Earl of Suffolk sent him a timely warning to refrain from meddling in what did not concern him.

Despite wounded dignity over the matter of precedence—which Dr Gooch settled in 1612 by pushing the mayor bodily from his seat on the bench—the dominant mood of the town was constructive and conciliatory. In 1610 the 'New River' from Nine Wells, first suggested by Dr Perne in 1574 (30 to 40 years was an average time for getting anything done in Cambridge), was made by the joint enterprise of town and university. This brought a stream of pure water through the town, along the King's Ditch (not very effectively) and eventually, in 1614, to a conduit in the market-place, erected by Henry King and Nathaniel Cradock. In 1613 an agreement was made between the town and Trinity College whereby the latter, in exchange for 16 acres of pasture west of the river, several other plots of land and £50 in cash, granted the town 25 acres in one piece, formerly in the tenure of Edward Parker, to be converted to grass and used as common pasture for ever. That was the origin of *Parker's Piece*. Millions have admired it and used it; few know that it is an abiding memorial to an act of sanity in an era of strife.

Relaxed vigilance in control of the market in 1615—the VC had held the office of Clerk of the Market since the charter of 1561—placed the university in the unusual position of having to come to the rescue of the country butchers and provided another instance of university interest coinciding with that of a section of the public. There were, according to the Registrary, no less than 40 butchers coming in on a Saturday to sell their meat in the market. The town authorities decreed that they should stop selling at 4 pm in winter and 5 pm in summer. The rather lame reason given was that it was difficult to detect bad meat sold by candle-light. The effect of the order was that, just before the bell rang at four o'clock, the country butchers had to sell off their meat, good or bad, quickly and cheaply. It was not bought by the townspeople—they had not yet left work or got their wages by that time—but by the town butchers, who later in the evening sold it at their shops and houses, at their own price. The interesting feature is that the Registrary was not sure whether the university had the right to interfere, or who ought to ring the bell, which at the time was kept locked up out of reach of the Taxor's man. No definite settlement was made and market-management remained a contentious issue for the next two centuries.

The visit of King James in March 1615, apart from providing both sides with the opportunity to do a bit of innocent and costly showing-off (it cost the university £414, John's £450) had two interesting features. Mr Brakyn's speech of welcome at the boundary included a recital of the 'history' of the town which, according to popular belief at the time, had been founded before Christ by Duke Cantaber, son of the King of Spain, who was entertained in England by King Gurguntius, and the materials of its 'castles, towers and walls' had since been converted into colleges. King James, who had an appetite for that sort of thing, no doubt swallowed the rubbish with pleasure, or at least a wry smile. He enjoyed much more the play performed for him at Trinity the next evening by the Clare Hall students. Called *Ignoramus*, it was a lively comic satire against lawyers in general and featured in particular a character who was easily recognisable as Francis Brakyn, the Town Recorder, who had incurred unpopularity by his part in the dispute over precedence a few years earlier. The play pleased the king so much that he came back in May on purpose to see it again.

The point of Brakyn's strange speech of welcome became clearer when in 1616 the town again petitioned the king to be granted the status of city. A similar request had been made in 1610, when the university—no lack of vigilance here—had 'got a secret view of their book (ie charter) and perceived our best charters neerely touched'. When asked by the university to be kept informed of the present petition, Mayor Pottall took care that there should be no leak—'they slight us, saying that were but to part the lion's skin'. But, of course, the proposed charter could not be kept secret for long and when it was made public the worst fears of the university were realised. The object of it was manifestly to have all the original liberties of the town restored—'city' status meant nothing of any real value—plus the abolition of some of the university privilege, despite lip-service in the form of a 'saving' clause tacked on at the end.

The two vital clauses were:

1 That the mayor, 'for the better government of the city, shall have authority to punishe all obstinate, uncivil, stubborne, unruly, sawcy and disordered persons within the Citty which are under the rule and government of the Maior, by imprisonment of their bodies'.

2 That the City may be freed from the necessity of taking prisoners committed by the VC 'which of late times have been imposed upon the Corporation of the town to their great perill, charge and losse'.

The VC Dr Lyell, and Heads despatched letters at once to the Earl of Suffolk, Sir Francis Bacon, Attorney General, the Bishop of Winchester, the Dean of St Paul's, the Lord Chancellor and HM King James. The gist of those letters was this:

There is a manifest daunger of loosing some of our liberties . . . and encroaching uppon others . . . by late secret working of friends and plotting to rayse money . . . They pretend honour and favour to us by this their project, but . . . we are verily persuaded it is but a trayne to draw us into some inconvenience, for as yet wee could never find that the University ever received dignity or honour by any Act or wish of theirs . . . When they were at their lowest, they ever showed themselves unkind neighbours . . . we cannot expect peace amongst them when their thoughts and wills shall be winged by that power which the very title of a city will give unto them.

The king agreed that there could be no question of city status for the town if it damaged in any way the pre-eminence of the university 'which is the glory of the town'. And so the ambitions of Brakyn, Pottall and a few others were nipped in the bud. I do not think many of the townsmen cared much one way of the other.

What they cared about was money. That was at the root of their objection to the plans now being discussed for the drainage of the Fens, a scheme which they—and the university—thought would ruin the river-commerce of Cambridge. Money likewise was the reason for some of the leading townsmen buying up as many properties as they could and as many vacant plots as were available for the building of tenements, and conversion of existing houses into tenements, each to house three, four or five poor families. Increasing numbers of labourers and artisans were coming into the town, hoping to find work of some kind, even at pitifully low wages, provided by the university. Whole areas of the town were being converted into slums, and the balance of the population being upset, infringing, in the process, the recent regulations regarding thatched cottages and houses presenting a serious fire hazard. One of the chief culprits, incidentally, was the famous carrier, Thomas Hobson.

Hobson's name has become part of the English language in a way that illustrates the triviality of fame and is, with dubious justification, attached to the only civic 17th century 'building' still surviving in Cambridge—the conduit at Lensfield Road corner. He would be more aptly remembered as the man who, in 1628, gave his farm (recently purchased from Parker) in St Andrew's parish, outside the Barnwell Gate, to a charitable trust—six privileged persons named by the VC and six burgesses named by the mayor—for conversion into a house where the poor should be set to work (a stock of wool and flax being provided) and also a house of correction for sturdy rogues and beggars. Endowed later with various other lands, this became known as the *Spinning House* and was to play a role in the history of Cambridge, both town and university, which many would prefer to forget.

Meanwhile (the date is uncertain, but it must be around 1625) the town authorities had embarked on what looked like the prelude to an outbreak of hostilities, on the scale of 30 years before, in the form of a long list of 'Complaints' sent to the Privy Council. It lists 23 items, here summarised and simplified. 'They', of course, refer to the VC Heads and university officers.

They claim 'mecanicall' men as privileged persons. Like other privileged persons, these men stand bail for others and so prevent the mayor from doing his duty as a magistrate; are not allowed to do jury-service at Sessions or act as constables, so that

poor men have to do extra service; do not pay rent for waste sites; do not pay rates—
not even for the late re-building of Garret Hostel Bridge.
They do not make contribution monthly to the poor, only at Christmas, and then
only as a charity, not as a duty.
They punish townsmen already punished by the mayor.
They claim sole right to punish unlicensed victuallers as well as licensed—'of both
which sorts the Towne swarmeth'—and take £20 a year in fines from brewers who
supply them.
They make us pay twice to have our bushels sealed, and stop us doing business by
taking away our bushels at the height of the fair.

But the main burden of complaint came from the corn-dealers:

They will not allow us to take corn to neighbouring counties when we have a surplus.
Licences are only to be had for bribery. They will not let us buy corn within five
miles of Cambridge, though the charter was supposed to protect us as well as them.
'Yet if we brought it into Cambridge they would not let us carry it out, but there
Informers would come into our boats and eat a mouthful of the corn and so by virtue
of it would seize all of the corn and arest the boat, which caused much fighting and
quarrellinge haserding the losse of men's lives; and it was Rye, such as the university
used not. But it was sent to relieve Yorkshire and Lincoln that were in want, the
Corne being much under the price.' They will allow Petty foggers and give them
licence to buy corn within five miles of Cambridge, if it be above the price, but they
will not allow any free man of Cambridge . . ..

So corn smuggling was added to candle smuggling, with similar effect.
Nothing whatever was done about those complaints. As far as I know, it was
the last time ever that such a list was drawn up. Much of that corn, which
was the subject of dispute, was undoubtedly barley used for brewing beer.
The number of pubs in the town was increasing week by week—'dayly'
according to the VC—giving rise to such disorder that the university
officials could not cope. 'I have done all I can to cure this disease,' wrote
the VC to the Lord High Treasurer, but regulations, removal of licences and
suppression were all of no avail. Young students were being enticed into
pubs 'where many of them are overthrowen and give occasion of much
scandal'.
      Candles had more than once set part of the town alight—literally. They
brought about a flare-up of tempers in 1629. The VC fixed the price at 4½d
per lb. Four chandlers—Almond, Balls, Scott and Oliver—exceeded it and
three of them were gaoled. The fourth applied to the Court of Common
Pleas, his costs being borne by the town, and secured a ruling that the
university had no jurisdiction as regards candles because they were not
'victuals'. The other three then sued for wrongful arrest and imprisonment,
prompted and abetted by the mayor, John Sherwood, and were discharged.
The Senate then discommoned all four and also discommoned Sherwood
and John Hurst, bailiff, for securing the release of the chandlers. Then the
VC and Heads sent a petition to the king, who referred the matter to the
Privy Council, who agreed with the university that candles *were* 'victuals'.
      It might interest you to know just who were the august personages who
sat round a table in Whitehall on December 4 1629 discussing this important
topic. They were His Majesty The King, the Lord Keeper, the Archbishop
of York, the Lord Treasurer, Lord President, Lord Privy Seal, Lord High
Chamberlain, Earl Marshal, Lord Steward, Lord Chamberlain; the Earls of

Suffolk, Dorset, Salisbury, Bridgewater, Holland, Danby, Kelley; the Lords Dorchester and Grandison; the Bishop of Winchester, the Master of the Wards, Mr Vice Chamberlain and Mr Secretary Coke. But do not regale your imagination with a picture of 23 of the highest in the realm nibbling ruminatively at candles manufactured in Cambridge with a view to determining their edibility, or observing the reactions of a bevy of London mice lured from behind the wainscot by that delicacy. The debate concerned *focalia*, translated (wrongly) as fuel; whether it was covered by the terms of the charter of 3 Elizabeth and whether it included candles.

The Council ordered the mayor, bailiff and errant chandlers, by setting their hands to the Order in Council, to submit themselves to the jurisdiction of the university, to pay the fines imposed by the VC and make public confession of their fault. As for the discommoning, it was ordered that 'peace and agreement shall be settled between both parties according to performance of that Respect and submission which is due from the Inhabitants of the said Town of Cambridge to the said University'. Never before had the townsmen been so weightily snubbed. Or snuffed.

Actually it was the discommoning rather than the candles which caused temperatures to rise. Sherwood protested bitterly against the sentence, its timing and the manner of its publication, and the injury done to him personally and to the mayoral office—'as no mayor was ever so used before'. The VC and Heads, in justifying their action to the Privy Council, were able to cite precedents for discommoning a mayor, at both Oxford and Cambridge, and pointed out that Sherwood was doubly deserving of punishment for his 'unkind and contemptuous acts' in that he was a scholar of the university (he had matriculated at Emmanuel in 1612, but left after one term) and traded from premises leased by the university. An interesting feature of the case is that its legality was earnestly debated by the VC, Dr Matthew Wren and Heads, three of whom considered that Sherwood should not be discommoned during his mayoralty.

There had been a violent outbreak of plague in 1610 when over 400 people had died. A similar outbreak, lasting through the summer of 1630, though resulting in fewer deaths, highlighted the appalling poverty amongst the bulk of the population and again showed that in times of real hardship and distress the town and university officials could act together. Many of the students went home from May until November; others remained in their colleges in a state of siege. The heroes of the drama were the VC, Dr Butts, and the mayor, John Sherwood, who met twice weekly to organise the feeding and relief of the sick and poor. Nearly 3,000 persons were in receipt of poor-relief. Only 140 townsmen were there to bear the cost of relief and carry out the work (a strange situation, explained presently). A national appeal for help was launched by the king and met with generous response, especially in London and Norwich. Pesthouses for the isolation of infected families were built on Midsummer Common. Riders were sent into the countryside to prevent the poor from going out of the town to do harvest-work and so spread infection. Surrounding villages banned all movement to or from the town, but farmers were ordered by the Privy Council to bring in corn when famine was imminent.

All this was the result of the organising genius, courage and compassion of Dr Butts. He found out, by enlisting a squad of 12 men of the town and district, how much corn the farmers had, how much the brewers and bakers had, how much they needed, then saw that it was delivered; and kept a strict control on the brewers. The fairs were cancelled; the Assizes held at Royston. Thanks to timely and sensible precautions and whole-hearted co-operation a major disaster was averted. But the town had been badly hit and the numerical strength of the university was reduced for several years. The next three petitions to the king and Privy Council were sent by the VC and Heads and the mayor and bailiffs acting in unison and all were concerned with measures to be taken for the relief of the poor. It is a pleasure to record that.

Now about that figure of only 140 men available to bear the cost of poor-relief ('not above 100' according to Dr Butts). How could that possibly be, in a town with a population of over 5,000? The answer had been hinted at more than 30 years earlier, but no one had taken any notice of it then. The situation was far more serious now and it was brought to light, firstly by the awful affliction of 1630, then by information from two other unusual sources.

In 1635 the town was required to furnish £100 of 'ship-money', part of the cost of a ship of 350 tons for the King's Navy. The mayor and aldermen petitioned the Privy Council, not for a reduction in the amount, but to have the exemption of 'privileged persons' cancelled, because '*More than one third of the inhabitants of Cambridge*, being men of the greatest ability in estate, *have purchased to themselves the privilege of being Scholars servants* in the university, and under that pretext are now seeking to be exempted from bearing their portion of the assessment'. Among those claiming exemption from payment of ship-money were Mr Crane, apothecary, worth £1,000 a year; Mr Thompson, brewer, worth £4,000 a year, according to the mayor, but only £2,000 according to the university registrary; and Mr Farley, vintner, worth £4,000 although he had 'come a very poor man to the town'. They were the only ones in a list of 17 supplied by the town who were really wealthy.

The Council wrote to Dr Beale and suggested the withdrawal of exemption in this instance. He replied that the university was a separate corporation, and should not be assessed with the town and referred to the charters since the time of King John—stretching a point there!—granting exemption from such dues. So much for law. In equity, he said, the town should be charged with ship-money and the university exempted because: *a)* What the masters and scholars earned annually went back to the townsmen in payment for goods and services: *b)* The town had an income of £1,500 a year from tolls, customs and other profits of fairs, 'from which we are barred and which they convert to their own use' and *c)* Until 35 years ago the town maintained a trained band of militia. For 30 years and more they have wholly neglected it, converted the armour and storehouse for it to another use and have not now one man ready to perform that service.

Even by letting that last cat out of the bag, Dr Beale had not made out a very good case and I think he knew it. The Privy Council refused to amend the order. Some of the privileged persons did contribute and the town's quota of £100 was promptly paid.

Six months later, Hugh Grove, under contract to the Admiralty to supply saltpetre for making gunpowder, and requiring horses and carts to get his materials to and from the king's saltpetre-house at Barnwell, ran up against the same difficulty. '*The greatest part of the inhabitants of that town pretend themselves to be privileged because they belong to some of the colleges* and the other part of the same pretend they are not able to do the work.' The VC claimed exemption for all the servants, their lands and animals. The mayor sent constables with requisition-warrants for carts and carriage, but many able men refused absolutely to do the work.

So there we have the absurdity explained. Just as for centuries outsiders had been encouraged—and still were—to purchase the freedom of the town in order to enjoy the commercial advantages of it, now freemen of the town were being encouraged to purchase university privilege in order to enjoy exemption from all the obligations of burgesses. These were exemption from military service, from payment of subsidies and taxes, from requisitioning for State purposes. It was bad enough that the Navy should be short of ships, and those ships short of powder; moral or political scruples might have come into play on those issues—as indeed they did. What made the Cambridge situation a disgrace was that this exemption claimed by privileged persons extended to liability for paying the rates for the relief of the poor. The exact proportion of rate-dodgers cannot be known; it was probably somewhere in between 'more than one third' and 'the greater part'—perhaps about a half. The VC and Heads could never have envisaged or intended that such a situation would arise, surely. Or was it part of a long-term plan to get the town completely in their hands? If so, nobody ever put it in writing.

And those townsmen—they must by now have numbered hundreds—who were well-enough off to be liable for rates but had opted out by becoming 'privileged', were they all selfish, greedy and heartless? Not all of them, for sure. Some were known to be charitable and some had seven or eight children to support. Many no doubt subscribed to the doctrine upheld by the university that caring for the poor was an act of charity, a matter for the individual conscience—with the ultimate reward of benefit to one's own soul, as in medieval times—not a social duty to be imposed by statute. Most of them, for one reason or another, evidently believed in the wisdom of the adage—'If you can't beat 'em, join 'em'.

I do not know whether the learned doctors ever debated this problem of the poor and their consciences; they must have done. They certainly discussed the reasons for the increase of the poor in Cambridge and came up with a solution to that problem. It was this:

1 Ban all poor people from grazing their animals on the commons. If they resist, put them in gaol.

2 Compel all poor people and their children to learn to spin or work at some other trade to earn a living.

3 Make all owners of cottages, and divided tenements where the poor live, indemnify the other people in the parish against their tenants, being a charge on the rates.

4 Force the tradesmen to take their apprentices and servants only from the town; especially the lace-makers and innkeepers.

The suggestions were not adopted. Neither side did anything to improve the situation.

On the contrary, it got worse. A few years earlier a survey had revealed that, in six parishes alone, there were 1,728 persons living in newly erected houses, cottages and divided tenements. In 1636 there was reported a further influx of poor people, due, it was said, to an intensification of the practice of crowding families into already overcrowded accommodation. Houses were built in the churchyards, in gardens, on every bit of waste ground, even on part of the market-place. The VC and mayor asked for a total ban on more outsiders coming into the town and that some already there should be sent back whence they came. In St Mary's parish alone there were 80 families with 350 children and servants making no contribution to the rates. Despairing of any help from either town or university authorities, the parishioners themselves petitioned the justices of King's Bench for relief from the poor-rate, which was costing them £4 a month and bitterly blamed the rich men of the town. The justices appointed a joint committee of university and town to look into the matter and nothing was done.

Civic pride, in all but ceremonial posturing, was dead, dulled by apathy and sedated by self-interest. The ever-present threat of the plague only served to increase the apathy. The mild outbreak of 1638 was only noticed because it resulted in a two-year suspension of the fairs. The ban was lifted—it had been ignored in any case—in response to the agonised cry from the corporation that it could not pay its annual £70 rent. Bickering and brawling became the order of the day once more. Bushel measures were broken without good reason given, a bedell's head was broken without warning and doors and windows were broken by pretended proctors. In 1640, 300 pressed men from the county, billetted in the town, added to the tension by staging a mutiny.

Oliver Cromwell's heart can scarcely have been uplifted as he contemplated the town which he was to represent in parliament, having been elected freeman a few months earlier. King Charles' heart was heavy when, on March 14 1642, he passed through the town on his way to York, despite the enthusiastic cries of *Vivat Rex*! from the scholars, the Latin speeches, the 'light' refreshment which included apricots, lemons, oranges, cherries, damsons, grapes (in March?) and a pound of tobacco. The sole acknowledgement of his presence by the town was a crowd of weeping women following his coach and beseeching him to return to his parliament. Six months later the Civil War had begun.

That war, except in so far as it affected the other one, is no part of my theme. The university suffered most, paying for its loyalty; it gave most of its plate to help the king, but about half of it fell into the hands of Cromwell. Some colleges were used for billeting troops, who did consider- able damage; some masters were removed from office and gaoled. Yet on the whole it was fairly treated by parliament and allowed to maintain a superficial neutrality in spite of its known royalist sympathies. The attitude of the townsmen towards the war was that which circumstances rather than their own feelings dictated. The town was a parliamentary garrison and headquarters, most of the time under Cromwell's direct orders. Mayors and bailiffs, when they could be persuaded to take office, were under military orders. The town was fortified with massive new earthworks at Castle End and a ditch round the eastern side; all bridges across the river except the Great bridge were destroyed. The fortifications were never put to the test, but they served their purpose. Under those circumstances it is difficult to believe that the fairs and markets operated as usual, but they did, or that anybody cared about the oath-taking by the mayor or the precedence of the VC, but they did.

The attitude of some of the townsmen towards the university during the war years was, as one would expect, neither tolerant nor fair. They began by getting hold of some of the muskets sent for the defence of the town and using the college windows as targets on which to practice, subjected any students rash enough to walk the streets to insults and stoning, assisted the soldiers in plundering the colleges until the Earl of Essex put a stop to it, brutally assaulted students who offered cups of beer to Royalist prisoners being marched through the town and so on. But all this, let it be stressed, was the doing of a minority. The majority of the populace were as anxious to see the war ended as was the university. Both sides fêted Colonel Fairfax with equal enthusiasm when he visited the town in 1647. When the king was captured in June and taken to Newmarket, he did not pass through Cambridge because it was feared that the townspeople might show him respect. As late as June 1648 there was a 'Tumult and Insurrection' in which royalist townsmen and scholars united against parliamentarians of both sides, the object and the outcome of which were equally vague. In fact the whole war was vague. The impression one gets of it, at Cambridge especially, is that it was rather farcical, a foolish mistake.

If it had any effect at all on Town/Gown relations, I would say that it probably brought the two sides nearer together. During the war the mayor and bailiffs had inevitably usurped some of the VC's privileges and the oath-taking ceremony had suffered neglect. In 1644 the mayor had denied the VC's right to administer the oath, said it was 'against the liberties of the subject and contrary to Magna Carta' and that the Corporation had 'beene a longe time in subjection and bondage under the VC, and now they resolved to shake off that yoake'. That spirit of revolt was short-lived. After 1649 we hear of no more antagonism for nearly 20 years. On the other hand there was active co-operation as regards the university's contribution towards the relief of the poor (£120 a year) and another joint petition on Fen drainage. When, in 1653, the Barebones Parliament seriously considered the idea of suppressing the universities and all schools, in fact all learning except the Scriptures, the town gave no support whatever to the idea. Opposition to the Quakers in 1659 came largely from the students— naturally, for the Quakers wanted to abolish the university—but the townsmen joined in the fray alongside the students and the mayor only acted as host to George Fox out of courtesy.

The proclamation of King Charles II on May 10 1660 presented a good opportunity for permanently burying the hatchet and inaugurating a new era of peace and harmony. The VC, Dr Ferne, sent an invitation to the mayor, Edward Chapman, to join him in the jollification and ceremonial proclamation. He declined, saying he would make the proclamation next day on horseback. So the university went ahead without the civic dignitaries, making the proclamation twice, to the accompaniment of loud music in the market-place and on top of King's Chapel. Bells rang all day; bonfires were lit and garlands paraded in the streets at night. Next day the mayor made *his* proclamation, seven times over, and again the bonfires blazed.

Chapman's ungracious refusal to join the VC in the celebrations is easily explained. Two months earlier he had had to make this apology:

Whereas I, Edward Chapman, Mayor of the Towne of Cambridge, did upon the XXVIth day of ffebruary 1660 by error send my warrant for releasing of William Land, John Devole and James Delamot out of the Tolboothe Gaole, to which they had been committed by the then Vice-Chancellor, Dr Ferne, I therefore, in satisfaction to the University, hereby acknowledge the error and doe promise not to doo or to my power suffer anything hereafter to be done that may anyways infringe the liberties or privileges of this University to my knowledge. In witness whereof I have sett my hand the second day of March in the year of our Lord God 1660.

Edw Chapman

That 'yoake' was very firmly in position.

Chapter 14

Corruption and stagnation 1660-1820

For more than 150 years the 'war' at the higher level virtually disappeared. The university statutes were all restored, the ejected masters and fellows were re-instated and all was as if the Civil Wars had never happened. In March 1665 the mayor and aldermen made their customary fishing-trip in three boats, drawing the pools between Newnham and the Sturbridge fairground, where they had a snack of bread and cheese and wine, and three of the doctors accompanied them. If traditional enemies could get together in the same boat for a bit of innocent amusement, that was surely a sign that reason had prevailed at last, and a new era of progress had dawned.

Subsequent events gave to the occasion a certain symbolic significance in that both sides henceforth conducted themselves as though acknowledging that they were all in the same boat and neither wished to upset the other if it could be avoided. As for reason and progress, that is open to question. Defoe aptly summed up the situation in 1723:

Tradesmen get their bread by the colleges, and this is the surest hold the University may be said to have of the Townsmen, and by which they secure the Dependence of the Town upon them and subsequently their Submission. Thus, I say, Interest gives them Authority; and there are abundance of Reasons why the Town should not disoblige the University, as there are some also on the other Hand why the University should not differ to any Extremity with the Town; nor, such is their prudence, do they let any Disputes between them run to any Extremities, if they can avoid it.

He might have added, though he may not have known, that one feature making for the avoidance of clashes was the fact that so many of the leading townsmen—even mayors, bailiffs and aldermen—were now also privileged persons of the university. The latter firmly and, as it seemed, irremovably, entrenched in its position of privileged superiority, made the most of it. The town, resigned to its inferior status, made the best of it.

Occasionally, for as long as was necessary, they co-operated. They joined forces to combat another serious outbreak of plague in 1666, when nearly 800 people died (not all plague victims) and pesthouses were again erected, this time further out, on Coldham Common, where they remained until 1703 and were never needed again. They combined in 1703 to found Charity Schools, which flourished with some success, and a workhouse in 1732, which eventually merged with the Spinning House, part of which was used solely for the confinement of 'lewd women'. The act for the better Paving, Lighting and Cleansing of the streets in 1788 was jointly promoted and financed, though the Corporation disbursed on its implementation a mere

£10 a year. Niggardliness—the mayor and bailiffs called it 'poverty'—of the Corporation in financing public undertakings was an outstanding feature of the period. When the Great Bridge was rebuilt in 1754 at a cost of £1,327, the Corporation contributed £50, the rest coming from public subscription. The new Guildhall in 1782 was paid for entirely by public subscription and the election of a number of honorary freemen at a fee of 30 guineas each. Towards the end of the period the town was obliged to call upon the university—a favour, not a right, as was firmly pointed out—for considerable financial assistance. The university's contribution to the poor-rate, for instance, was increased to £200 in 1791. The town even had to borrow sums of £100 or more to meet the cost of royal visits, of which there were no less than 15 in this period.

The townspeople and civic dignitaries could not be kept entirely out of the picture when royalty visited Cambridge. On one occasion the jubilant populace replaced the horses of the royal coach; the visitors were usually met by the mayor and aldermen at the town boundary; the townsfolk were entertained with fireworks and sometimes the conduit in the market-place ran, briefly, with wine. But each and every visit was primarily a university occasion. Mayor Samuel Newton in 1671 described in his diary the homage paid to King Charles II when the Corporation officials met him on Christ's Piece. The king touched the town mace offered to him, accepted the purse of a hundred sovereigns without so much as a word of thanks and, Samuel noted sadly, 'His Majesty came not out of his coach'. That visit cost the university £1,000. The town spent £300, half of it on the 'very plentiful dinner' at the Town Hall, which His Majesty did not attend.

The town had become a sort of base-metal setting for the architectural and academic jewel in its midst. The jewel became more resplendent as the 18th century progressed and 'Cambridge' acquired its reputation as a place which ought to be seen. The fact that its academic standards declined in the same proportion as its architectural glory increased, passed largely unnoticed for a very long time. As for the appearance of the town, this is how a visitor described it in the late seventeenth century:

The town is so abominably dirty that Old Street, in the middle of a winter's thaw, or Bartholomew's Fair, after a shower of rain, could not have more occasion for a scavenger than the miry streets of this famous corporation, and most of them so very narrow that should two wheelbarrows meet in the largest of their thoroughfares they are enough to make a stop for half an hour before they can well clear themselves of one another to make room for passengers. The buildings in many parts of the town were so little and so low that they looked more like huts for pigmies than houses for men.

Exaggerated, no doubt, but confirmed by a later visitor: 'The place is not at all large, and about as mean as a village, and were it not for the many fine colleges it would be one of the sorriest places in the world.' There was some improvement after 1788 but, although the population had increased to just over 10,000 (inclusive of the university) in 1801, the built-up area of the town at that date was much the same as it had been in Elizabethan times, when the population was only half as great (See Map 5 on page 141).

Mainly, then, it was a case of town and university each going its own sweet way, free from outside interference for the most part, as parliament and Privy Council increasingly had more important things to do than resolve the differences of opinion in this small town. Even Sturbridge Fair, a major contributor to such prosperity as the town enjoyed and no mean source of revenue for the university (by 1723, according to Defoe, it was the largest fair in the world, dealing in many hundreds of thousands of pounds worth of commodities from all over England, but nothing from Cambridge!) failed to bring them together in any sort of amicable relationship. They took turns at making the official proclamation to open the fair and when it was the mayor's turn to do so, full advantage was taken of the opportunity to show the townspeople and visitors that the Corporation officials could make a splash—of colour at least.

The procession was headed by the town-crier, followed by 28 constables, three kettle-drums, a host of children bearing banners, then the Grand Marshal on horseback, followed by two trumpeters, the town band of 12 in full blast, and two French horns. After that came the bellman, then four mounted sergeants and the Head Sergeant, bearing the mace, the Town Clerk in full robes, the Mayor in full regalia, the two Members of Parliament in sober black, 12 aldermen in scarlet robes (each attended by a henchman), the 24 members of the Council (in order of seniority), eight dispencers, the four bailiffs and, lastly, the Town Treasurers, considering in silence the cost of it all.

It was the cost that put an end to this display of civic pomp in 1758. A more modest procession took its place and even that had to be discontinued in 1790. The banquet at the fair ceased at the same time, partly because of the cost, more because the famous fair itself was fast declining. 'Of late it has suffered, in common with others, on account of the great houses in these trades (wool, horses, hops, pottery, etc,) employing riders who go about the country and buy those commodities at the proprietors' houses.'

Meanwhile the university continued to exploit the fair in its own way. There were no ceremonial processions and less and less actual work to do, for one could not check weights and measures which were not there. However, it was a splendid opportunity for getting together and doing in style what the university officials had always been good at—ceremonial stuffing. Here is a shortened account of one of them, Dr Henry Gunning, of the proceedings following the proclamation of the fair in about 1780:

At the conclusion of the ceremony the carriages drew up at the Tiled Booth where the company alighted for the dispatch of business . . . and of oysters; and passing through an upper room . . . to what was called the University Dining Room . . . a narrow bench, next that the table formed from rough materials and supported by tressles and casks; on this table, which had no cloth of any kind, were placed several barrels of oysters, with ale and bottled porter in great profusion . . . We then left the dining-room that the waiters might remove the shells and cover the boards with a cloth . . . We took two or three turns in Garlic Row and then returned to the Tiled Booth . . . Before the Vice-Chancellor was placed a large dish of herrings, then followed in order a neck of pork roasted, an enormous plum-pudding, a leg of pork boiled, a pease pudding, a goose, a huge apple-pie, and a round of beef in the centre. On the other half of the table the same dishes were placed in similar order (the herrings before the Senior Proctor) who sat at the bottom. From 30 to 40 persons dined there, and although the wine was execrable, a number of toasts were given, and mirth and good humour prevailed, to such an extent as is seldom to be met with at more modern and more refined entertainments. At about 6.30 the dinner-party broke up, and, with scarcely an exception, adjourned to the theatre.

Gluttony and self-indulgence were the order of the day, not just that one day, every day, and not just among the upper university ranks, but equally in those of the town. What the poor townspeople thought of these orgies— of which, if not actually spectators, they must have been well aware—is not on record. They occasionally made known their feelings, however, in desperate fashion—clamouring, not for oysters and legs of pork, simply for bread.

In June 1751 a farmer brought 30 sacks of wheat into the town, refusing an offer of 9s 6d a bushel for it, and saying he would hold it until he got 14s or 15s. 'A mob arose, chiefly of women, and broke open the storehouse where the wheat was lodged and carried it all off. The Mayor caused the proclamation to be read . . . This had very nearly cost the farmer his life as well as the loss of the grain, for he was attacked by part of the mob with stones and brickbats . . . Taking to his heels and running into one of the colleges, he hid himself in the kitchen, and the gates of the college being immediately shut, the man was preserved and the mob dispersed.'

In July 1765 a mob assembled to 'make a riot in respect of the high price of corn' was prevented by the vigilance and resolution of the magistrates. The next day further tumult was prevented by many of the principal gentlemen, attended by the constables reading the Riot Act in the market-place and 'everything was restored to its usual tranquillity'. Three of the ringleaders were arrested and sent to the house of correction.

On July 17 1795 an angry mob seized a lighter laden with flour on its way to Ely and prepared to dole it out among themselves. The local magistrates intervened and had the flour taken in a waggon to be locked up in the Town Hall. The deputy mayor, Mr Mortlock, bought the flour and he and the VC promised an ample supply of bread at 6d a loaf. The mob assembled again the next day and seized meat, and again Mortlock averted serious trouble at the expense of his own pocket—that pocket having been frequently filled at the expense of the poor and not-so-poor.

The poor were becoming a more serious menace to the tranquillity of the town than were the students, with whom on several occasions they combined in defying authority and demanding justice or in airing a grievance. In 1732 a riot ensued when the body of a man was taken from Ditton churchyard to be used in the School of Anatomy. A party of townsmen got a warrant to search Emmanuel College, where the body was lodged, but were refused entrance by the students. The VC and Heads, armed with another warrant, were likewise refused admission and had to break down part of the college wall to get in. The students stoutly defended the inner court against their superiors and the Town Clerk was summoned to read the Riot Act to disperse the mob; next morning the corpse, which was the innocent cause of the tumult, was found in the pond in the college close. Again in 1773 the students defied their superiors by noisily interrupting the sermon of an unpopular senior proctor in Great St Mary's then, in the ensuing fracas, knocked him down as they made a wild escape, and hissed at the VC and the Bishop of Peterborough.

On two occasions at least the students got away with murder, not by the intervention of the VC in defence of university privilege, as had happened so often in the past, but by having recourse to the normal process of law. In 1665 the butler at Pembroke died as a consequence of a quarrel with four students. The town coroner, Thomas Fox, landlord of 'The Bull', empanelled a jury which found them guilty of murder. The VC and Heads debated whether to invoke the charter of 1561 giving them power to deal with the case—not to try it, but to nominate the judge who could. The terms of the charter were not absolutely clear to them in the light of later legal developments—this was a difficulty to be encountered again and again as time went on—and appeal to the Lord Chief Justice produced the ruling that the High Steward, not the VC, should nominate the judge. Meanwhile the friends of the students had pressed for the case to be heard at the assizes, a move which would have been unthinkable even 50 years earlier, and Dr Sparrow waived his claim. The students were tried by jury at the Assizes and acquitted 'very justly', as the judge said.

In July 1788 two 'Gentlemen of the University' were declared by the coroner's inquest to be guilty of the wilful murder of a drayman in 'a Town and Gown Row' in the previous March. They elected trial by a grand jury but the indictment was quashed. Then they requested trial by inquest; the judge heard counsel on both sides and quashed the charge 'and the Gentlemen were immediately discharged'. It was becoming decidedly unclear as to who was fighting on which side in this war.

Only once in this period, as far as I can discover, were shots exchanged between the two chief adversaries, and then with weapons only half-loaded, as it were. In 1705 there was an exchange of rude remarks and a slight scuffle when the VC, Dr Ellys, claimed precedence over the mayor in the seat at the upper end of the Town Hall when the Black Assembly was held. The mayor, two aldermen and the deputy recorder, John Welbore, were discommoned in consequence. The burgesses apologised at once and were re-instated in the university's good books. John Welbore, with less to lose by the discommoning, held out for five months, but was eventually persuaded to put his neck under the yoke. On March 29 1706 he read and signed in the chancel of Great St Mary's, in the presence of the VC, proctors and Registrary, this document:

Whereas I, John Welbore, Esq, Deputy Recorder of the Town of Cambridge, not fully understanding the rights and privileges of the University of Cambridge did upon Michaelmas Day last past [when Dr John Ellys the Vice-Chancellor came to the Town Hall according to the ancient charters of the University to administer the usual Oath to the Mayor and Bailiffs of the Town] by my opinion then declared, encourage the refusal of the Chief place to the said Vice-Chancellor in the said Hall, which I am now convinced that of right the Vice-Chancellor ought to have; I do hereby freely acknowledge my error in that particular, which proceeded wholly out of mistake, and not out of malice to the said University or to any Member thereof, and promise that I shall not be guilty of any such like indignity for the future; all which I declare with the same sincerity that I now desire to be restored to the good will and favour of the said University.

John Welbore

I feel sorry for John Welbore, an old friend and fellow Foxtonian, and known to be a man of integrity and kindly disposition. Even though he was a graduate of Trinity, he should not have been subjected to such humiliation. Some of the masters evidently shared my sentiment for, as the century progressed, the Black Assembly was held less and less frequently and finally just petered out. An attempt by Dr Wood to revive it in 1817 was politely ignored, even though his invitation to the *Magna Congregatio* did include a threat of withholding the university contribution to the poor-rates if the charters and Ancient Customs were not complied with.

   The old argument as to who had the right to supervise the weighing of hops at the fair was revived in 1733; a decision in favour of the university was accepted by the mayor and bailiffs without demur. Issues which a century earlier would have been bitterly contested as a matter of principle were now allowed to be settled by default or indifference. Neither side had any firm principles by which to be guided, only self-interest. The oligarchy of the town—they numbered less than a hundred—was gradually reinforced by the county gentry who bought or were given the freedom of the town and, for nearly half a century, was dominated by one noble family. Election to municipal and parliamentary office became wholly a matter of bribery, fraud and often violence; the bribery usually in the form of beer for the lower order, lavish dinners for the upper. First blatantly evident in 1708, this situation steadily worsened throughout the period under review. By the end of it, the state of corruption in the civic affairs of Cambridge provoked this astonishing observation in a *Times* leading article of 1833, referring to conditions over the past 30 years:

Probably no judicial investigation into a public trust ever brought to light more shameless profligacy or more inveterate dishonesty, more bare-faced venality in politics, a more heartless disregard of the claims of the poor in the perversion of the funds left for their benefit, or a more degrading subserviency to the views of the rich when they appeared in the shape of patrons or distributors of places, a more insatiable cupidity in the corporate officers to enrich themselves with the corporate property, or a more entire neglect of their duties and functions as magistrates, than are presented by the evidence now before us.

Strong words, but amply supported by the facts, and incapable of dismissal as 'mere journalism'. To what extent, if any, could that state of affairs be blamed on the university? If the VC and Heads in, say, 1660 had relinquished all their privileges in so far as they affected the running of the town, and devoted all their time and energy to the management of the university, would things have been altogether different? Would both town and university have been better managed? I think it is right to ask the question. You probably think it obligatory of me to answer it, so I will. My answer is 'yes'.

   The VC and Heads did, I believe, carry out their 'municipal' duties to the best of their ability. They did have the interests of the town at heart—when those interests coincided with their own. They did strive—perhaps too assiduously—to maintain standards of 'morality' as they saw it. That, to them, meant largely the suppression of illicit sex and excessive drinking.

   The campaign for the restriction and reform of the numerous ale-houses—their number has been variously estimated as between 100 and 170, nobody could really count them—continued unabated and quite ineffectually. Surety of between £5 and £10 was required of every new applicant for a licence and strict conditions were laid down as to the conduct of the premises, but still the pubs increased in number and no sooner was one unsavoury haunt suppressed than another took its place. The spread of the now fashionable coffee-houses did little to mitigate the situation, though the original ban on students frequenting these new establishments was tacitly allowed to lapse.

The proctors still kept up their search for 'lewd women', well knowing by now that they were fighting a losing battle, yet still hoping that the occasional burst of zeal would clear this 'menace' from the streets and ensure the moral purity of their pupils. In February 1675 they swooped in force on Barnwell, apparently with some success, for the following order was issued soon after by the VC and Heads:

Whereas there hath been lately much complaint of disorders committed at Barnwell and divers houses there are become infamous for harbouring lewd women, drawing loose scholars to resort thither. It is Ordered and Decreed by the Heads of Colleges . . . that hereafter no Scholar whatsoever (except Officers of the University performing their duty in searching houses) upon any pretence whatsoever, shall enter into the house of Francis Harvey, or William Butler, or William Larkin, or Edward Davies, or John Clark, or into any other house of bad report in Barnwell; and that if any Scholar shall presume to disobey this Decree he shall for his misdemeanour and contumacy be immediately expelled from the University.

The Barnwell raid was followed by a visitation of the pubs. The 'Green Dragon' in Holy Trinity, the 'Three Feathers' in St Edward's, the 'Saracen's Head' on the causeway to Queens' and 'Boot' in Trumpington Street, the 'Salutation' near the Castle, Widow Grigson's house in Little St Mary's Lane, Challis Gardens by Pembroke and the 'Carpenters' Arms' by Peterhouse—all, it seems, were supplying customers with more than drinks. Nothing is said about scratched faces, torn gowns or crumpled wigs, so perhaps the naughty ladies all went in a quiet and dignified manner to the Spinning House. If so, their attitude changed before long, as the town-crier earned ten shillings for whipping ten of them.

Even if they had succeeded in abolishing all the brothels and beer-houses, the VC and Heads would still have been left with their biggest headache of all, which was the high spirits of the students themselves. The university existed in order that they might study Latin, literature, theology, mathematics, some Greek and a little anatomy—so they were told. They thought differently, and that is what kept the Town/Gown war alive, for the activities which they preferred inevitably brought them into contact, and usually conflict, with the townspeople—cock-fights, billiards, bathing, circuses, hunting, driving tandems and four-in-hands, etc, all banned, all therefore more alluring. Students' pranks were such a commonplace that they were no longer 'news'. A few examples will serve to illustrate the tone of the 18th century:

1740: Order by the Master of St John's—'If any scholar *in statu pupillari* shall, when the gates are shut by order of the Master, break open any door, or by scaling of walls, leaping of ditches or any other ways get out of the limits of the college, he shall be *ipso facto* expelled'.

1751: People said it was futile to put up more lamps because the students so often smashed those already installed.

1751: VC and Heads issued a decree stating that 'great terror and apprehension is caused by students who walk the streets with lighted torches and links'.

1756: Thomas Gray, poet at Peterhouse, was horrified at the behaviour of some of the students who 'placed women upon their heads at noonday, rioted in the town and ran up heavy bills at inns and coffee-houses which they had no intention of paying'.

1774: A crowd of students gathered on Market Hill and refused to disperse. Colonel Lord Montfort lined up the militia, fixed bayonets and charged, inflicting several wounds. The same thing happened the next day. In subsequent years the militia was dispersed to other towns in the county. (The people of Cambridge wanted the students curbed, not killed.)

1790: Gunning, writing about the Pot Fair on Midsummer Green on a Saturday night: 'Amongst the company, groups of MAs, consisting of four or five in a party, who had evidently dined, were to be seen linked arm-in-arm, and compelled all they met with to turn out of the way. Difficult of belief as it may be at the present time, amongst them you might discover many Fellows of Colleges, and not a few clergymen'.

That last example suggests that some of the senior members of the university had also adopted the motto—'If you can't beat 'em, join 'em'.

Cambridge in 1798
Comparison with the previous map will reveal an astonishingly static quality in both town and university. In the last two years, it is true, the colleges have been enlarged and two new ones established. However, the town still stops at the limits it had in Elizabethan times, Castle End in the north and Spital End in the south. Barnwell is still an outlying suburb, Chesterton still a neighbouring village; both separated from the town proper by open country.

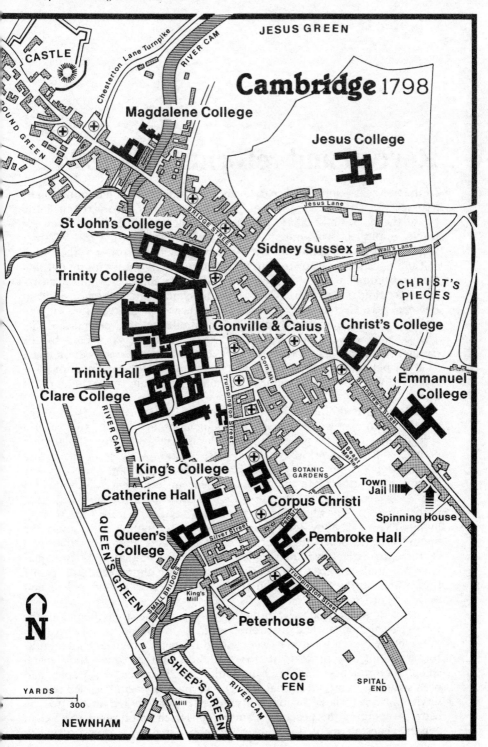

CASTLE

ROUND GREEN

JESUS GREEN

Chesterton Lane Turnpike

RIVER CAM

Cambridge 1798

Magdalene College

Jesus College

Jesus Lane

St John's College

BRIDGE STREET

Sidney Sussex

Wall's Lane

Trinity College

CHRIST'S PIECES

Gonville & Caius

Christ's College

Corn Mkt

Trumpington Street

St Andrew's Street

Trinity Hall

Emmanuel College

Clare College

RIVER CAM

King's College

Beast Market

BOTANIC GARDENS

Town Jail

Catherine Hall

Corpus Christi

Spinning House

Queen's College

Silver Street

Pembroke Hall

QUEEN'S GREEN

SMALL BRIDGES

King's Mill

Trumpington Street

Peterhouse

N

SHEEP'S GREEN

COE FEN

SPITAL END

YARDS

300

RIVER CAM

Mill

NEWNHAM

Chapter 15

Revival and reform 1820-1894

Of the two evils—subservience to an apathetic university and domination by a corrupt corporation clique—many Cambridge people considered the latter by far the worst and realised that nothing much could be done about the former until their own house had been put in order. As early as 1783 there had been a public meeting at 'The Rose' which sent a petition to the House of Commons pressing for reform of the electoral system, pointing out that the two borough members represented only 180 freemen, of whom just over half were residents of Cambridge. Nothing came of it. More non-resident freemen were elected on payment of a guinea each to keep the Rutland faction in power; neglect and corruption continued on an even greater scale. The rateable value of the borough was £25,000; the rates paid by the freemen were less than a tenth of that. In 14 years the corporation spent £480 on public services; it spent 15 times that amount on litigation. For nearly 40 years the rot continued with many lamenting, none doing much else.

In April 1820 another public meeting was held, against the wishes of the mayor, again expressing 'sorrow and indignation at the continuance of a corrupt system' and pressing for reform. The mounting indignation permeated to the lower ranks and gave rise to rioting—the term 'Town and Gown Riots' comes into general use at about this time—without any specific cause other than the release of pent-up feelings. On November 5 1827 occurred the first—it is the first I know of associated with that particular date—of what was to become a regular feature for the next hundred years. The low-level war had once more found a pattern. On the pretext of celebrating the failure of the Gunpowder Plot more than two centuries earlier, crowds of people—students predominating at first, but later outnumbered by town youths—flocked into the streets and let off fireworks, mostly 'squibs' used as missiles directed at the police and university officials.

Thanks to an ironical twist of human perversity, the strengthening of the forces to maintain law and order only served to provoke even more breaches of the peace. Seven townsmen were gaoled for between one and 12 months for assaulting the proctors in the execution of their duty and several students reprimanded. In 1820 an additional 250 special constables had been sworn in to meet a special emergency; many of them declined further service. Five years later the university successfully promoted an Act 'for the better keeping of the peace in Cambridge' which empowered the VC to appoint constables of the university; the force was never officially recognised by the civic authorities and was not very effective (at least it was not as disastrous as the 17th century 'police-force' of students) but it remained in being until 1856. Finally, in 1836, the Borough Police Force was created: a superintendant, two inspectors, four sergeants and 24 constables. From that time on the students were able to recognise with greater ease their chief opponents; uniformed, helmetted and bearing truncheons, the constables were prominent and inviting targets. Knocking off a helmet was a distinction more coveted by some students than the award of a degree.

Meanwhile, in January 1831, yet another public meeting was held, this one convened and presided over by the mayor, protesting that 'this populous town is degraded into a rotten borough' and urging support for the Reform Act then in progress through the House of Commons. The resolution, like the Act, met with considerable opposition from both town and university but, on June 7 1832, the Act became law and the way was at last open for forward progress. Every male householder worth £10 a year got the vote, non-resident freemen were excluded from the franchise and a greater proportion of the Cambridge population from now on had a say in the choice of those who represented them in Parliament. This, let it be said, did *not* abolish bribery and corruption at a stroke—those features were still in evidence 20 years later—but it was a step in the right direction.

I said earlier that the university was in some measure to blame for the state of affairs in the town. It would perhaps have been more accurate to say that they had taken unfair advantage of it. When it became clear that the tide of reform was rising, the VC and Heads adopted an attitude of caution. They continued to discommon traders who defied university regulations, such as an innkeeper who allowed students to play billiards; and fined bakers who sold short-weight loaves, like Joseph Chapman in 1827. However, in his case—as presumably in others—the fine was small (only 12 shillings) and instead of the money going into the university account, half of it went to the informer, half to the poor of the parish. On all matters of general principle, it was now deemed prudent to get learned counsel's opinion before taking a firm stand. Usually they found a legal expert who was on their side, but in 1817 they were firmly advised that, whatever the charter of 1382 and subsequent charters might have said, more recent Excise Laws debarred the university from retaining fines imposed on brewers and innkeepers—hence the 'one half to the informer, etc'. That is the earliest instance I know of university privilege being diminished by legislation. It was not the first time it had been tested—50 years previously the right to search premises for prostitutes and confine them in the Spinning House had been submitted for counsel's opinion and fully vindicated in all aspects, even including the absence of evidence given on oath.

Similarly in 1827, when the Bill for the new gaol was going through, the VC and Heads behaved with discretion, abandoning their original claim to total exemption from rate contribution to pay for the gaol, which cost £12,000; although 12 years later they obtained counsel's opinion in favour of retaining their right to commit prisoners to it, irrespective of whether they helped to pay for it or not—and that opinion was based on charters two and a half centuries old. What the town called 'antiquated' and considered as a defect, the university called 'ancient' and considered as a merit. Again in 1830, the matter of market-tolls was in dispute; the charge for a stall prior to 1814 having been one penny per week, it had recently been increased to one penny per day, and a market was held every day. Although the corporation was taking £120 in a year, it was only spending £10 of that on lighting and paving, did not repair the market-place and had not built a market-house. The VC and Heads wanted to know whether they could enforce the terms of the Composition of 1503; counsel said they could, but prudence caused them to refrain and things remained as they were.

Then, in 1837, arose the question of paying for the new police force. This was tied up with the centuries-old right of the VC to have sole control over the students, and complications were bound to occur. On the one hand, policemen were arresting students in the normal course of their statutory duties; on the other, the proctors were having to call on the police for assistance in carrying out *their* duties, particularly the search of 'houses of ill fame'. After ten years of wrangling, no satisfactory compromise had been reached. A syndicate (university term for 'committee') of the Senate did at last agree to pay one quarter of the cost of the police force, up to an annual limit of £600, provided that: *a)* the police shall at all times show respect to proctors and Masters of Arts and refrain from interfering with them in the lawful exercise of their academical duties (the proctors for their part shall endeavour to prevent any breach of the peace); *b)* if a student is arrested, his college and the proctors shall be informed and *c)* all regulations of the watch committee, and the appointment of police constables, shall be subject to the approval of the VC and Heads.

This satisfied neither side. The Senate rejected the syndicate's proposals as too conciliatory; the town officials were equally firm in their rejection of them as too arrogant. Their position had been greatly strengthened by the Municipal Corporation Act of 1835, whereby the old corporation was dissolved; in its place a new corporation was created, styled 'The Mayor, Aldermen and Burgesses of the Borough of Cambridge'. No more bailiffs. Burgesses consisted of all male occupiers of houses, counting-houses, shops or warehouses rated at £10 annually in the borough or within seven miles of it. Government was by a Council consisting of 10 aldermen and 30 councillors, from whom the mayor was elected annually on November 9, and each of the five wards was represented by councillors elected by the burgesses; one third of the councillors were to retire each year and half of the aldermen to retire every third year. That was the biggest step yet in the putting in order of the civic house.

It was a long step away from a settling of the matter of university privilege and its crippling hold over civic affairs. For the Act expressly stated that no college property should be rated, no powers of trusteeship vested in the university by the Paving Act of 1788 should be transferred to the Council without the consent of the VC, masters and scholars and nothing in the Act should alter the rights and privileges of the university. Similarly the Highways Act of August 1835 and the Weights and Measures Act of September 1835 both contained clauses safeguarding those privileges. The university, for all its caution, was in no mood yet for capitulation.

The students were as militant as ever, especially on November 5, now firmly established as their 'Field Day'. A full press report of one typical incident is quoted in the Introduction of this book. It is typical in the sense that these incidents were mostly much ado about very little. Sometimes they were reported, sometimes not, depending on supply of material or reporters and the number of arrests or broken windows. When a reporter was sent to get a 'story', he made sure that he got one. It was unusual for more than half a dozen arrests to be made and the fines imposed did not usually exceed £2. Some of the incidents took an ugly turn due to over-excitement, especially when the cry of 'Gown to the rescue!' was raised, but the overall impression given is that of a boisterous 'rag' (a term first used about 50 years later). The accounts generally show a bias in favour of the 'gownsmen', except in the matter of attacks on the police or the 'Station-house'.

The attitude of the university authorities towards these disturbances was clearly stated by Dr Philpott, Master of St Catharine's, speaking in court after the hearing of the charge against two students of assaulting the police at a riot in the Town Hall when an anti-tobacco lecture had been violently disrupted in 1852:

I regret exceedingly to see two members of the University placed in the position of the two young men at the bar, which reflects great disgrace upon the body to which they belong. It was their duty, instead of acting as they did, to have assisted the police in the maintainance of order. I repeat, I regret the matter exceedingly, and I hope their punishment will serve as a warning to all members of the University present . . . . [The report ends]: It is almost ùnnecessary to state that the fines (£5) were immediately paid and we are informed were soon made up to the defendants by a 'whip' among sympathising undergraduates.

That, then, was the situation in 1852—solidarity in the ranks, circum-spection in the high command, as the town came in to the attack.

For the final assault—or what was intended as such—by the town upon the citadel of privilege was even then being made. There had been a probing attack 15 years earlier, when a Bill to secure drastic reform of the universities, mainly by revision of their statutes, was debated in the House of Lords, but the petition in favour of it secured only 136 signatures as against 753 on that urging its rejection, and rejected it was. The struggle continued, both locally and nationally, the scores being roughly equal. The rapid growth of the town (its population had reached over 24,000 by 1841, nearly 28,000 ten years later) made it perfectly obvious to all but the most hide-bound traditionalists that the university was going to be swamped if it tried to cling to its control much longer.

Yet cling it did. When the Railway Act of July 1844 was finally passed— 19 years after a line from London was first proposed—the university secured the insertion into it of these clauses:

1 That the VC and Heads, proctors and other university officials should have free access to the station at the arrival and departure of trains and the right to demand of the railway officials information concerning any university personnel travelling on the trains.

2 That the railway officials should forbid any university members unauthorised by the university officers to travel, even though the fare had been paid.

3 That passengers so excluded should have no claim on the Railway Company.

4 That the setting-down of passengers within three miles of Cambridge between 10 am and 5 pm on Sundays be forbidden to the Company on pain of a penalty of £5 for every person so set down.

I find that one of the most remarkable displays of arrogance in the whole history of the railways—or the university.

It is not true, as has been often stated, that university opposition to the railway was responsible for the siting of the station so far from the centre of the town—in fact, at the time of its construction, in open countryside. Geology and engineering considerations were responsible for that; and it did not matter all that much, for the town soon expanded up to and well beyond the railway. What really worried the university authorities was the prospect of hordes of 'lewd women', quickly and cheaply conveyed, descending on the town, especially on Sundays, to corrupt the youthful innocents in their charge or, alternatively, those chaste youths being quickly and cheaply conveyed to the metropolitan den of vice where no proctorial surveillance could shield their virtue. In 1851 the VC, Dr G. Corrie, wrote to the directors of the Company expressing pain that they 'had made arrangements for conveying foreigners and others to Cambridge on Sundays at such fares as might be likely to tempt persons who, having no regard for Sunday themselves, would inflict their presence on the University on that day of rest', adding that 'the contemplated arrangements were as distasteful to the University authorities as they must be offensive to Almighty God and to all right-minded Christians'.

Whatever the views of the Almighty on cheap Sunday excursions may have been, those of the new Chancellor—Prince Albert, elected in 1847—on the proper functions of a university were much clearer. He wanted reform and progress and was the first Chancellor to recognise the anachronistic nature of many of the university privileges. A commission was appointed in 1850 to inquire into all aspects of university government, finance, discipline, studies and resources. It was the signal for centuries-old grievances to be brought out into the open and thoroughly aired. For a time it looked as though the Town/Gown war might assume the nature it had had in the late 16th century. The same issues which had been fought over then were now fought over again, only this time the university was in the position of last-ditch defence.

In 1847 Mr Death, a horsedealer, had been discommoned for failing to report a student who had incurred a debt of more than £5; he had sued the VC and Heads in the High Court for damages and had lost the case. From 1852 all aspects of discommoning were closely examined by the Senate and its frequency declined sharply. In 1850 the junior proctor, The Reverend John Fenwick, and his two assistants were charged before the borough magistrates with 'assault' on Emma Thompson, whom they had arrested on suspicion of being a prostitute. The proctor's claim to be outside the court's jurisdiction was overruled and fines of 20s and 10s were imposed on him and his 'bulldogs'. When payment of the fines was refused, a warrant was issued for the arrest of all three. They were in fact taken into custody and the fines were then paid.

In the spring of 1850 a syndicate of the Senate and a committee of the

Town Council got together and agreed a whole list of proposals for peaceful co-existence—concerned mainly with finance, the police, and the procedure for charging students—by the modification of Acts already in force; the arrangements to remain operative for 14 years. This sort of thing had been tried before; it would have been as futile now as it had been then, merely postponing a permanent settlement and giving rise to endless argument in the meantime. It was firmly rejected by the Senate, strongly opposed by a large number of the townspeople and totally ignored by the Commissioners in their inquiries. Prince Albert, apart from expressing the view that there should be no outside interference in the affairs of the university—although there clearly had to be if change were to be effected—took little part in the debate in so far as it concerned relations between university and town, being more interested in the modernisation of the curriculum.

The Town Council decided to strike out on their own while the iron was still hot, ie, before the Commissioners issued their report. At a meeting in February 1852 a memorandum was compiled, stating the Council's views on every major point at issue:

The oath: We recollect with deep regret for how long a period feelings of hostility prevailed between the Members of the University and the Inhabitants of the Town. Believing firmly that the true interests of the two bodies are identical. [They asked for the oath to be abolished. Oddly enough, they quoted it.] You shall swear that you shall observe and keep, so far forth as in you lieth, the liberties and customs of this University as concerning the keeping of the peace, and also the Assize of Bread and Ale and other victuals, and that you shall not unduly or of malice impugn the other liberties and due customs of the said University as far forth as you shall have knowledge thereof. So God help you through Jesus Christ. [Oddly, because the authority given was a charter of 1317, quoted nowhere else, it is doubtful whether that form of the oath was used then and anyway the oath had not been taken for the last 50 years.]

Search for common women: We have lately obtained a local Act, incorporated in the Town Police Clauses Act of 1847, giving magistrates the power to punish every common prostitute or night-walker, etc. The police are vigilant, and offenders are daily punished by the magistrates; but the proctors still exercise the powers given them by their charters. Mistakes have been made. This practice puts all women of the class referred to on a level with the lowest [the first admission ever made in this context that there were high-class prostitutes]. It creates strong popular feeling against the university, costs the university money and the task can be done better by the police. We do not suggest that the proctors are wrong in the way they carry out their duties, but we must suggest that there are doubts whether duties of this kind are strictly compatible with the clerical character; the proctors are, with few exceptions, all clergymen.

Licensing of wineshops and alehouses: The VC still claims the right of licensing, even after the Act of 1836. Since then there have been two licensing bodies. (The VC of Oxford did not have this right.)

Inspection of weights and measures: This has been neglected for many years. It would be better done by the police.

Markets and fairs: The proclamation is still made annually, though the powers are practically obsolete and it would be no loss to the university if they were abolished.

Theatres, etc: The ban on theatrical performances within 14 miles of Cambridge, except with the VC's permission, includes the towns of Newmarket, Royston and St Ives. But theatrical performances do take place in the long vacation, without any licence granted, the manager of the theatre paying 10s 3d a year to the university.

Discommoning: This has been used to punish traders for centuries. It is a most serious form of punishment exercised by a secret and irresponsible tribunal; it injures the character and credit of respectable traders, without serving as a deterrent to the disreputable.

Trade regulations: These encourage the idea among students that, having contracted debts, they cannot be compelled to pay them. Decrees are made to curb extravagance, it is true, but in practice they have the opposite effect. The town has been overrun with non-resident traders soliciting orders from undergraduates. It is not the students but the traders who are punished.

University courts: These are obsolete and should be abolished. They are held in secret, with no jury and no professional counsel. The judges do the cross-examination and there is no appeal from their verdict.

University constables: These are appointed under the Act of 1827 and should be abolished.

Taxation: The university pays Land Tax of £100; the town pays £2,707. The town raises by parochial rates, poor rates, borough rates, church rates and highway rates £18,000 a year. The university and college buildings are not rated for poor rate, but they contribute £240 a year as a voluntary contribution. They have not contributed to the cost of the police.

The Town Council had struck the iron a little too hard for the Commissioners who, incidentally, were the Bishop of Chester, the Dean of Ely, Sir John Herschell, Sir John Romilly, Attorney General, and Professor Adam Sedgwick. They raised objections to every one of the town's suggestions and commented: 'If universities are to exist at all, some means should be taken, by the legislature if necessary, to *protect them from the contamination and evils incident to towns* in general'. It was rather late in the day to put forward such an idea, as regards Cambridge at least, but there was wisdom in it and future foundations would see it put into practice.

In August 1852 the Commissioners made their report, a vast document of 127 clauses, only about a dozen of which (those at the head of the list) concerned the town. Their recommendations, briefly, were that:

—the inefficient university courts be considered for reform;

—the VC's court, in cases involving townsmen, be made open and public;

—the Great Assembly be abolished;

—the oath be discontinued—mainly because it was a cause of jealousy;

—the VC should give up granting licences for ale-houses, but retain the power of revocation in the case of resort by loose women and gambling;

—discommoning should be retained;

—proctorial powers as regards prostitutes should be exercised with judgement and discretion. Charges against proctors should be heard in higher courts, not before local magistrates;

—weights and measures should be controlled by the town magistrates.

An interesting comparison with the financial position of three centuries earlier (page 82) was provided in the report. The annual income of the university in 1852 was £7,966; that of the colleges £146,525 (Peterhouse £7,317, Pembroke £12,000, Trinity Hall £3,917, King's £26,857, Queens' £5,347, Christ's £9,178, John's £26,116, Trinity £34,521, Magdalene £4,130, Emmanuel £6,516, Sidney Sussex £5,392, Downing £7,239). The list is not complete—no reason was given. The town authorities certainly did have a case when they clamoured for greater contribution by the colleges towards municipal expenses. They also had reason to be dissatisfied with the findings, which they were, and the dispute continued as fiercely as ever.

Arbitration had been used in the past to restore something like peace. It was the answer now. Sir John Patteson presided over a committee which thrashed the matter out over the next two years and, eventually, in 1856, the Cambridge Award Act was passed. It was the most momentous piece of legislation affecting Town/Gown relations since 1561 and largely demolished the rock on which university privilege had been based since then. The oath was abolished, as was the VC's power to license pubs, supervision of weights and measures became the responsibility of the borough magistrates and the VC's right to try all cases involving university members was abolished. College and university property in the town, with certain exceptions, was to be assessed for rates like any other property, assessment being done by three valuers, one appointed by the VC, one by the mayor, the third by the other two. The Watch Committee was to consist of 15 members, ie, the mayor and nine councillors and five university members. The borough accounts were to be audited annually by three university members and three of the town. The sum contributed by the university for the purpose of the Improvement Commission was to be one quarter of the whole.

It was the nearest thing yet to a peace treaty but it did not end the war. Neither side could really claim a victory. The VC retained the power to prohibit theatrical and other entertainments, except during the long vacation. He could still discommon tradesmen although this was limited to the one offence of failing to report students' debts. He still held the monopoly of granting wine licences. Most significant of all, the proctors still had the power to search for and arrest loose women and the VC still had the power to send them to the now abominated Spinning House, recently adapted to accommodate more of them. Furthermore, as if to underline the fact that there was to be no real alliance between the two parties yet, one clause in the Act precluded members of the university from being registered as electors in the borough or being enrolled as burgesses and exempted them from municipal or parochial duties. It was not until the Local Government Act of 1889 that the university was represented on the Town Council by six councillors, two of whom were aldermen.

I would not say that the students deliberately set out to destroy whatever prospects of peace there may have been, but the behaviour of a small minority of them—let me stress that it *was* a minority—during the next 20 years certainly did not help to foster good relations. I am not even sure that it was really part of the war, because it is fairly certain that many of those who took part in the disturbances knew little or nothing of the past history of the conflict. The following extracts from the *Cambridge Chronicle* illustrate my point:

(1856) They were followed as on former occasions by scores of dirty little boys supposed to represent the 'town', who treated the gownsmen to a miscellaneous concert of howling and yelling . . . Of this no notice was taken, until certain individuals designated by the gownsmen as 'cads' stood in the way, and these being considered fit objects of wrath, although profoundly ignorant of what it all meant, an onslaught was made upon them . . . the party cries of 'gown, town' were freely emitted, and blood (nasal of course) flowed rather copiously.

On this occasion one of the students wrote to the *Chronicle* to give his version of the affair. He charged the police with needless violence and gross partiality in that 'in every case where a contest occurred between a university man and the town, the university man was taken and the townsman was left'. There is a modern ring about that and the court proceedings tended to justify the complaint—of the ten people arrested, six were students, one a prostitute, two townsmen and one a country lad; all were dismissed with a caution except three undergraduates, who were fined £2, £2 and 10s.

(1859) A party of freshmen opened the ball by walking arm-in-arm along the principal streets, with defiant expression of countenance and sleeves turned up as if ready for battle . . . there was a large number of country lads in the town . . . the boys of Barnwell and other 'scum' . . . as dirty a mob as one would choose to set eyes on was soon at the heels of the gownsmen . . . Groaning and shouting . . . running away and shouting 'town', a cry in which the 'yokels' heartily joined the mob, though no doubt entirely ignorant of the cause of the squabble and unversed in the traditional history of these feuds . . . flying skirmishes commenced; sticks were used by both parties, and stones were thrown . . . a member of the University is said to have had an arm broken, and sundry black eyes and damaged noses were received . . At 10 o'clock most of the 'gown' party had been sent home by the proctors; but the 'roughs' continued to prowl . . . one of the proctor's men was knocked down and mauled by the mob, but the police came to his aid . . . .

Only three arrests were made; two townsmen were fined 5s and 2s 6d.

Elizabeth Ison, a prostitute, was sent to gaol for seven days for using bad language in the streets. She was following the mob . . . and being recommended to 'move on' by a gentleman in blue, she refused to do anything of the sort for such a ✶✶✶ cad, and told him she would see him [further] first.
(1863) Immediately a cap and gown appears, the war cry commences on the part of these boys. The air is filled with the most terrific yells, shouts and groans, and upon the electric summons of 'Town! Town! Town!' these ruffians, armed with sticks and stones, mix with the boys and surround maybe one, two, three or four University men, watching their opportunity to fall in, commit a brutal assault, and rob their victims of whatever they can lay their hands on . . . .
(1868) A small army of boys . . . paraded the streets, shouting in pot-valiant accents . . . their war cry of 'Town! Gown!' . . . whenever half a dozen of the 'knights of the mortar-boards' appeared . . . took to their heels with surprising celerity.
(1871) . . . the 'Gown' were the originators of the disturbances . . . running fights and attendant uproar for two or three hours . . . a serious collision not only between 'Town' and 'Gown' but with the lawful authorities . . . on the Market Place at about half-past nine nearly 200 of the 'Gown' in a solid and compact company . . . received by frantic yells . . . somebody shouted 'The Proctor!' . . . they fled ignominiously in disorder in all directions . . . .

And so it went on, gradually getting less violent and ugly, more hilarious and harmless. Noise, movement and artificially-induced excitement were really what it was all about; by the morrow it was merely a hazily remembered 'night out'.

The other surviving war-area was rather different, though at times overlapping with those noisy occasions, resulting in what came to be called 'Proctorial Rows'. In them, feelings ran deeper and lasted longer. A prostitute—if such she was—in a manner of speaking started the whole war nearly 700 years before. It was around prostitutes—or those deemed to be such—that the last real battle was fought; and this at a time when, one might have thought, few people would have been found to champion them. It was not, of course, that many people felt strongly in favour of prostitution—though no doubt some of the undergraduates did—rather that they felt strongly against the university authorities using its attempted suppression as a means of asserting their prerogative of power.

On several occasions at least in the last two centuries (perhaps many more than are known about) the proctors had slipped up badly by arresting as 'prostitutes' women and girls who were, if not perfectly respectable, not wholly deserving of classification as members of that ancient profession. (There is a story, which I cannot trace to its source, and of which the details differ each time it crops up, to the effect that on one occasion they arrested the VC's daughter.) Every such incident caused smouldering resentment to be fanned to a blaze of anger. When a blaze of publicity was added to the conflagration, then the heat became really intense, as in January 1860.

Because the Bachelors' Ball, a 'delightful resort of youth and beauty', had been discontinued, a number of students decided to stage a 'base imitation' of it in the form of a party to be held at the De Freville Arms at Shelford, to which each male guest was expected to bring a lady partner. Transport was arranged and a good supply of eats and drinks ordered, including, it was said, provisions for breakfast the next morning. A horse-drawn omnibus made the round of the picking-up points and was soon filled, mostly with excited young ladies. Do not misunderstand my use of the term 'picking-up'—the ladies were all invited. Unfortunately one young lady who was not invited, but who thought that she ought to have been, showed her resentment by writing an anonymous letter to the proctor. As a result, when the horse-drawn load of charmers was passing the Town Hall, its progress was barred by the proctors, their bulldogs and about a dozen policemen. After minimal inquiries, it was driven straight to the Spinning House. There the students on board were dismissed to their respective colleges. The girls were hustled inside. Five of them, after a brief hearing by the VC next morning, were kept there. The others, one a girl of 16, were sent home. All described themselves as dressmakers; some of them probably were, said the *Chronicle*, 'though that is an honest occupation frequently assumed for concealing a worse'. Only four students turned up at the rendezvous; the rest had all been warned off.

The rights and wrongs of the affair—there were some of each—were lost to sight in the ensuing storm of passions, which supplied the *Chronicle* with copy over the next two months. Emma Kemp, one of the girls imprisoned, and sister of the 16-year-old, was released after five days and later brought an unsuccessful action against the VC. At a meeting held at the Hoop Hotel on February 12, a resolution was passed condemning the action of the proctors as 'opposed to the spirit of the English constitution, subversive of the liberty of the subject, repugnant to the feelings of the inhabitants of the town and wholly inoperative in achieving its object'. A public subscription was launched to raise funds for a campaign for the abolition of the proctorial system of dealing with prostitutes. The *Chronicle* condemned the committee, its subscriptions, pamphlets and posters, and violently attacked *The Daily Telegraph* for printing an article attacking the system.

While that storm was still raging, 'There was a disgraceful row in the streets on Saturday night. One of the proctors was taking a notorious prostitute to the Spinning House, when a mob collected, attacked the proctor and his men, and succeeded in rescuing the girl from their custody'. A similar incident occurred in the following November. The proctors took the hint and arrests of prostitutes became quite rare for a number of years.

Then once again it was the irresponsible conduct of a minority of undergraduates that brought the matter of Town/Gown relations into the limelight of the national press and so gave it an 'importance' it did not really possess. It happened on Monday, November 10 1875. A party of about 50 students went to a concert in the new Corn Exchange for the express purpose of 'indulging in a lark', knowing that the event would be graced with the presence of all the notable citizens of the town, including the new mayor. Lateness in starting was made the excuse for a demonstration of stamping, hissing and shouting. Disapproval of this was the reason, apparently, for the students invading the reserved enclosure. Then all reason departed. The students danced a sort of war-dance in the centre of the hall, surrounding groups of terrified women, some of whom had their clothing torn off, and panic took possession. When the police arrived, they were the targets of the student activities. 'Riot' and 'lawlessness' were the words used later to describe what had happened. Yet 'riot' it was never meant to be; just a 'lark'.

Hurt at the lack of a sense of humour on the part of the populace, the students gathered in force in the market-place on the Tuesday evening to burn an effigy of Alderman Death, the retiring mayor, who was chairman of the magistrates who would hear the case against the seven students who had been arrested on the Monday night and released on bail.

On the Wednesday a huge crowd gathered in front of the Guildhall to await the verdict of the court. All the cases had been adjourned. The crowd of students evidently expected them to be dismissed (they were later, except for one man who was fined £15) for immediately the cry 'To Death's house!' was raised and off they rushed to the ex-mayor's residence. Although it was defended by a dozen policemen, the students managed to pull down part of the fencing then, driven off by the vigorous use of police truncheons, they went round to the back and broke most of the windows. 'It was a wanton and vindictive act.' The police had no support whatever from the townspeople; later in the market-place one of them was knocked down by a student and injured. No arrests were made.

That occurred just at a time when the local people were beginning to feel confident that such things were of the past. The reaction was a tremendous surge of anger, disgust and disappointment, which a great many of the students shared. It needed no stoking by the *Chronicle*, though that eminent journal made hundreds of column-inches out of it, and the theme was taken up by the national press. The *Evening Standard* carried an interesting commentary, not just on this latest incident, but on the whole subject of Town/Gown relations, part of which I must quote:

It is only in human nature that Town and Gown should not like each other. The former is nourished, to a very great extent, by the expenses of the latter. If Gown sometimes does not pay its debts with regularity, Town, on the other hand, does not always do its best to make reckless extravagance difficult to the undergraduate.

Temptations are thrown in his way, some people are very subservient to him and between fawned on and fawners there are always grounds for contempt and hatred. This is not a healthy, nor, of course, by any means a general, state of relations between the pupils and the tradesmen of the Universities but it is out of centuries of such relations that the traditional animosity has grown up. The same dislike is well known in Germany between students and Philistines, and even the quiet Scotch Universities sometimes indulge in a riot with the townspeople. All this is no excuse for the bearish rudeness that has long prevailed on the side of a certain kind of undergraduate. It is in the intolerable insolence of men who insult the citizens and the wives and daughters of citizens by their arrogant bearing at places of amusement that the present riots have their origin.

That is fair comment, and largely true, but my main reason for quoting it is that it illustrates very well the general state of ignorance prevailing then— and now—as to the *real* history of the Town/Gown conflict. Failure of students to pay their debts was, it is true, a cause of trouble; it always had been, but only *one* of a host of causes, and by no means the chief. The shop-keepers and traders had generally managed to offset their losses from this cause by overcharging or withholding discount, as I dare say they still do. The history of Cambridge is studded with examples of traders who made a modest fortune out of dealing with the students; the famous Hobson was one. Anyway the university authorities had got that particular cause of the war well under control by this time. The practice of discommoning traders was retained solely to coerce them into reporting students who ran up debts, so that their tutors could deal with them. It worked so well that on average only one or two, mostly tailors, were discommoned in any one year.

Publicity was now a major factor in the campaign. It—and two girls— decided the final battle. Jane Elsden, aged 17, was arrested by the proctor on February 2 1891, charged with being a prostitute and committed to the Spinning House for seven days. On February 11 she was back on her beat in Petty Cury. Spotted by the proctor, she fled, only to be caught by the bulldogs a few streets away. Back to the Spinning House, this time for a period of 21 days. That afternoon she escaped through a window into St Andrew's Street and went home to Dullingham. Instead of leaving her in peaceful, if somewhat dull, rustication, the VC, Dr H.M. Butler, had her arrested by the police on a charge of prison-breaking. He was perfectly entitled to do so, but it was an imprudent step, for the charge had to be heard, not in the VC's court, but at the Assizes.

Her counsel, Mr Livett, first challenged the right of the VC to make arrest as he had done, or to hear the original charge, but this was countered by the Registrary of the University producing the original charter of James I dated March 9 1645 (I assume that to be a reporter's error, though charters often were misquoted). Mr Livett then asserted that the offence for which Jane had been detained was not one known to common law or the charters. He was overruled, but he had come to strike a resounding blow, and strike he did, in his summing-up:

The prisoner has been subjected to a cruel persecution and dragged through three courts. She was first arrested by men who have acted more in the character of Russian police [applause and calls of 'Silence!'] than in a way that is recognised in a state where civilisation exists. The trials in the Vice-Chancellor's Court savour rather of the Inquisition than of a Court in England. It combines the secrecy of the

Inquisition with the severity of lynch-law almost. Whilst it exists no woman is safe in Cambridge, and ladies of the highest respectability in the town have been subjected to the indignity and annoyance of detention. [Loud applause in the galleries.]

But the jury found Jane guilty and the judge sentenced her to three weeks in prison not, however, before he had made the observation that the VC's court 'if the Legislature thought fit to do so, could be swept away tomorrow'. Jane was released by the Home Secretary after five days. Publicity such as she can never have dreamed of was coming to her aid.

The editor of the *Chronicle*, ever a staunch supporter of proctorial powers, warned its readers:

The University contributes an addition of 3,500 inhabitants to our population for a great part of the year [24 weeks out of 52, in fact] who spend on an average £200 per annum in our midst. It is not too much to say that many parents would hesitate to send their sons to Cambridge if there were not proper measures of protection there for maintaining an observance of authority.

The Senate proposed a conference with the Town Council which accepted the invitation, subject to the proviso 'that no settlement of the question raised by the recent Spinning House case will be satisfactory which does not abolish the jurisdiction at present possessed by the University authorities, on any subject, over persons not members of the University'. Meanwhile the tide of correspondence flowed through the columns of the press as it had done 30 years before in the affair of the dressmakers, only stronger. It ranged in sentiment from amusement through moral indignation to utter disgust, embracing politics, religion and Empire. 'A looker on' concluded a lengthy epistle with 'this is no matter merely of Cambridge local government, but one which the remotest corners of the Empire are concerned'.

Poor little Jane! I wonder if she enjoyed it. I wonder if she even *knew*. I am sure she did not understand. She had become a symbol, a martyr. There was little likelihood of her becoming a saint, though if the cycling distance had been shorter, or the trains more frequent, there was a strong possibility of Dullingham becoming a place of pilgrimage—not under the patronage of the Church, of course.

In July the VC wrote to the mayor to say that the Senate had decided:

1 That the town authorities were not capable of maintaining order and decency in the streets; though the VC's procedure would be modified and certain structural alterations made to the Spinning House.

2 That in the interests of discipline among students and townsmen, the

Cambridge in 1863

This is based on the Cambridge Chronicle *map, drastically simplified. The enclosure of the common fields early in the 19th century, then the coming of the railway, and the exploitation of both, resulted in rapid expansion of the town on all sides except the west, where the university was in sole possession. Expansion since 1860 has gone on at an ever-increasing rate, made possible by the absorption of the neighbouring parishes of Chesterton, Trumpington and Cherryhinton. The area shown on this map is considerably less than one quarter of that of modern Cambridge, yet the situation it portrays has not appreciably changed.*

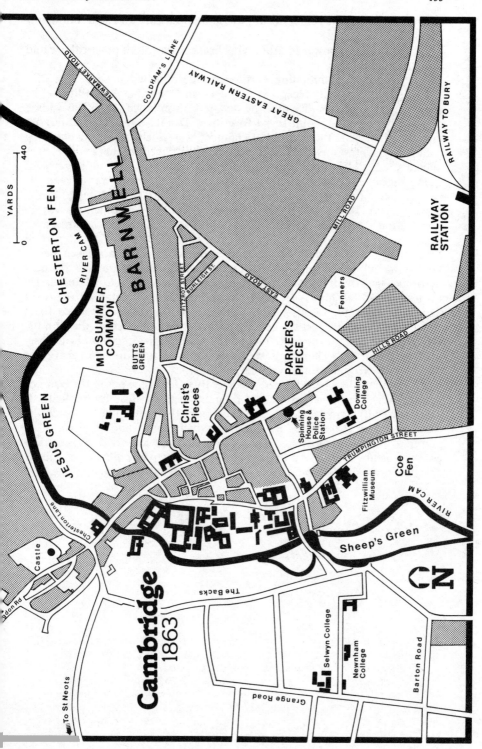

NEWMARKET ROAD

COLDHAM'S LANE

GREAT EASTERN RAILWAY

RAILWAY TO BURY

CHESTERTON FEN

440
YARDS
0

RIVER CAM

BARNWELL

MILL ROAD

RAILWAY
STATION

MIDSUMMER
COMMON

FITZROY STREET

BURLEIGH ST

EAST ROAD

Fenners

BUTTS
GREEN

PARKER'S
PIECE

HILLS ROAD

JESUS GREEN

Christ's
Pieces

Downing
College

Spinning
House &
Police
Station

TRUMPINGTON STREET

Coe
Fen

Chesterton Lane

Fitzwilliam
Museum

RIVER CAM

Castle

Sheep's Green

N

on Rd

The Backs

Cambridge
1863

To St Neots

Selwyn College

Newnham
College

Grange Road

Barton Road

power of the VC to refuse to authorise amusements and entertainments should be retained.

3 That the VC's power to grant wine licences was of no practical use and could be abandoned.

4 As regards discommoning, further consideration was needed.

This got a very chilly reception in the Town Council and hostilities—the courteous kind of hostility used by debaters—continued. Jane was fading into the background, soon to be forgotten. Debate centred on university jurisdiction which, the university claimed, was solely aimed at checking immorality, yet somehow the economic advantages to the town always managed to slide into the argument, and somehow the superiority of Cambridge over Oxford was frequently inferred. The town was as ready as ever to back its convictions with its cash—some of it now contributed by the university. A Bill for the Abolition of Proctorial Jurisdiction was in preparation. Then, in December, Daisy Hopkins appeared on the streets.

Daisy was another 17-year-old. She had appeared on the streets several times before and was well known by sight to the proctors, even better known to numerous undergraduates. She appeared before the VC next morning, smartly dressed in a navy-blue costume with gold edging and a fawn-coloured felt hat. A singularly unsusceptible VC sentenced her to 14 days in the Spinning House. Daisy, advised by her counsel, applied for a writ in the Court of Queen's Bench, and was released after six days on the grounds of a flaw in the indictment—the words 'for an immoral purpose' had been omitted. Then, less well advised, she sued the university for damages for wrongful imprisonment, and lost.

But the flame had been fanned sufficiently to bring the pot to the point of boiling over. The university wanted no more of this distasteful publicity. It was by friendly agreement, not legal coercion, that both sides accepted the Act, eventually passed on June 18 1894, which finally abolished the VC's power to send women to gaol and also ended his control over theatrical entertainment. In 1901 the hated Spinning House was pulled down and a new police station built on the site. A new era had dawned.

Chapter 16

Peace in our time 1894-1982

The war at the top level was well and truly over by the end of the 19th century. This chapter is wholly concerned with the aftermath. No more money was to be spent by either side on litigation, defending or attacking university privilege in so far as it affected the government of the town. Both sides had better uses for their money and the university in particular was rather short of money for what it had to do. All the contentious privileges had been relinquished, in practice. The bitter lessons learnt over the centuries, however, had instilled the university with caution and the principle of privilege was maintained. When the Local Government Act of 1889, providing amongst other things for university representation on the Borough Council (six members out of a total of 36), was passed after some opposition from the town, its final clause stipulated that:

Nothing in this order contained shall affect the exclusive rights and privileges of civil and criminal judicature and trial in the courts of the University as the same may have been granted by the charter of the University and confirmed by divers Acts of Parliament to the University and to all persons matriculated therein or being members thereof, nor any other of the respective rights, privileges and franchises of the University and their successors and the several bodies politic, corporate, collegiate or sole of the University and their successors, except so far as the same are hereby expressly altered.

It was partly force of habit, no doubt, partly customary legal caution, but also, I think, a warning to the town that this was no abject surrender; rather a settlement entered into because it suited the university's purpose, like all the other concessions of the preceding 40 years, and the few still to come.

That purpose from now on was to develop into a world-renowned international seat of learning and research, especially in the scientific field; an aim which the university could only hope to achieve if untrammelled by involvement in petty squabbles like the Daisy Hopkins affair, and if it were seen to merit the considerable financial grants now accruing from the State and from private benefactions. The university was not and is not the fabulously wealthy institution which some people imagine it to be. Neither are the colleges, despite their endowments. After the 1889 Act they, as corporate bodies and 'charities' (by virtue of the nature of their foundation) paid half the normal scale of rates. Since 1968 they have paid full rates. Their members, as private citizens, have paid the same rates as anyone else.

The presence of the university in the town does not deprive the civic corporation of any revenue nor, despite the assertion of some people to the contrary, has it cost the ratepayers one extra penny for the provision of amenities which they themselves do not enjoy. Up to and including the 1930s there might have been some substance in the complaint, still heard occasionally from ill-informed quarters, that the university was financially 'exploiting' the townspeople. It was one of the major employers of labour; people were still coming in from outside the town in search of work there. Established college servants clung doggedly, loyally to their posts, willing to accept relatively low wages in return for security. Part-time employees, of whom there are still a fair number, accepted the laying-off during vacations as part of the job. With the change in economic circumstances, the vast growth of the city population and the expansion of light industry, the importance of the university as an employer has declined considerably in recent years and the provision of seasonal employment hardly constitutes 'exploitation'.

At the same time there has been an expansion of another 'industry', one in which it is the university's turn to be 'exploited', although the strongest term I have heard used in protest is 'a feeling of irritation'. Large numbers of tourists, especially Americans, visit the city every year. They come to see the colleges, kept attractive at considerable expense yet open to all and sundry free of charge. They spend their money in the shops, hotels and restaurants of the town. The colleges derive no financial benefit whatever from the invasion and the satisfaction of being one of Britain's major tourist attractions is somewhat marred by the disturbance it causes to normal working life. The recent development of the conference trade, still an expanding 'industry', has restored the balance to some extent both as regards the employment situation and college finances.

I have dealt with money matters first because they have been a primary element in the 'war' from the very beginning. There are still minor disagreements about money; there always will be. It can no longer be said to be a major bone of contention between Town and Gown. Nor could it be said that the university wanted to 'rule' the town. One sixth representation on the Council hardly constituted undue interference in civic affairs. Indeed it proved to be an arrangement satisfactory to both sides. Since 1896 various university aldermen have held the office of mayor, bringing to it a distinction often lacking in the past. The university councillors, though generally by nature of right-wing tendency, have sometimes upset the balance of parties on the Council by maintaining their independence in political issues. Sometimes, too, they have caused frustration by their difference in attitude, particularly on matters of town-planning and have contributed still further to the delays which always seem to have characterised civic undertakings in Cambridge. One notable instance of recent years was the Lion Yard development plan, which must have dragged on for over 20 years. The university would have liked to see a really imposing civic centre on the site, whereas the town was more concerned with commercial premises of high rateable value. Relations as regards planning policy are still not as amicable as they might be. Not because of university intervention on the Council— their representation was ended in 1974 by yet another Local Government Act, with no recrimination on either side—but simply by virtue of the fact that the colleges own so much land and property in the town.

It is this fact which causes many people, including some students, to assert that the town is too much dominated by the university. That it *is* dominated is an undeniable fact, though far less so now than, say, 50 years ago; whether it is still 'too much' so is a matter for debate. The domination is largely confined to the centre of the town, and is largely just a physical fact, arising from centuries of progressive development on the one hand set against near-stagnation on the other. You can scarcely move 50 yards in the centre of the town without being in the shadow of a college or university building, to the delight of visitors. You can hardly tread one yard west of the river which is not university or college property and what virtually amounts to a new university is steadily growing up in that area, almost unnoticed by the townspeople.

The town, likewise, is growing in a way that the university members hardly notice. Physical expansion to the north, east and south has been enormous in the last 60 years and still goes on; the population topped the 100,000 mark some years ago. A high proportion of these people would laugh at the suggestion that they were 'dominated' by the university. As one taxi-driver put it: 'They don't even know that the university exists'.

Town (I find the change of title to 'City' difficult to adapt to after writing about 'Town' all through the book and it clashes with my title) and university have grown apart for reasons wholly unconnected with the circumstances which bound them together in bitter hostility for so long. The former no longer feels any sense of deprivation at the prospect of the university flourishing independently of it. Just over two years ago the *Cambridge Evening News*—successor to the *Cambridge Chronicle and University Journal* which a century ago placed its loyalty heavily on the second element of its title—carried an article showing clearly a shift of emphasis and no doubt spoke for a majority of its readers in declaring that Cambridge had become:

. . . a city where the citizens are quite capable of forming themselves into organis- ations, institutions, committees and bodies of all sorts, with or without the assistance of the university . . . Various members of the university have described Cambridge as having either more bookshops or men's outfitters to the square mile than anywhere else. Members of the city could make the same claim by citing different bodies and organisations which abound in all side streets and centres of education. Cambridge might remain a predominantly university city, but it is quite clearly evolving and becoming a more lively place in its own town right.

One eminent and elderly member of both town and university has commented on the 'slightly acid note here'. He and others, of whom there are more than one might suppose, would like to see town and university more fully integrated as one community. The chief obstacle to that ideal is, in their view, what they call the 'arrogance' still displayed by the university in such matters as the formation of a 'Cambridge Society' which excludes from its membership all members of Cambridge society who are not members of the university. The Society was formed in 1978 with the main object of keeping past and present members of the university informed of developments in the university. It has now about 4,500 members. What my informant objects to most strongly is its title and constitution, with the implication that 'Cambridge' *is* the university. One must face the fact that the outside world largely holds that view, and has done for a very long time, but I would have thought that the charge of arrogance could be easily refuted by changing the society's name to 'Cambridge University Society'.

There are perhaps other lingering traces—I know of none—of the attitude engendered by centuries of tradition and strife which can only be called 'arrogance' on the part of the university. They are, however, a mere nothing compared with the situation at the beginning of the period under review. I know of several instances, but quote only the silliest. Just before the First World War, a university don and his wife met a well-to-do Cambridge couple on holiday at an East Coast resort and spent a pleasant fortnight in their company at the same boarding-house. On the morning of their departure the don's wife said to the other lady: 'It has been very nice meeting you, but of course we shall not know you when we are back in Cambridge. You're not university'.

Such stupid snobbery as that must have been a hangover from the 19th century. It was vanishing during the inter-war years and had, I think, completely gone soon after the Second World War. Nevertheless, despite the upsurge of egalitarianism in the 1960s, there persists in the university ranks a certain sense of 'superiority'. It has nothing to do with 'snobbery'. True, it is fostered by tradition, but it is firmly based on achievement. A student who wins a place at a Cambridge college, particularly if he comes from a grammar or comprehensive school, has every right to feel 'superior'; he undoubtedly is, anyway, in the academic sense. College fellowships and professorial chairs are no longer gained by knowing the right people, having the right accent or by scheming patiently for years before stepping into a dead man's shoes. There still exists an 'Old Boy network', but every year sees its strands increasingly severed by intellectual worth. There are still schools where 'MA Cantab' automatically takes precedence over 'BA London', regardless of what each represents in the way of work and ability; but the world of industry and commerce has learnt better ways of assessing fitness for appointment. The graduate of Cambridge University today knows that his 'superiority' has to be demonstrated before it is accepted and that nothing is to be gained by offensively asserting it.

Because a lot of people are slow to realise that fact, it is not difficult to sustain the illusion that bitter hostility between Town and Gown still persists and that it is caused by the unfair advantages enjoyed by Gown and claimed as of right in the name of 'superiority'. Those who stoke the fires of passion thus roused will usually be found to have an iron of their own in the fire—or an axe to grind, if the metaphors are not too incompatible.

In 1968 the student newspaper, *Varsity*, carried an editorial aimed mainly at the university authorities, accusing them of a 'negative attitude towards town-student relationships' and pointing out a 'desperate need to integrate town and gown. One way of doing this would be to throw open and advertise university activities to the town—open our discotheques, our clubs and societies and as many of our facilities as possible'. The article then referred to the menace of assaults by 'bored' city youths on undergratuates— 'It is no longer possible to walk through the streets at night without fear'— and suggested as a remedy 'a large entertainment centre where both students and townspeople can enjoy themselves together'.

The local paper heartily approved the gesture, but rightly viewed the suggested remedy with some concern. 'The only difficulty is that some of those most responsible for causing trouble will probably be little interested in clubs or societies. They might well be interested in discotheques. But here the basic rivalry that feeds all others (over girl-friends) would be more marked, rather than less.'

This happened in the early stages of a brief period of student protest against their own authorities; by no means the first one in which Town/Gown relations had become involved, but the first in which students had championed the interests of town youth. One feature of the protest, according to a police officer, was 'a pseudo sympathy with the townies'. Several hundred students staged a 'sit-in' at the Old Schools for three days in January 1969. This passed off peacefully enough but tension continued to mount and, after a meeting of the Students' Union in October 1970, attended by over 1,500 students and demanding reform of the disciplinary system, an inquiry was held. It dragged on for weeks, and was so marked by noisy interruptions, some verging on the obscene, that proceedings were transferred to Mill Lane and police protection was requested.

This was regarded as 'provocation', though in fact the only provocation was that suffered by the police, whose sole concern initially was to prevent the total obstruction of Mill Lane, which did occur. A violent skirmish ensued in which ten students, including a girl, were arrested. All the men were fined £20 for obstructing the street and the police. The ringleader, one Tizard, who had 'kicked a bulldog in the goolies'—'kicked a University constable in the stomach' according to the Devlin Report—was fined an additional £5 for that and for 'dishonestly handling a policeman's helmet'.

Meanwhile the Student Representative Assembly had rejected by 18 votes to three the idea of forming a Town/Gown relations study group, although one speaker had said: 'Our own student problems are important, but the real priority should be the way the university has exploited the town'. Reference was also made to the proposed use of the University Library by townspeople and ways of increasing wage-rates for employees of the university—a strangely incongruous pairing of aims.

The upper echelons did not stand aloof from participating in the debate now raging. 'Don calls for Town/Gown co-operation' was the headline under which the local paper reported the speech of Mr R.F. Bennett, Fellow of Magdalene, in the Senate House. The discussion was about the university's planning procedures, but Mr Bennett (who played a leading part in the abolition of gowns a few years before) gave it a broader significance with the remark, referring to town and university: 'We are not so much the employers and the employees as co-citizens'. Dr Glyn Daniel rowed in with a plea for integration, in the form of town representation in the administration of the university, participation by graduate townspeople in university social life and a system of civic fellowships.

These were idealistic sentiments, seeds which were doomed to fall on stony ground. The borough MP was on even stonier ground when he used the issue of Town/Gown divisiveness as party political fodder. The *Cambridge Evening News* reminded him and its readers: 'Clearly the difference exists, but by talking about town and gown as distinct entities one may run the risk of perpetuating a theory which is no longer entirely accurate'. Mr Lane was on firm ground when he said 'town and gown must draw together, not drift apart' but he lost his balance slightly when declaring in the market-place that part of his policy was that the colleges should offer their facilities to the townspeople. A Caius don who heard him came down from his rooms, identified himself, and pointed out that the colleges *do* make their facilities available to the townspeople and have done for a long time; their sports-grounds *are* used by local clubs, their concerts are open to the public, their courts are public promenades. 'What more,' demanded an exasperated don, 'can we be expected to do?'

Two years later the prospective Labour candidate adopted the same line, alleging 'widespread resentment' among Cambridge people that they cannot make full use of college sports-grounds when they were making such a 'generous contribution' from the rates towards the maintenance and upkeep of the grounds. In 1975 the *Evening News*, under the headline 'Town/Gown gulf wide as ever', quoted the left-wing student *Broadsheet* in an attack on 'blinkered university-based nonchalance'. And in 1981 the borough MP, Mr Rhodes James, warned students of the city's 'resentment' against their presence in the city. (He was speaking at Coventry.) 'What are these expensive institutions for? What use are they? Why is it that they are used for such a relatively short time every year? Is the tax-payer to be expected to go on paying for such institutions without explanation?'

I dare say that kind of talk will go on, as will the 'niggling'. 'People bring up petty grievances against the university at the slightest excuse'—like the watering of the Senate House lawn during a period of drought or the burial of anthrax-infected horses on waste ground, on the very edge of the town, which 25 years later happened to be within yards of the back gardens of a housing estate.

I was not surprised when a university servant of long standing, asked to comment on the lingering hostility between Town and Gown, declared hotly: 'It is a myth, fostered by the media with the object of sensationalising and perpetuating something that doesn't really exist. Any vestige of the old enmity exists only in the minds of those who talk about it'. Others have described the conflict as 'a non-event' and one police officer stated with conviction: 'Town and Gown animosity has totally gone'.

On the positive side, and in contrast to the above, is to be set the excellent record of public-spiritedness shown by countless members of the university who could have turned their back on the town's problems and retired into the comfort of their academic shell, but chose to play a leading part in civic and social affairs. The tradition in fact goes back for centuries—as far back as Dr Perne—and has been either overshadowed by the strife and turmoil amidst which magnanimous individuals endeavoured to perform their duty as good citizens, or overstated in an effort to minimise the extent of that strife. On an ever-increasing scale since the 1930s, dons and their wives have furthered the educational, charitable and welfare services of the town and district. Maybe at times there has been an element of patronage about their activities. Maybe some of them would merit the term of 'do-gooders' bestowed on them by detractors to whom anything savouring of 'charity' is anathema. Be that as it may, I have no hestiation in quoting an eminent, now retired, official of the Local Health Service: 'Cambridge in the last 50 years would in my opinion have been a much poorer place but for the contribution to public welfare made by University men and their wives acting as public-spirited individuals'. He cites Lord and Lady Adrian as notable examples. A full list of those who by their services freely given have earned the gratitude and affection of their fellow citizens would fill a book, and then some names would be inadvertently omitted because no publicity attended their efforts, so I will not attempt it.

It is to be noted that this participation in the social welfare of the town is largely 'as individuals'. Not that the university as a body does not also make its contributions; the foundation of the Arts Theatre and that of the Cambridge Preservation Society are examples of joint enterprise in recent years. The general gloom of my story over the centuries has been brightened—and might have been much more so—by instances of compassionate action promptly taken by the university to relieve distress and counter the effects of disasters such as fire and sickness.

But there is not a great deal in that line that the university as a body *can* do. Generally speaking, it is Vice-Chancellors, Masters, professors, dons and their wives who *do* things. Yet when brickbats are to be thrown, they are nearly always aimed at 'the university'. Only a few weeks ago a city councillor remarked: 'The university does not care about the town'. It is one of the penalties of tradition, I suppose. As one don put it: 'The university is still a prisoner of ancient tradition'.

All things considered, then—or all the things I can think of—there is no good reason why any real animosity should still persist between Town and Gown at the higher level. There are complaints—disagreements would be a more apt term—that crop up from time to time at what might be called the 'middle level', a stratum to which the bulk of both university and town people feel that they belong. Such disagreements would occur anywhere. Shopkeepers complain that their rents are too high, the majority of premises in the centre of the town being college-owned. The rents *are* high, but no higher than they would be if someone else owned the property. What aggravates the situation—and this applies equally to lodging houses—is that some colleges allow 20 years or so to elapse before they revise the rents to keep pace with inflation, then find that they have to make what seems like an enormous increase. There are huge discrepancies in lodging-house rents, some pay over £1,000 per annum whilst others of the same capacity pay only £500 and at least one is as low as £130.

Lodging-houses in fact constitute one of the very oldest links between the modern situation and that of old. They, or the charges made in them, were a subject of complaint in 1231. They still are, only now the complaint oddly comes from the opposite direction. Some city officials object to the use of private houses altogether for lodging students, on the grounds that their use in that way diminishes the rateable value and restricts the accommodation available for visitors. Some landladies invite criticism by treating their students as of secondary importance. It used to be the custom to have no guests in the Easter vacation, when spring-cleaning was done, and none at Christmas, reserved for the family, taking in foreign students and visitors only in the long vacation. Now, it seems, the 'Bed and Breakfast' notices go up in the windows as soon as the students can be conveniently got out of their rooms, all the year round.

An interesting development of recent years is that two landladies serve on the Lodgings Syndicate and their views carry considerable weight. I am told that 'landladies are a dying race'. More and more students are being housed in colleges and college hostels. One can see the wisdom and practicality of this, yet many will regret the passing from the Cambridge scene of what, I believe, has been a considerable agency in cementing good relations between students and townspeople over the last 80 years. Some landladies have been 'dragons'; far more have been substitute 'mums' in homes from home. They are the ones who really know their students. Which brings me to the point towards which I have been heading all this time—students and their behaviour.

If this whole business of 700 years of 'warfare' were to be considered on a 'cause and effect' basis, like the old-fashioned history examination question, then student behaviour would surely rank high in the list of causes. What the Vice-Chancellor, Senate and Masters were getting up to behind closed doors was often only a matter of hearsay to the man in the street. Student behaviour was what the Cambridge public saw, heard and felt every day and night of every term. So let me now review this aspect of the affair from 1894 on, thus restoring this chapter to something like chronological order.

The situation was already easing in the last decade of the 19th century and the years before the 1914-18 war, but was still too lively for comfort. It was an age of jingoism and patriotic fervour; an era when a large proportion of the Cambridge students were affluent aristocrats with more patriotism than prudence, more money than sense. Not content with drawing Lord Kitchener triumphantly in his carriage from the Senate House to Christ's when in 1898 he came to receive an honorary degree, the students in the evening celebrated the occasion with a huge bonfire in the market-place. It had been done before as an official civic event, but not by feeding the flames with market-stalls, trestles, doors, shutters, fences and anything else combustible within reach. The damage was all paid for by the perpetrators of it—that too had become a tradition—and there was no great amount of ill-feeling engendered.

The relief of Ladysmith (or was it Mafeking?) was celebrated in similar fashion. This time the police made several arrests and the culprits were fined by the borough magistrates. Reference to the latter as 'pro Boer' probably contributed to the students being later pardoned, but the police still deemed it prudent to guard the mayor's house for several nights.

It soon became evident to the students that they had a role to play as entertainers of themselves and the public, and the phase of elaborate hoaxes and 'rags' began. One of the earliest was the official reception of 'The Sultan of Zanzibar' by university and civic officials, which only ran into difficulties when the hoaxers had either to enter King's Chapel wearing their turbans—and a jest could not be carried that far—or remove them and reveal their true identity.

The war put an end to that sort of thing. In the first year the number of students in residence fell from 3,200 to a quarter of that, and a year later to less than 600. The ghastly tragedy of young lives cruelly wasted during those years made the public and the authorities more sympathetic towards those who came back to resume their studies. They had left as boys and came back as men, impatient of paternalistic discipline and slightly contemptuous of those who had stayed at home. Hence a period of rowdyism and ragging which strained relations perhaps more than it need have done.

Then for about 15 years, from 1920 on, came what was perhaps the jolliest and most harmonious period ever in student activities as affecting the populace. It was marred only by the over-popularity and over-use of the latest status-symbol, the motor car. As early as 1909 its use by students had been restricted, on account of the noise and danger to both people and horses. In 1925 the Senate imposed a ban on students' cars before 12.30 and after 8.30 pm, as much out of consideration for the feelings of the townspeople as in the interests of their own peace and quiet. It appears that the students made a habit of driving round the town and making an awful din. More sinisterly, they 'used cars to pick up lewd females and indulge in immorality'.

The first Poppy Day Rag took place in 1921, when the students were given the monopoly of collecting for the Earl Haig Fund and nowhere can it have been done with more zeal, more efficiency or with more entertainment given in return for the money collected. The students not only collected a huge sum of money each year, they amassed a huge fund of goodwill. In particular they established a friendly rapport with the police which was to last throughout the whole career of some policemen who have only recently retired. Many readers will recall incidents such as one that occurred on Rag Day in 1923, when a group of students played ring-a-ring-o-roses round PC Fell as he controlled the traffic in front of the Round Church and continued with his task totally unperturbed. Of course traffic then was not what it is now. Others may remember the discovery and excavation of 'Toot and Come-in's Tomb' in the underground lavatory in the market-place in 1924.

There was sometimes a good deal of nuisance in these pranks. The college authorities were not at all amused by the night-climbers who risked life and limb to place inappropriate objects in seemingly inaccessible places—chamber-pots on the pinnacles for King's, for instance. There was a good deal of nonsense, but no malice. In this same period the May Balls (held in June), instead of the sour recriminations they now excite, aroused admiration of the ladies in their finery, and amused speculation as to what went on between 4 am and breakfast at Grantchester or Ditton, but never an adverse comment to my knowledge.

In those days the proctors and their 'bulldogs' were a familiar sight in the streets. I never heard of any of them being involved in an unseemly scuffle. Towards the townspeople they always behaved with exaggerated politeness and there was an unwritten code which decreed that a student, fairly and squarely cornered after an attempted evasion, surrendered with the same politeness as that used by his captors, and paid the 6s 8d fine (usually for being out after dusk without his gown) with good grace the next day. I have heard of one instance where a student accompanying a young lady was stopped and requested to introduce her to the proctor—this would be in about 1926—to the young lady's intense indignation at the implication that she looked like a tart. (Proctorial authority over the students had not been abolished by the Act of 1894. In fact it has never been abolished, though its abolition has been seriously discussed several times of late. Proctors to this day have the statutory authority to apprehend prostitutes and hand them to the police; an authority, let me hasten to add, which they never use.)

With the outbreak of the Second World War all frivolities ceased, and many people thought, not without relief in some quarters, that they had seen the last of Guy Fawkes Rags and the like, for again the numbers of students were drastically reduced, this time to just over half the normal; and those who were there were actively involved in fire-watching and similar duties. Then in 1944 there was an almost unbelievable reversion to a state of affairs which many had forgotten. On November 5 several hundred students gathered in the market square to let off home-made fireworks and make a bonfire of paper, straw and the trestles used for the stalls. They were joined by a number of British and US servicemen—on whom some people later put most of the blame. Excitement overcame common sense; four cars were overturned, apparently to get the petrol from their tanks to feed the bonfire. Police and specials were hastily called to the scene and cleared the square with difficulty. The proctors tried to intervene, but could not be heard above the din. The 'raggers' then spilled out into King's Parade, Petty Cury and St Andrew's Street, where they damaged notice-boards, traffic-signs and smashed the windows of two buses. Two students were arrested, one of whom, charged with disorderly conduct and assaulting a policeman, was fined £15.

The outcry, as reflected in the local and national press, was out of all proportion to the seriousness of the affair. The word 'riot' was carefully avoided, lest it should have political or military repercussions, but a wave of anti-student indignation swept the country. It was said that these irresponsible young hooligans were dodging military service—a grossly unfair and untrue assertion—wasting national resources, etc, at a time when others were giving their lives for their country. The university authorities, and many of the students themselves, were prompt to speak out in condemnation of the senseless behaviour of a few of their number. Yet the volume of correspondence sympathising with the raggers was considerable and no one, to my knowledge, associated the affair with Town and Gown riots, although the resemblance was pretty close.

The return of the matured students after the war was marked by far less rowdiness than that of 1918—too much preoccupation with rationing, accommodation and the like—though there was another shock on Guy Fawkes Day 1948 when a home-made 'bomb' shattered much of the glass in the Senate House windows. Then came another brief period, about ten years, of happy relations. Although I was working in Cambridge at the time I knew nothing of what was going on. My information on this period comes mainly from men who were young policemen at the time, in the 'front line' when students were on the rampage. Here is the substance of what one of them has told me:

My job was to deal with crime, but the doings of these lads had nothing to do with crime. There was no malice on their part and no ill-feeling on ours. On November 5 they would be trying to knock our helmets off; a week later, on Rag Day, we would be shaking hands and sharing jokes, joining in the fun.

On one occasion when I was on point-duty outside Sainsbury's a group of undergrads dressed in police uniform were playing ring-a-ring-o-roses round me. It was just harmless fun. We often came off duty with our uniforms covered in flour or soot, but nobody minded that. They were old uniforms anyway.

On November 5 there was a certain amount of damage done, but it would be promptly paid for the next morning, either by the culprits or their pals or tutors. They had more money in those days and they wore gowns, with their name inside;

our tactic was to grab the gown and so identify the miscreant. The main objective of the students was to put the street lamps out. The corporation used to send men round in the afternoon to grease the lamp-standards to make it impossible to shin up them, but they succeeded in spite of that.

On one occasion there was just one light still left on. The police cordoned it off and were determined to save it, but one undergrad broke through and climbed up as far as the greased part. There he was slowed down sufficiently to allow two of my colleagues to dash forward and grab his trousers, which split down the middle. They were left holding a trouserleg each, while the young monkey was streaking across the square in some embarrassment, to the huge delight of everybody else.

As regards minor offences, like being tiddly or 'borrowing' a bike, we always showed clemency and discretion, preferring to report the matter to the student's tutor rather than bring a formal charge, because we knew it might seriously prejudice the rest of a man's career. Even now, years afterwards, we get graduates coming and asking if a certain PC is still around, because they want to thank him for some former kindness.

A high-ranking police officer confirmed all that:

The proctors in those days kept a low profile and worked in close liaison with the police. We agreed not to exacerbate the situation. For instance, we did not go into a college in uniform. We had a gentleman's agreement that we would only go in at all when invited, or if there was a major disturbance. On November 5 the police wore old uniforms, of which a supply was kept for the occasion. A lot of helmets were stolen, but most of them were returned by the college authorities.

He went on to refer to the ugly change which came over the situation in about 1954, when good-natured high spirits gave place to vicious hooligan-ism; not, he hastened to add, on the part of the students, but townies, who from then on played an ever-increasing part in the disturbances.

Extra police were called in from the county. The market-place was cleared and ringed by police, with a crowd of students and townies behind them. Home-made bombs were being tossed by the townies. A solitary student on a legitimate errand crossed the empty square. Five yobbos broke through the ring of police, ran up to this one youth and savagely attacked him in full view of the crowd. There was a rush of police to make arrests and a general mêlée ensued. The square was eventually cleared again. Then from the back of the crowd in St Mary's Passage a brick was thrown. It struck PC Bush, a big dour man, on the side of the head. With blood streaming down his face he advanced menacingly upon the crowd, muttering 'Who threw that bloody brick?' The crowd dispersed hurriedly. After that the November 5 affair was strictly controlled, and disturbances were almost wholly caused by townies with fireworks.

The fun was over for students and police. A new 'sport' was coming into existence; or rather a very old sport was being revived. It soon acquired the name of 'grad-bashing'. With minor variations it generally took the form of a gang of five or six youths, usually 14 to 18-year-olds, unemployed and of low intelligence, attacking without provocation a single student in an unfrequented spot between 11 pm and the early hours of the morning. Sometimes it was accompanied by robbery, usually of quite trifling sums— as little as ten pence. The victims were punched and kicked and often quite seriously hurt. On rare occasions they were able to give as good as they got, like the Scots laddie in King Street who was riding a super bike which was apparently the bait attracting the 'skin-heads'; he managed to remove the chain from the bike and used it as a defensive weapon.

I had hoped to find out precise details of these grad-bashings and make a detailed study with a view to reaching a decision as to whether they were or were not a survival of the Town/Gown war. It simply is not possible. The Chief Constable's annual report, based on records not available to the general public, gives statistics of all crimes committed, but does not distinguish between attacks by skinheads on students and all other attacks. Many of the attacks were not reported. Many of the assailants were not identified, though it was known that some gangs would perpetrate as many as six or seven attacks a year. The local press in the main only reported those cases which resulted in a prosecution. A reliable police estimate puts the number of attacks as high as 25 to 30 in the year 1971. Yet the *Cambridge Evening News* did not report a single case for that year, and only five cases for the years 1967-73.

Practically every student I spoke to had heard of grad-bashing and knew of at least one instance. Only one had actually experienced it. He told me it was far worse at Oxford, where the students have to take such precautions as not wearing college ties and scarves, and adopting a speech other than their famous 'Oxford accent'. An ex-proctor actually witnessed an attack in the middle of a Saturday afternoon in Trinity Lane and just missed another one night when he was on duty. According to him the incidence of the attacks was causing grave concern in 1978-79. The menace is still going on; two cases were reported in February 1982.

It is certainly tempting to view this phenomenon as a resurgence of the Town/Gown conflict. Some people do so regard it but far more, including the police, share my own view that it is something different. What is it then? Just an ugly feature of our times, a symptom of the sickness of modern society. The skinheads—punks, yobbos, hooligans, underprivileged adolescents, call them what you will—are bored, idle (perhaps not their fault), vicious and senseless. The only reason they can give for their behaviour is 'He gave me a funny look' or 'We just wanted to have a laugh' or a sullen 'Don't know' or even a sullen silence. Many of them are not city youths at all, but come from outlying villages, or from other towns. The same youths would as readily attack old ladies if old ladies roamed the streets at midnight. If they were in other towns they would amuse themselves with 'Paki-bashing' or 'nigger-bashing'. It just happens that in Cambridge the students are there to be attacked; by no means always university students, any young person who looks as if he might be a student is liable to attack.

I was told, by several students among others, that these attacks on students were one of the main reasons for the abolition of the wearing of gowns after dusk. It sounds plausible, for a gown is an unmistakable badge, and would to a skinhead be rather like a red rag to a bull. But it is not true. The wearing of gowns was discontinued in 1965 because of 'the difficulty of distinguishing undergraduates from other citizens, with consequent annoyance to townspeople; the inconvenience to undergraduates who live at a distance from the centre, and danger to those who use bicycles; the embarrassment of trying to enforce a regulation which a large number of undergraduates find irksome and unreasonable, and many senior members of the University think to be out-moded; and finally the fact that the existence of a requirement which cannot be satisfactorily enforced is likely to make the maintenance of undergraduate discipline in general more difficult'.

And so, 35 years after Oxford had set the lead, the gown—that 'dusty relic of a clerical past' or 'one of the subtle factors that contributes to the flavour of a great university and helps to keep it so', according to age and point of view—was blown away by the wind of change. (Not entirely; it is still obligatory for certain internal ceremonial occasions.)

The Guy Fawkes revel was as good as finished. Soon afterwards (1968) the Poppy Day Rag was discontinued, to be replaced by a Rag Day in February in aid of various charities; a shadow of its former self and unlikely, it seems, to survive much longer. The proctorial system still exists, even more of a shadow, and few proctors regret the change. The modern proctor's function is what it always was, namely to impose compliance with the disciplinary regulations of the Regents, but there are virtually no 'trivial' regulations left now. 'In recent years the only cases involving discipline have been cheating in examinations and the stealing of manuscripts'.

The proctors still 'walk' (patrol the streets) not as a matter of routine, but rather to maintain their ancient right to do so, 'when they feel like it'. The proctor, when he does walk, still wears the 18th century robe and ruff and carries the chained Book of Statues dated 1785. His constables or 'bulldogs' still wear top hats and on ceremonial occasions still carry the rather gruesome-looking weapons which in times past must have inspired a good deal of respect. Proctors still have the statutory right to enter pubs, which they do—to stand their constables a drink.

The question of lewd women, that second oldest and longest-lived bone of contention between the Town and Gown, 'does not exist'. I am not even sure that lewd women exist any longer. There were, according to press reports, at least three in the Pound Hill area 12 years ago and one of my police informants says there are still some in private houses, catering for visitors and soldiers. Anyway, it is something the students do not wish to know about and do not need to.

Time was—I am thinking back to the 1930s now—when a lot of students, at Cambridge as elsewhere, either regarded all town girls as potential prostitutes or hoped that they were. Today, town girls might as well not exist for all the notice the undergraduates take of them. At least that is what they say. Some of those die-hard dons of 60 or 70 years ago who steadfastly refused to acknowledge the presence of girl students at their lectures and stoutly opposed the conferring of degrees on women would turn in their graves if they could see what has happened to the colleges in this 'permissive' era. All but two of the colleges—and they, I understand, will soon fall into line with the rest—are 'mixed', ie, with male and female students sharing the same premises. The sexes are not everywhere equal in numbers, though tending more and more that way; Girton, for instance is now 40 per cent male.

Being debarred by age and temperament from membership of the permissive society, I might have been excused if I had skated round this topic. But it is an important topic. I believe it is one of the most significant developments in the whole history of the university—the ultimate shedding of the cloak of monasticism which had hampered progress for centuries—and certainly the most startling change in the last 50 years, which is saying something. However, I will be as discreet as I can.

Life in college—and in lodging-houses, which are likewise mixed—is *not* one gloriously endless round of sex, as the reverend doctors of old would have supposed. Of course it goes on, but it 'is not indiscriminate and not wholesale', according to a pretty Girton girl. At one of the smaller colleges the girls divide roughly equally into 'those who do and those who don't' and the two categories do not mix. There are landladies who, against the wishes of the college, have insisted on a student leaving because a girl has stayed the night in his room, declaring: 'I will not allow that sort of thing in *my* house'. There are others—not many—who turn a blind eye. The result of it all—permissiveness, having one's own key, absence of 'gating', etc—is that there are fewer breaches of discipline now than ever before. Come to think of it, there would be. If you do away with rules, you do away with breaches of rules.

Are the students any the worse for being given their 'freedom', being treated as responsible adults? Does unrestricted opportunity to indulge in 'immorality' lead to an increase of vice? What are today's students like, and what do the townspeople think of them? It depends very much on whom you ask. A taxi-driver had this to say: 'Anybody who lives in the centre of the town will tell you the students are a bloody nuisance, up all hours of the night making an infernal noise with their record-players, getting drunk at parties; they're a lot of idle layabouts, they don't work, they're just here to have a good time at the tax-payer's expense. I get no trade at all from them. Of course I'm biased'.

A college bursar, asked to comment on that: 'I can understand it. Ten years ago I would have agreed with him, but things are improving now. They can be infuriating, but they do bring the place to life. Some of them do stay up all night. Some of them work all night and sleep by day. They are adults and are now treated like responsible persons. Some have come from restrictive environments and they want to break away from that. Since the war, maintenance grants have relieved the students of financial worries, but they do not have money to squander. They do not have the sense of belonging that they used to have. It was different in the 1930s. Security is now one of our major worries; the doors are locked at midnight and we have two porters on duty all night, one to patrol the premises and one to let in the late-comers. We do get break-ins and some of them are by students'.

A landlady, also asked to comment on the taxi-driver's remarks, was 'horrified'. 'My students are an extremely hard-working lot. They get up in time for lectures at nine o'clock and work all day. I have to urge some of them to take more part in social activities. They each have a key and can come and go as they please, on the understanding that they cause no disturbance, and they don't cause any. Friends are expected to leave by midnight, and the rules forbid parties of more than five people at any one time.'

Although there are more students than ever before, their impact on the town is less noticeable than ever before. Numerous people have commented on the impossibility of distinguishing undergraduates from other young people. They dress alike, look alike and speak alike. The 'Cambridge accent' has almost vanished. The term 'student' is used of those at the College of Arts and Technology, sixth-formers in schools and all those foreigners who come to Cambridge to study the language, so that it no longer means necessarily those *in statu pupillari.* The best way to observe the latter en masse is to drive, or attempt to drive, along Mill Lane, Downing Street or Tennis Court Road just before a lecture is due to begin. They ride bicycles less recklessly than used to be the case, but efficient brakes are still not the universally accepted thing and one-handed riding still the norm, the other hand being full of books.

Hats and coats, raincoats especially, are still shunned by students, as they always were in my memory. Umbrellas are still carried, though less frequently since they were found to provoke some of the grad-bashing. There is nothing like the amount of drinking and pub-crawling that there was formerly; most students simply do not have the money to do it. Several pubs—'The Mill', 'The Fort St George', 'The Eagle' among them—are regarded as popular student resorts, mainly perhaps because food is served there, and the regular customers may find themselves crowded out during term-time. Disturbances are extremely rare, 'virtually non-existent'. Nearly half the Cambridge student population is still drawn from 'public' and 'independent' schools; acceptance depends on academic merit, not social standing or wealth. They are here to work, and work they must, or go.

My own opinion? Twelve years ago I was appalled by the personal appearance and dress of many of them. I had heard of students 'in revolt' and thought that they did not really have to *look* so revolting. Now I do not notice their dress, so it must have improved. I do notice their behaviour, and have no fault to find on that score. All those I meet are polite, intelligent, friendly, and quite charming—especially the girls.

Finally, what are the chances of a complete integration of city and university? The idea is not new; Lord Burleigh first suggested it more than four centuries ago. Will it ever come about? I think not, nor do I think it should. It is a vast subject calling for debate on a scale beyond my intellectual capacity. I will make one observation only. Seven centuries of strife must take some time to forget; but both city and university are thriving now. Leave well alone.

Glossary

Advowson The right to present a clerk to the bishop for institution as parson of a vacant church. Originally connected with ownership of the land on which the church stood; later often separated from it and given to religious houses and colleges. It became a commodity of considerable value. For instance, Trinity College sold the advowson of Papworth Everard in 1897 to E.T Hooley for £2,000.

Aid Under the feudal system, a monarch or lord could request financial aid from his subjects or tenants in special circumstances such as the knighting of his eldest son, marriage of his daughter, ransom of his person, etc. Not of legal right, rather of grace and favour. No specific sum was named; it had to be 'reasonable'.

Angel Gold coin varying in value between 6s 8d and 10s; so called because it bore the image of St Michael slaying a dragon.

Assize or Assay Here referring to bread and ale. Feudal lords and borough officials had the statutory duty to hold session twice a year to see that bread and ale were being sold at the right price and conformed with accepted standards of quality. As regards ale, it was mainly a matter of checking measures. The price varied with the price of grain; even so it did not vary much from a penny or two-pence per gallon for centuries.

Badgers and Kidders Hawkers, ie itinerant traders carrying small quantities of merchandise in bags or bundles.

Basons ringing Those found guilty of marital infidelity were subjected to the indignity of being carried round the town in a muck-cart followed by a band of pots and pans being bashed with fire-irons, to draw attention to the spectacle. Originally a punishment imposed by the consistory court of the Vice-Chancellor, it developed into a cruel popular entertainment, such as the 'skimmington ride' described in *The Mayor of Casterbridge*.

Bedell Ancient term for university official whose duty originally was to serve writs, collect fines, etc. Still used, though his duties since the mid-19th century have been ceremonial only.

Benefit of clergy A clerk, parson or student could be arrested and charged with felony in a civil court but still had to be tried and convicted in the bishop's (or chancellor's) court, which never imposed the death penalty, but could and did impose banishment, imprisonment, whipping and degradation.

Bill A weapon carried by night-watchmen; a short curved sword-like blade on the end of a four-foot handle, with a straight axe-like blade on the back. Later adapted as a hedge-trimming tool.

Chattels Belongings, usually of a personal and movable nature; but it could also refer to cattle. The chattels of a convicted criminal were forfeit, nominally to the Crown, but in practice to the authority imposing sentence.

Church ale The forerunner of the modern church fête. A periodical event organised by the church-wardens to raise funds for the upkeep of the church by the sale and consumption of ale in the churchyard, in the days before a church-rate was introduced (mid-16th century).

Cognisance The Vice-Chancellor had civil jurisdiction which excluded the jurisdiction of the courts of the realm; he could send his representative to any other court and 'crave cognisance' of a case in which a member of the university was involved; ie claim the right to deal with the case himself.

Compurgators A number of people, usually 12, but as few as three or as many as 72, prepared to come into court and support the accused by 'purging' him, ie, by swearing that what he said was true.

Cordwainer Shoemaker. So-called because he handled Cordovan leather. Market Street was formerly called Shoemakers' Lane or Cordwainers' Lane.

Cucking-stool More commonly 'ducking-stool'. A sort of chair on the end of a pole pivoting and swivelling on central support and placed beside a river or pond. The offender, usually a scolding wife, was secured in the chair and ducked several times in the water. The practice had more to do with lynch-law than with legal process.

Dispencers Minor municipal officers, of uncertain function; probably to do with the handing-out of poor relief.

Excommunication Ecclesiastical outlawry. A person excommunicated by a bishop (or chancellor) could not be spoken to, eaten with, or prayed with; could not sue in a court of law. If he did not seek absolution within 40 days he could be imprisoned by a civil court until he made submission to the Church.

Fee-farm To hold property or land in fee-farm was to hold by inheritance, perpetually, on payment of an annual rent. The burgesses of Cambridge held their town in fee-farm of the king. (The 'farm' element actually means 'rent'; but I have added or substituted the word 'rent' for the sake of clarity.)

Forestalling Buying commodities on the way to market or before the official opening-time in order to establish a part-monopoly and so be able to put up the price. It was forbidden under the by-laws.

Franchise Two meanings. (1) Liberties or privileges granted to a corporation by charter. (2) The right, conferred by certain qualifications, to vote in elections. Connected with 'freedom' and 'freemen' in each case.

Freeman Originally one who was not a serf or villein, ie, bound to the service of a manor. When Cambridge became a free borough, all men of the town, subject to property qualifications, became 'freemen'. Others were able to purchase that status. Later it was conferred upon or sold to outsiders as well.

Grace A resolution of the Senate, governing body of the university. Term also applied to the granting by a college of permission to take a degree.

Habeas corpus, **writ of** (Latin—'you shall have the body'.) Two uses: (1) A man who considered himself wrongfully imprisoned could apply for the writ and have himself brought to trial and liberated if found innocent. (2) Magistrates could use the writ as a means of compelling a suspected wrongdoer to present himself for trial.

Hagable and Landgable Various spellings. Rents paid for houses and land; very small amounts, tokens rather than indications of true value. Origin uncertain.

Haling Pulling, dragging by force.

Hue and cry Anyone witnessing a crime or discovering evidence of one was by law bound to 'raise the hue and cry', ie, shout. What he actually shouted is not very clear; probably the French *'hue'* (now meaning 'Gee-up!' if addressed to a horse, or 'boo!' if used by a heckler) or perhaps 'Out! Out!'. The bystanders and neighbours on hearing it were required to turn out with bows and arrows, knives, pitch-forks, etc, and begin search or pursuit. The horn-blower passed on the alarm to the next parish. Originally the criminal, if caught red-handed, met with prompt and rough justice. Later he did get a fair trial.

Hundred An area of land, usually about ten villages, or a whole town and its environs, considered as an entity for administrative and judicial purposes.

In statu pupillari (Latin—'in the status of pupil'.) Undergraduate.

Ipso facto (Latin—'by that very fact'.)

Itinerant justices or **Justices in Eyre** In addition to the local assizes held by local magistrates, two itinerant justices were commissioned to go on circuit from town to town, and their courts took precedence over all others. They used local juries and sat in the county-town, sometimes for months at a time, hearing cases of all kinds. They usually held court in one place only once in seven years.

Link Torch of pitch and tow (coarse flax) used for lighting people along dark streets. Origin dubious; probably French: *lin*—flax.

Loggets Kind of skittles, using bits of wood.

Manciple University servant whose function was to buy provisions for a college or hostel.

Mortmain, Acts of Various 'parliaments' in 1258, 1259, 1267 and 1279 made ordinances, later referred to as 'Statutes of Mortmain', forbidding the Church to acquire more lands, unless licences were applied for and granted by the Crown. Such licences were quite easily obtained, on payment of a fee. Latin *mortua manus*—'dead hand'; an allusion to the fact that land held 'in mortmain' was not held by a person, but by a corporation, which could not die, so did not have to pay fees for inheritance.

Pantables Variant of 'pantaloons' and 'pantalettes'. Sort of breeches or bloomers, considered rather clownish.

Papist One who acknowledged the Pope as head of the Church, ie, a Roman Catholic. A term of abuse after the Reformation in England.

Petty foggers Similar to badgers and kidders. Small-scale dealers of dubious integrity. Usually applied to lawyers, but of general application.

Pledges Those who gave surety for the appearance in court of one charged with an offence, and were prepared to suffer loss if he defaulted.

Pollerers and Pillerers Another way of saying rogues and swindlers.

Preferment Appointment to office or ecclesiastical living.

Promoter One who brought a law-suit for his own gain.

Quarter Measure of corn. Two sacks; eight bushels. Five quarters made a ton, more or less.

Rape seed Seed of plant grown mainly as food for sheep. Now mainly cultivated for the oil obtained by crushing the seeds; used for cooking.

Regrating Similar to forestalling. Buying up food-stuffs with a view to retailing at more than a fair profit. Forbidden by ancient law.

Sallet A sort of 'tin hat' or helmet worn by watchmen.

Sanctuary Ancient custom whereby a criminal fleeing from justice or an irate mob could seek safety in a church. Neighbours were bound to prevent his escape and summon the coroner. At the end of 40 days, if not before, the fugitive had to choose between submitting to trial or leaving the realm for good, forfeiting all his possessions. If he did return, he was an outlaw.

Scot-ale A money-raising device adopted by officials, sheriffs mainly, when short of cash for official purposes. Attendance at the drinking-feast was compulsory, as was the purchase of a stated quantity of ale, on pain of incurring the host's displeasure, which might be even more expensive.

Shillings and pence (For the benefit of younger readers there were 20 shillings to the pound, and 12 pence to the shilling.)

Tallage One of the many forms of taxation under the feudal system, imposed by a lord of a manor on all tenants, usually once a year, sometimes twice in seven years. Supposedly to meet contingent expenses. Abolished in the 15th century.

Taxor University official; assessor and collector of taxes, tolls, fees, etc.

Tenths and Fifteenths Medieval money-raising practice resorted to by impecunious monarchs, especially when war was imminent or intended. One tenth or one fifteenth of a year's income was demanded from religious houses, corporations, merchants, and the Church in general. It was extremely unpopular, and gave rise to much falsification of accounts.

Tippler Publican, taverner, ale-house keeper. Later came to mean a habitual heavy drinker.

Tithing Group of males, usually ten, of the age of 12 and upwards, collectively responsible for the conduct of its members.

Toll A small fee, usually pence or half-penny, exacted for the use of a road or bridge, stall in the market, passage of animals, etc.

Vivat Rex Latin—'Long live the King!'

Waits Band of musicians and singers employed by the town for special occasions, such as the mayoral banquet.

Wall, to take the To walk on the side of the street, so avoid having to step in the central gutter, which was usually full of filth. Common courtesy demanded that females be given this privilege ('the weakest goes to the wall'). In the case of males, one gave way to rank and status, or risked a sharp and painful reprimand.

Wattle and daub The spaces between the upright timbers forming the walls of a timber-framed building were filled with a lime plaster daubed on to a foundation of interlacing sticks. A certain amount of clay or clunch was mixed in with the plaster, also chopped straw and cow-hair.

Writ of error Local justices were not legal experts, and often made mistakes, in which case a plaintiff could sue for a writ of error and obtain a re-hearing, usually in a higher court.

Index

Adrian, Lord, *162*
Albert, Prince Consort, *146, 147*
Ale, alehouses, pubs, *112, 116, 119, 126, 138, 147, 149*
All Saints Church, *14, 23*
Andrew, Richard, *63*
Andrews, William, *118*
Arbitration, *67, 69, 85, 113, 149*
Archdeacon of Ely, *31, 110*
Ascham, Roger, *85*
Ashwell, John, *46*
Assizes, *23, 49, 128, 137*
Atkins, Thomas, *105*
Audley, Lord, *77, 80*
Aylsham, John, *30*

Bacon, Sir Francis, *124*
Ball, John, *45, 49*
Barebones Parliament, *131*
Barber, John, *46, 65*
Barber, John, chandler, *108*
Barnwell, *30, 52, 96, 109, 129, 139, 150*
Barnwell, Prior of, *16, 37, 56*
Barnwell Priory, *27, 35, 49, 54, 58*
Barrington, *39*
Bateman, Bishop, *42*
Battisford, John, *123*
Baylham, Robert, *46*
Baynard, Thomas, *35*
Bear-baiting, *100, 120*
Bear Inn, *106*
Beale, Dr, VC, *128*
Beaufort, Lady Margaret, *67, 69*
Bedell, *41, 47, 58, 68, 73, 78, 100, 118*
Benefit of clergy, *20, 24, 33*
Benet College, *42*
Bennett, Mr, R.F., *161*
Berke, John, *46*
Bilney, John, mayor, *57*
Black Assembly, *28, 57, 72, 75, 82, 102, 111, 114, 137, 138*
Black Death, *42*
Blancpayn, John, *46, 48*
Blankgreen, Roger, *47*
Boot Inn, *139*

Brakin, Francis, *114, 124*
Brakin, Thomas, mayor, *76, 79, 80, 82*
Brasyer, Henry, *46, 50*
Bridge, Great the, *24, 62, 63, 130, 134*
Brigham, John, *46, 52*
Brigham, Robert, *47*
Buckingham College *64*
Buckingham, Duke of, *50*
Buckmaster, Dr, VC, *75*
Bull Inn, *137*
Bullring, *110, 120*
Bungay, Henry de, *42*
Bury, Robert de, *37*
Bury St Edmunds, *46, 49, 52*
Butchers, *68, 96, 109, 116, 123*
Butetourt, Roger, *38*
Butler, Dr, VC, *153*
Butts, Dr, VC, *127*
Byngham, William *64*

Caius College, *162*
Caius, Dr, *63*
Cambridge Award Act, *149*
Cambridge Chronicle, *9, 149, 151, 152, 153, 159, 160*
Cambridge Society, *159*
Candles & chandlers, *54, 74, 108, 126*
Candlesby, Hugh, *48, 49, 50*
Caning, *20, 100, 123*
Cardemaker, John, *46*
Carpenters Arms Inn, *139*
Castle gaol, *14, 36, 53, 62, 82, 83, 89*
Cavendish, Sir John, *45, 49*
Cecil, Sir Robert, *116*
Cecil, Sir W, (Burghley), *89—115*
Chancellor of University, *18, 31, 36, 40, 67, 70, 77, 89, 116, 146*
Chapman, Mr, mayor, *75, 76*
Charters, *14, 26, 35, 36, 39, 46, 80, 84, 89, 104, 120*
Charles I, King, *130*
Charles II, King, *131, 134*
Chapman, Edward, mayor, *131*
Chesterton, *35, 56, 69, 82,*

99, 104, 120, 123
Christ's College, *10, 64, 69, 87, 92, 164*
City status, *124*
Civil War, *130*
Clare Hall, *39, 115, 124*
Clark, Henry, mayor, *109*
Clubs, *87, 95, 106*
Coals, *68, 80, 118*
Coffee-houses, *139*
Commons, abuse of, *73, 86, 103*
Conduit, *96, 123, 125, 134*
Corn supplies, *44, 93, 103, 112, 126, 136*
Cooper, Robert, *55*
Corpus Christi College, *42, 43, 48, 71, 118*
Corrie, Dr, VC, *146*
Corruption of officials, *34, 92, 116, 138*
Corruption of University officers, *73, 75, 110, 111, 114*
Cotton, John, *46*
Cotton, Sir John, *119*
Cranmer, Archbishop, *83, 85*
Crayford, Thomas, *117*
Cromwell, Oliver, *130*
Cromwell, Thomas, *75, 76, 77*
Crooke, Dr, VC, *71*
Cumberland, Earl of, *106*
Cutts, Sir John, *106, 119*

Danes, *13*
Daniel, Glyn, Professor, *161*
Death, Ald, mayor, *146, 152*
Defoe, Daniel, *133, 135*
Depedale, Master John, *25*
Description of town, *16, 30, 96, 134*
Discommoning, *65, 74, 98, 103, 126, 137, 143, 146, 148, 149, 153*
Dissolution of Colleges, Act, *79, 80*
Dissolution of monasteries, *77, 79*
Dolphin Inn, *66, 87, 105, 106, 113*
Draper, William, *48*

Driffield, Master Robert, *24*
Dullingham, *153*
Dunmow, Henry, *62*

Edmonds, John, mayor, *102*
Edward I, King, *28, 32*
Edward II, King, *35, 39*
Edward III, King, *39, 42*
Edward IV, King, *64*
Egerton, Sir Thomas, *121*
Elizabeth, Queen, *89, 90*
Ellys, Dr John, VC, *137*
Elsden, Jane, *153*
Ely, *26, 53, 136*
Ely, Bishop of, *19, 21, 32, 66*
Emmanuel College, *107, 127, 136*
Essex, Earl of, *115, 131*
Excommunication, *31, 62, 70, 72*

Fairs, *16, 56, 74, 128, 140, 147*
Falcon Inn, *106*
Fee-farm rent, *14, 16, 40, 43, 51, 54, 60, 130*
Fen drainage, *125, 131*
Ferne, Dr, VC, *131*
Filthy streets, *26, 54, 56, 96*
Fires, *53, 98*
Fish & fishing, *34, 60, 73, 74, 76, 133*
Fisher, John, Chancellor, *67, 70*
Fletcher, James, mayor, *83*
Football, *99*
Fortescue, Sir John, *121*
Fourbissher, Thomas, *47, 48, 49, 52*
Fox, George, *131*
Foyster, George, mayor, *71*
Freemen, *47, 53, 60, 66, 110, 129, 134, 138, 142*

Games & gaming, *93, 117*
Gaol (town), *24, 36, 67, 78, 84, 89, 122, 143*
Gaunt, Nicholas, mayor, *104*
Gibbon, John, mayor, *44, 47, 48*
Gifford, Nicholas, *105*
Godshouse, *64, 69*
Gogging, Bartholomew, *33, 40*
Goldsborough, John, *110, 115*
Gooch, Dr, VC, *123*
'Grad-bashing', *167*
Grantchester, Jakes de, *47, 49*
Gray, Thomas, poet, *140*
Green Dragon Inn, *139*
Grey, Lady Jane, *86*
Guildhall, *44, 54, 134*
Gunning, Dr Henry, VC, *135, 140*
Gunville Hall, *42, 56, 70*

Hammond, William, *103*
Harleston, Roger, *48*
Harrison, Thomas, *83, 109*
Harvard, John, *107*
Harwedon, Master Henry, *40*
Hasleden, Sir Thomas, *47*
Hastings, Henry de, *35*
Hauke, Nicholas, *59*
Hede, Nicholas, *46*
Henry I, King, *14*
Henry III, King, *19*
Henry VI, King, *64*
Henry VII, King, *65*
Henry VIII, King, *76, 78, 82*
Herries, John, *50, 63*
Herry, John, *46*
Hierman, Thomas, *58*
High Steward, *70, 77, 87, 121, 137*
Hobson, Thomas, *125, 153*
Holt, Master John, *45*
Holy Sepulchre Church, *30, 36, 98, 106*
Holy Trinity Church, *115*
Hoop Inn, *151*
Hops, *135, 138*
Hopkins, Daisy, *156*
Hosier, Simon, *47, 49*
Hospital of St John, *32, 54, 70*
Hue and cry, *23, 86*
Hundred Rolls, *28, 30*

Income of colleges, *77, 82, 148*
Integration of town & university, *95, 161*
Ipswich, *44*

James I, King, *124*
Jegon, Dr, VC, *111—119*
Jesus College, *66, 103*
'Jetting', *58, 75, 87, 122*
John, King, *14, 128*

Kemp, Emma, *151*
Keymer, John, *101, 109*
King's College, *64, 86*
King's Ditch, *14, 17, 27, 40, 67, 96, 123*
King's Hall, *39, 62, 75, 82*
Kymball, Mr, mayor, *94*
Kynne, Master John, *48*

Lancaster, Duke of, *42, 47*
Lane, David, MP, *161*
Latimer, Hugh, Bishop, *85*
Laurence, Richard, *33*
Laurence, Robert, *112*
Leicester, Earl of, *101, 102*
Lighting of streets, *98, 139*
Lincoln, *32, 126*
Lister, Edmund, mayor, *45, 46, 50*
Lister, Thomas, *48, 49*
Local Government Act 1889, *149, 157*

Lodging-houses, *19, 28, 30, 163*
Lolworth, Peter, *46*
London, *40, 50, 54, 62, 66, 76, 79, 84, 93, 119, 127, 145*
Lyell, Dr, VC, *124*
Lynn, *14, 30, 53, 74, 80, 93*

Magdalene College, *64*
'Mainprise', *56*
Marshall, John, *46, 50*
Martin, Richard, *49, 52*
Mascall, William, *65*
Mashrelle, John, *55*
Maysterman, Richard, mayor, *50*
Merton College, Oxford, *32*
Michaelhouse, *39, 56, 63, 70, 82*
Mildmay, Sir W., *107*
Militia, *80, 84, 89, 94, 128*
Mill Street, *39, 42, 48*
Morice, Stephen, *44*
Mortlock, Mr, mayor, *136*
Mortmain, Statues of, *33, 39, 79, 121*
Municipal Corporation Act 1835, *144*

'Nationalities', *24, 58*
Newmarket, *109, 131, 147*
Newnham, *23, 30, 90, 133*
Newton, Samuel, mayor, *134*
Nicholson, William, *136*
Noreys, John, *48*
Norfolk, Duke of, *71, 89, 94*
Norgate, Dr, VC, *101*
North, Lord, *87, 89, 94, 100, 105, 107*
Northampton, *25, 40*
Norwich, *47, 127*
Norwich, Bishop of, *42, 49, 64*
November 5th, *142, 166*
Nowell, Mr, MA, *106*

Oath-taking, *28, 62, 69, 72, 79, 82, 98, 114, 131, 147, 149*
Oxford, *17, 18, 22, 24, 25, 38, 51, 86, 90, 115, 127, 147, 156, 168, 169*
Oysters, *68, 116, 135*

Paget, Sir William, *81, 83, 85*
Paris, *17, 19*
Parish, Richard, *100, 104*
Parish, Thomas, *99*
Parliament, *32, 34, 54, 114*
Parleben, Roger, *25*
Parker, Archbishop M., *81, 102*
Parker's Piece, *9, 123*
Parr, Catherine, Queen, *81*
Patteson, Sir John, *149*
Pavage, *34, 62, 80*
Payne, Benjamin, *116, 122*
Payne, Stephen, *118*

Peasants' Revolt, *45*
Pembroke College, *42, 137*
Perne, Dr Andrew, VC, *92, 95, 102, 123, 162*
Peterhouse, *32, 38, 102*
Petty Cury, *48, 106, 153, 166*
Pigs, *66, 96, 102*
Pillory, *16, 19, 26, 31, 94, 111*
Plague, *42, 93, 95, 96, 127, 130, 133*
Plays, *115, 124, 147*
Police Force, *142, 144*
Poor-relief, *99, 115, 117, 119, 127, 129, 131, 134*
Popham, Lord Chief Justice, *115*
Population, *30, 70, 112, 128, 44, 134, 145, 159*
Porthors, John, *33*
Post-horses, *84, 89*
Pottall, Mr, mayor, *124*
Pound, *103*
Pourfisshe, John, *37*
Privileged persons, *43, 67, 94, 104, 111, 120, 125, 128, 133*
Privy Council, *75, 76, 77, 80, 82, 83, 91, 92, 115, 123, 125, 126*
Proctors, *30, 70, 73, 83, 100, 109, 112, 119, 123, 147, 151, 165, 169*
Prostitutes, *36, 37, 58, 65, 83, 84, 139, 147, 149, 151, 165, 169*
Pryme, Benjamin, *118*
Pump Tavern, *75, 77*

'Rags', *145, 164, 165, 169*
Railway Act 1844, *145*
Raleigh, Sir Walter, *101, 102*
Rande, Henry, *46*
Reading, *18*
Recorder, *66, 114, 121, 124*
Redingfield, Roger de, *33*
Redmedowe, Edmund, mayor, *48, 49*
Reepham, Simon, mayor, *37*
Reform Act 1832, *143*
Resham, John, *48, 62*
Rhodes James, Mr, MP, *162*
Richard I, King, *14*
Rikinghale, Master John, *60*
River trade, *14, 53, 125*
Robinson, Richard, *108*
Robinson, Robert, *65*
Robson, James, *109, 118*
Rose Inn, *142*
Royal visits, *26, 27, 90, 124, 130, 134*

Royston, *95, 128, 147*
Russel, Christopher, *92*
Russell, John, *47, 49*

St Andrew's Church and parish, *30, 98, 115, 125*
St Benet's Church and parish, *14, 17, 30, 118*
St Botolph's Church and parish, *98*
St Catherine's College, *65, 112*
St Clement's Church and parish, *24, 77, 91*
St Edward's Church, *14*
St Giles Church and parish, *17, 47, 115*
St Ives, *35, 53, 147*
St John's College, *70, 103, 106*
St John's Church, *39*
St Mary's Church and parish, *23, 38, 39, 47, 48, 60, 67, 74, 82, 98, 123, 136, 137*
St Michael's Church, *31, 33, 38, 75*
St Peter's Church, *14, 17*
St Peter's, ex-Trumpington Gate, *32*
St Radegund's Priory, *65*
Salle, Sir Robert, *49*
Saltpetre, *128*
Salutation Inn, *139*
Saracen's Head Inn, *139*
Seditious speech, *49, 77, 78, 79*
Senate, *88, 90, 98, 112, 126, 144, 146, 165*
Sergeant, Adam, *46*
Serle, Henry, *91, 110*
Servants, *67, 68, 71, 94*
Shaxton, John, MA, *106*
Shelford, *96, 151*
Sheton, Walter de, *37*
Sherwood, John, mayor, *126, 127*
Shingay, *47*
Ship-money, *44, 128*
Shirle, John, *49*
Sidney Sussex College, *107*
Sledmere, William de, *37*
Slegge, Edward, mayor, *72, 76, 79*
Slegge, Roger, mayor, *91, 94, 99, 105, 110*
Slums, *125, 130*
Smith, Sir Thomas, *85*
Smythe, Robert, *70*
Spinning House, *125, 133, 139, 143, 149, 151, 152, 153, 154, 156*

Stamford, *38*
Standish, Dr, VC, *80*
Stanton, Hervey de, *38*
Star Chamber, *79, 95, 114*
Starre, Margaret, *48*
Stationers, *43*
Stocks, *16, 75, 82*
Sturbridge Fair, *52, 62, 69, 76, 77, 79, 83, 96, 104, 135*
Suffolk, Earl of, *64, 123, 124, 127*
Sutton, Richard, *55, 58*

Tangmere, Henry de, *43*
Taverner, Alex, *46*
Thompson, Oswald, *73*
Thornham, Master Hugh, *25*
Three Feathers Inn, *139*
Tobacco, *123, 130, 145*
Tolbooth, *16, 37, 47, 56, 57, 78, 83, 107, 118*
Tournaments, *21, 28, 35*
Treveth, Thomas, *46*
Trew, Simon, *80*
Trinity College, *82, 86, 105, 107, 112, 123*
Trinity Hall, *9, 27, 42*
Trippelow, John, *46*
Trumpington, John de, *46*
Tyteshall, John, *49*

University Hall, *39*

Victuallers, *71, 90, 119, 126*
Vintners, *101, 128*

Walde, Matilda de, *33*
Wall, taking, the, *95, 107*
Wallis, Robert, mayor, *111, 116, 119*
Watch, *23, 87*
Watson, Dr, VC, *73*
Welbore, John, *137*
Wendover, Roger de, *17*
Wendy, Mr, JP, *119*
Wering, Thomas, *58*
Whaley, Leonard, *113*
Wharton, Martin, *109*
White Hart Inn, *66*
Wigmore, William, *47, 48*
Wine, *26, 40, 54, 101, 135, 149*
Withersfield, Roger de, *33*
Wolsey, Cardinal, *70, 71, 76*
Woodlark, Dr, Robert, *65*
Wren, Dr Matthew, VC, *127*
Wympol, Nicholas, *49*
Wyvelingham, William de, *40*

Yaxley, John, mayor, *116, 119*